NEVER STOP THE ENGINE WHEN IT'S HOT

David Lee

NEVER STOP
THE ENGINE
WHEN IT'S HOT

DAVID LEE

Illustrated by

Richard Lee

Thomas Harmsworth Publishing
London

By the same author:
Flight from the Middle East (HMSO)

ISBN 0 9506012 4 1

Printed in Great Britain by
The Pitman Press, Bath.

PREFACE

Much has been written about India under the British Raj, and particularly about the Indian Army. Life in the Royal Air Force has, however, had little mention. This is a light-hearted description of the experience of a young RAF officer serving on the North West Frontier during the early 1930s.

David Lee

CHAPTER 1

OFF TO THE NORTH WEST FRONTIER

SS *California*, flagship of the Anchor Line, hooted dismally as it floated out into midstream down the cold, grey Mersey on that depressing February afternoon in 1933. For a small party of twelve Pilot Officers huddled together by the starboard rail, heavily disguised in an assortment of civilian clothes, it would probably be their last glimpse of England for almost five years. No one spoke as the ship gathered speed on an ebb tide, each wrapped in his own thoughts, wondering perhaps what would befall him before he saw England again. Whatever unknown experiences lay before

1

him, one thing was certain, he would enjoy a great deal more sunshine and warmth than the Mersey was offering him that day, for the *California* was on her way to Karachi by way of the Suez Canal carrying the young officers to an overseas tour of duty in India.

Most of the silent party had been in the term which had graduated from the RAF College, Cranwell, during the previous July and now had come together again after an interval of six months during which their Cranwell training had been consolidated with a few months in various squadrons throughout the country. No 35 (Bomber) Squadron at Bircham Newton in Norfolk had had the doubtful privilege of my company for five months during which I flew the Fairey Gordon for 42 happy hours, learned to be an Orderly Officer, had inadvertently soaked the Station Commander during a fire practice, taken a severe beating on behalf of Bircham Newton in the Wakefield Boxing Championships (the only officer to be knocked out twice in one fight) and learned to drink more than two pints of beer without disgracing myself. Whether 35 Squadron heard of my posting to India with pleasure or regret is not recorded but my Flight Commander was good enough to put 'Above Average' in my flying log book, doubtless out of gratitude that I had not damaged any of his Gordons during my brief stay.

As the shoreline vanished in the mist, the silence was broken by Peter Lloyd saying, 'I wonder if he's sold my car yet?' It transpired that Peter had driven his old car up to Liverpool docks and, after unloading his luggage, had given the car keys to a helpful porter, telling the astonished man that the car was now his and that the registration book was in the glove locker. Being a more mercenary sort of chap, I had left my 1928 two seater Morris Cowley with my father to sell for what he could get, which subsequently turned out to be £12. This was entirely satisfactory and meant that I had had six months of reliable motoring since leaving Cranwell for a depreciation of £8. Putting the matter into this perspective and bearing in mind that my Morris was much more valuable than Peter's old banger, his gift to the porter was not quite so princely as it might at first have seemed. Nevertheless it was a parting gesture which somehow typified the feeling of leaving England for almost a lifetime, which most of us had.

We were fortunate to be given passages in the *California* instead of travelling by troopship which was the usual way of starting an overseas tour. All trooping to the tropics was carried out during the cooler months of the year and it was customary for two troopships to be allotted to the RAF each year between October and March. These ships, which were named after English counties such as *Somersetshire*, *Dorsetshire* and *Oxfordshire*, had an unenviable reputation for discomfort and overcrowding. They travelled to India by way of Iraq where, after a long voyage round to the Persian Gulf and up to Basra, they would disembark some airmen for a two year tour in Iraq, and take on others who had completed their two years there and were then destined for a further three in India. This always seemed a particularly harsh penance but it was well understood and accepted in good spirit. When the troopships were full or when a few officers and airmen had to be sent abroad outside the normal trooping season, civilian passages were booked. Our small party was in that happy position and we were all looking forward to a voyage of three weeks or more as first class civilian passengers, free from the chores of being Orderly Officer in a troopship, wearing mess kit for dinner every night and uniform all day.

After dinner that night and a few jugs of ale to ward off the seasickness, quietly checking over the female company meanwhile, I retired to the minute cabin which I was to share with one of my friends. The ship was ploughing through the Irish Sea by this time and beginning to roll and creak disconcertingly. As I lay in my bunk feeling slightly depressed and perhaps a little apprehensive, I could not help but think, 'What on earth are you doing here, on your way to defend some God-forsaken part of the British Empire called the North West Frontier, with little prospect of seeing home and family again for five years, or perhaps never again as you have only 179 hours and 55 minutes flying experience in your Log Book?' As I became increasingly conscious of the rolling and pitching of the ship and understood why bunks had such high sides, I began to question the wisdom of having joined the RAF in the first place. To this day I have never quite known what motivated me. I had received a classical public school education and my headmaster expected me to swell the school's records in classics at University. My parents were totally mystified at my choice of career: no other member of the family had ever considered such a dangerous form of livelihood and I was certainly not the daredevil character popularly identified with the RAF at that time. The only clue to my motivation was that one of my close friends was the son of a Squadron Leader. He was determined to go to Cranwell and his enthusiasm communicated itself to me. It was sad that he subsequently failed the medical examination whereas I passed without difficulty, and so found myself in the RAF on my eighteenth birthday without quite knowing what had hit me. The euphoria was soon dispelled by the hard reality of learning to fly but now in the pitching, rolling darkness of a cabin with no porthole, the old doubts about the wisdom of my choice arose again. Would not life have been more straightforward if I had obtained a classics degree and become a schoolmaster or a civil servant? With this mental conflict, doubltess increased by faint symptons of seasickness, I fell asleep on the first night I had ever spent out of England.

The less said about the Bay of Biscay the better, but it was soon behind us and the dining room began to fill up with pale passengers as we rounded Gibraltar and entered the Mediterranean. Port Said was to be our first call for a few hours while awaiting the formation of a south bound convoy for passage through the Suez Canal. By the time Malta was astern, the sun was shining, the decks were dry for the first time, shuffle board and deck tennis were in full swing and a much better view of life was being taken by everyone, including myself. I had made the right decision. There was no longer any doubt about it and I was going to enjoy this overseas tour to the full.

4

As the *California* steamed into Port Said we could see that the harbour was packed with ships which seemed to indicate that Port Said was an extremely prosperous and important place.

'Far from it,' said a seasoned traveller over a glass of beer at the bar. 'All those ships are merely waiting their turn to join a Canal convoy. Port Said itself is fairly unimportant and pretty squalid. Don't let yourself get led astray'.

I saw what he meant half an hour later when the ship tied up by the waterfront immediately opposite the huge department store of Simon Artz, the Harrods of the Middle East. We were besieged by a tattered collection of Arabs of all ages, some diving for pennies, some selling 'feelthy peectures' and inviting the passengers to follow them to haunts of unbelievable pleasure. The famous 'gulli gulli' men were there, producing day old chicks from impossible places, vendors of eastern brass work made in Birmingham and perpetrators of every kind of swindle imaginable. Even the ageless 'Mr Macgregor', a particularly plausible rogue, well known to countless British troops passing through Port Said over the years, was there offering a sightseeing tour which would never be forgotten. I could have watched this colourful and noisy scene in the bright Egyptian sunshine from the rail of the ship for hours, but there was serious work to be done, and little enough time in which to do it. Simon Artz had been strongly recommended as the best place to make good deficiences in one's tropical kit before entering the Red Sea which, even in February, could be quite hot.

Very little official guidance was given to officers before leaving England about their uniform and civilian clothing but, from other more experienced officers, I had picked up a few valuable tips.

'Take as little drill uniform as possible,' they all said, 'just enough to see you through the voyage and the first few days in India. You can get shorts, shirts, slacks etc run up quickly and much more cheaply on your new station by the local dhersi (tailor). Do, however, take stockings, socks and other woollen articles, shoes, mess kit and headgear.'

A visit to my London tailors who were the custodians of my overdraft at that time had produced the minimum amount of uniform that I needed for a troopship voyage. I did not know at that time that I was to travel as a civilian passenger or I would certainly have bought even less; the standard of tailoring and the quality of some of the material was extremely poor. Such items as white Mess dress, for which there was a strict pattern, were satisfactory but the same could not be said of shorts, slacks and khaki shirts. The shorts were festooned with five sets of metal buckles, all of which had to be removed daily before going to the dhobi: mine even had buttons for braces as did the slacks. The khaki shirts began to lose their colour after the first wash, turning into an attractive pink shade before finishing up so white that I could eventually use them for cricket and tennis. These low standards were astonishing considering that British officers had been equipped for India by the big London military tailors for centuries. Many of my colleagues subsequently sent some of these garments back often accompanied by examples made up locally, but it seemed to have little effect and junior officers continued to arrive in India with unsuitable clothing. My own tailors were, however, sufficiently ashamed of their shirts which turned white within four months to replace them. Another standard item of uniform which had to be bought at home was the Wolseley helmet. This large, heavy and all enveloping headgear had a substantial peak in front to shade the eyes and an even larger one at the back to protect the neck from the sun. Its large domed crown was held away from the head by an inner band of cork and leather and the whole structure was wrapped in many yards of puggaree cloth wound like a turban and held in place with a flash of RAF ribbon. This edifice, which bore a striking resemblance to the domes on Viceregal Lodge in Delhi, was most impressive when worn by a large and rubicund officer but it did nothing to enhance the respect of one with a small head and thin features, into which category I tended to fall. The fit was critical; if too large the sheer weight of the helmet would bring it down onto the wearer's ears and, in extreme cases, might even allow him to turn right round without taking the helmet with him, from which originated the expression – 'Good morning, Sir, are you coming or going?' It was even said by some that this piece of headgear was bullet proof although there is no recorded proof of this. The story probably originated from the undoubted fact that a number of Indian troops were saved from serious shrapnel injuries during World War I by the many layers of puggaree cloth wrapped around their heads.

With these accoutrements I had bought a uniform trunk and a topee case, both strongly built of japanned steel and proof against bugs, damp and rust. The uniform trunk measured five feet overall and would hold trousers at full length and a sword, with room to spare at one end for a full dress hat. Fifty years and four overseas tours later these two pieces of luggage are still intact and perfectly usable although far too heavy and cumbersome for modern travel.

The items which needed to be bought in Port Said for use during the later part of the voyage were tropical mufti and, in particular, a civilian topee. Had we been sensible, we young officers would have sought advice from the few more senior officers who were aboard. As was the case with uniform, such advice would undoubtedly have been to delay buying all but essentials until they could be made up by a station dhersi. However, we had to learn and it cost most of us a certain amount of hard cash and a good deal of embarrassment. Perhaps the worst mistake that a few of us, including myself, made was in the purchase of the topee. Nobody had volunteered the information that the type universally worn by officers in civilian dress was the 'Bombay Bowler.' This was a small khaki topee, shaped like an inverted pie dish – very light and comfortable to wear but somewhat fragile.

Without the expert information which was available for the asking, a small party of us made for Simon Artz, grimly pushing aside all the attractive alternatives offered to us at the foot of the gangway, pausing for only a moment while three day-old chicks were produced from Bob Carter's jacket. Shaking off numerous tattered escorts, we walked along the front to Simon Artz which proved to be a noisy, cheerful department store, thronged with shoppers from several other ships waiting to transit the Canal. Being winter, the hat department seemed to be selling mostly European style felt hats, straw boaters and panamas, but there was a fair range of topees available. Those who were buying them mostly favoured large white expensive models which, in earlier days, American lady tourists had covered with veils as a protection against mosquitos. Clearly these were the current civilian fashion and so, without a second thought, several of us bought them and returned to the ship well satisfied. Well satisfied, that is, until some days later when the *California* was steaming down the Red Sea with a following wind and a blazing sun. One of our party, who shall be nameless, felt that it was hot enough to try out his new topee and duly strolled around the promenade deck in it before lunch. He was somewhat disconcerted by the thinly disguised smiles and sniggers of some of the more senior officers until one of them took him aside.

'You know you can't possibly wear that hat on a station in India – you will be taken for a bloody box wallah' (a derogatory term for a European business man.)

'Oh,' said the Pilot Officer, 'all the civilians were buying them in Simon Artz.'

'Yes,' was the reply, 'but they were box wallahs or holiday makers. We all wear Bombay bowlers off duty. Not to worry,' he went on, 'you won't need a topee at this time of year on the voyage, and there will be plenty of time to buy another in Karachi.'

That night before getting into my bunk, I surreptitiously climbed up to the boat deck and dropped my brand new, unworn topee over the side. As I turned away from the rail, I caught a glimpse of what looked suspiciously like another white topee floating away from the ship. I have a strong feeling that a small trail of box wallah topees followed in the wake of the

California as she ploughed on down the Red Sea. This little incident was never discussed among us but at least six pristine white topees must have been quietly disposed of as no Pilot Officer was ever again seen wearing one.

The final week of the voyage past Perim Island and Aden, and across the Arabian Sea to Karachi was perfect. The sun shone brilliantly, temperatures were in the high 70s and the sea was calm. The swimming pool was filled, the girls looked prettier every day and, with gin at twopence a tot, I began to feel that the Air Ministry had shown great wisdom in selecting my colleagues and me to defend British India. Somewhat surprisingly shipboard romances did not flourish as much as might have been expected in these idyllic circumstances. We were very young and too excited at the prospect of flying on the North West Frontier and venturing into the unknown to form romantic attachments which might lead us into difficulties later. Also the few girls who were not the wives of more senior officers on board were closely chaperoned.

Young air force officers were regarded at that time with a certain amount of suspicion and they had the reputation of being irresponsible young daredevils who had adopted a risky profession. It was the era of the short service commission when some young men were told by their fathers to join the air force for five years to sow their wild oats before settling down and taking over the family business. 'Don't tell my Mother that I've joined the Royal Air Force. She thinks I'm still playing the piano in a brothel,' was a ribald comment at that time. This did not mean that young RAF officers were socially unacceptable: far from it, but there is no doubt that they were regarded with some reserve. They had strange sounding ranks, they belonged to a new Service which had only been in existence for fifteen years, and their whole way of life was something of a mystery. It was therefore prudent to protect one's daughter against the unknown, and this was particularly so when she was on her way to India as part of what was irreverently known as the 'fishing fleet'. We had never heard of this expression but it was one with which we were to become well acquainted during the coming years. Young women led very sheltered lives and did not enjoy the career opportunities or the freedom to meet young men of their own age as they do today. If a girl in her twenties had relatives or close family friends serving in India, her parents would often send her out to stay with them for several months during the cooler part of the year, usually between October and March. Ostensibly this extended holiday was intended to broaden her education but, if in so doing, she was attracted to one of the many thousands of young and eligible bachelors who were on military service abroad, so much the better.

Many of these girls did form attachments during their holiday but early marriage in the Services was discouraged and, in the RAF no marriage allowance was granted until an officer either reached the age of thirty or became a Squadron Leader. As the latter was almost impossible to achieve and, as 'living in sin' without a marriage allowance involved considerable hardship, particularly as few RAF officers had large private incomes, there were very few junior married officers in the Indian squadrons. It was usual for the squadron commander and perhaps his flight commanders to be married but the remaining fifteen to twenty officers would be bachelors. Consequently the girls of the 'fishing fleet' were popular and much in demand for dances, picnics, tennis and good company generally. But they were always carefully chaperoned as became evident aboard the *California* whose boat deck saw very little midnight activity, even on those warm moonlight nights in the Arabian Sea.

At Karachi all was bustle and serious business. No longer were we allowed to be disguised as civilian passengers, and a dozen slightly self-conscious Pilot Officers appeared for the first time in their khaki drill uniforms dominated by the Wolseley helmet and embarrassingly white about the knees. We did not at that time know our exact destinations although we all expected to go to one or other of eight RAF squadrons then serving in India, five of them being on the North West Frontier and one at Ambala. All officers were posted from the UK to the Aircraft Depot at Karachi which in turn allocated individuals to the various units. RAF personnel were loaned to the Indian Government who paid them and provided all their requirements throughout their stay in India. As its name implies, the Aircraft Depot held, distributed, stored and repaired all aircraft and equipment and administered all personnel on behalf of the Indian Government. This was a strange and unique system but it worked well enough and one had no serious complaint about the scales of pay and conditions of service. A Pilot Officer, for example, received about 400 rupees per month, which with the rupee standing at one shilling and sixpence, produced about £400 per year, a little more than the home rate of pay. Living in a Mess in India was cheap, and I found myself able to save about £100 a year without in any way stinting myself.

As soon as the ship had docked, all the RAF officers on board were summoned to the dining room where we met a Flight Lieutenant from the Aircraft Depot who had full particulars of our destinations. His announcement would decide my fate for several years ahead and I felt my old apprehension growing again as he worked his way down the list to Pilot Officers at the bottom. He came to them at last. Tom Gale to 39 Squadron at Risalpur, Kiwi Broughton to 11 Squadron on the same station, myself to 60 Squadron at Kohat.

I didn't listen to the rest of the list. What did I know about Kohat and 60 Squadron? Well, we had all done our homework with the help of some of the older hands aboard, and my first reaction was one of satisfaction.

Kohat was one of the three stations on the Frontier, the other two being Peshawar and Risalpur. It was a bomber station with two squadrons of Westland Wapitis – 27 and 60 Squadrons. The Wapiti was a single engined general purpose type of aircraft, powered by a Bristol Jupiter engine, and not unlike the Fairey Gordon which I had been flying at Bircham Newton. It was perhaps a little smaller and carried a pilot and air gunner.

11

Risalpur also housed two bomber squadrons and these had recently been equipped with the new Hawker Hart. Risalpur would certainly have been more exciting, but I was satisfied, particularly as 60 Squadron was a splendid squadron with a fine record in the Great War, including Albert Ball VC among its many distinguished members. I liked the sound of my new posting and my colleagues seemed equally happy with theirs. We just had time to celebrate before the duty-free drink was turned off in the bar, and it was time to leave the *California* which had been a happy home for the past three weeks.

As we turned to go, the Flight Lieutenant who had briefed us threw out the almost casual remark:

'Your bearers will be waiting for you on the quay, and there is also a troop train to take you up to the Frontier – the journey will take about four days and three nights.'

This last remark stopped me in my tracks.

'How long did you say?' I gasped.

'Today being Tuesday, you should reach Peshawar some time on Saturday. This is not the Frontier Mail, you know,' said the Flight Lieutenant, clearly enjoying the sensation he had caused. 'Even cattle and coal trains take precedence over troop trains but they are reasonably comfortable at this time of year.'

I clearly had to review my ideas about the size of India; I had expected a journey of about eight hours, and that was longer than I had ever spent in a train before. Now I was going to be incarcerated for four days. Obviously I was going to be a very long way from home by the time I reached Kohat and the need for a five year tour of duty was beginning to become apparent.

On the quayside the noise and activity was reminiscent of Port Said, but more orderly. A long, dusty train was drawn up close to the ship, with no engine attached to it and no sign of imminent departure about it. This was presumably the troop train which was to be our home for the next few days. As I stepped off the gangway, a young Indian, neatly dressed in white baggy trousers, khaki drill shirt worn outside the trousers and a khaki puggaree wrapped smartly round the head, stepped towards me.

'Lee sahib?' he enquired hesitantly. I nodded and he went on:

'Salaam sahib – your bearer, Hukmud Khan.'

I was not to know it at the time but Hukmud Khan, who was a young Pathan of about twenty years of age was to be my personal servant, and a most efficient one at that, for the next four years. He was on the staff of the Officers Mess at Kohat and, as was customary when new officers arrived, he had been sent down to Karachi to meet the ship and accompany me up to Kohat. I would eventually be asked to pay his rail fare – the princely sum of about £2 for the return journey.

Every officer had his own personal bearer and each one had been checked for security and character by the RAF before being placed officially on a station register. If any officer was posted home, his bearer reverted to the Officers Mess until a new master could be found for him. If, as often happened, an officer was posted to another station in India half way through his tour, he would take his bearer with him unless he wanted a good excuse to get rid of him. These Indian servants who were mostly Pathans, Punjabis or Sikhs in Northern India were intensely loyal to their officers, attended to their every need, waited on them in Mess and accompanied them on leave. Towards the end of my tour when I could afford a car, I even taught Hukmud Khan to drive it and obtained a licence for him. For all this attention I paid him the modest sum of 26 Rupees a month (about £2) and, in addition, always allowed him to pay my local bills for which he obtained a little 'baksheesh' from the traders.

One of my first thoughts on meeting Hukmud was how I would converse with him. His language was Urdu and it would take me some time to pick up even the rudiments of it. However, I need not have worried. Hukmud had already been a bearer for a few years and had picked up a good smattering of English. As the knowledge of our respective languages

13

improved we became fluent in a concoction of Urdu and English well known to all military men in India.

'Your bistra here, sahib' was the next comment from Hukmud. This threw me. 'Bistra,' – what on earth was it? It sounded like the feminine of a small French cafe. Hukmud pointed to a large green bundle bound with two leather straps and a carrying handle. This turned out to be my bedroll, issued by the Aircraft Depot and without which nobody in India travelled. On examination it consisted of a green canvas case over six feet in length when unrolled, containing a thin mattress, one blanket, two sheets and a pillow. A large pocket held the pillow and, indeed, any other luggage that one cared to cram into it. Inside the bedroll was a camp bed with a folding wooden frame, a canvas wash basin also with a folding trestle stand and a canvas bucket. The ability to 'pick up thy bed and walk' was soon to become a reality: bedding was not provided in resthouses, trains, our own quarters or even in hotels other than a few first class hotels in the big cities. One usually found in the bedroom only a simple bedframe strung with a coarse type of jute cord. This was the 'charpoy' and travellers or visitors simply placed their bedrolls on it and climbed into their own sheets. Although primitive in the extreme, the 'charpoy' was quite comfortable provided one had one's own thin mattress to prevent a permanent pattern from the jute lattice work appearing on one's body the following morning. I was to sleep on nothing other than a charpoy for the next four years and certainly suffered no ill effects.

I strolled over to the troop train. It consisted of about ten coaches, two dining cars and several luggage vans and there appeared to be three classes: First for officers, Second for other ranks and the Third for bearers and other servants. Each first class coach was divided into a number of four berth and two berth compartments, quite spacious and containing an icebox and a 'thunderbox' toilet. The windows, which were long and narrow with deep overhanging boarding to shade them from the fierce sun, were glazed but also had mesh mosquito screens and shutters. There were no corridors and this immediately raised the problem of how to reach the dining car for meals. Surely we were not expected to take our own food sufficient for four days. As I later discovered, we stopped for all meals and either walked along the track or along a platform when meal-times coincided with a station. No wonder the journey was to take four days.

And so the leisurely journey started a few hours later by which time I had found time to slip over to some nearby shops and buy a Bombay bowler to replace the topee which had been mysteriously lost at sea. As I entered the shop, Tom Gale strode out wearing just the hat I wanted and looking as if he had owned it all his life. The new purchase cost less than half the price of my earlier disaster which made it doubly irritating.

As we steamed out of Karachi, pulled by one of those British built locomotives which one sees all over the world, festooned with external steam pipes, cow-catchers and a large doleful sounding bell, the train passed close to Drigh Road, the home of the Aircraft Depot. We could see in the distance the airship hangar and mooring mast which had originally been erected for the ill-fated R101 and her sister ship the R100. Having been brought up near Cardington, I had always been intensely interested in these and earlier airships, and well remembered seeing the R101 set out on her last voyage, destined for Karachi but ending in tragedy at Beauvais in France a few hours later. The sight of the mooring mast brought back many memories.

Karachi receded and the train slowly puffed its way into the Sind desert, a desolate area of rock, scrub and sand which stretched for several hundred miles north of Karachi. I believe it was Wellesley who, in an earlier age, had sent despatches to London announcing 'I have Sind.' As far as I could see, he was more than welcome to it.

It was time to stop for the first meal – in the middle of nowhere. As the dining car staff walked the length of the train summoning the passengers to dinner, Hukmud Khan appeared from the rear of the train and announced that he would make up

15

my bed while I was away. A sweeper also appeared to sweep out the compartment and to empty the thunderbox. The first meal in India was curry, the first of about twelve hundred, I estimate. Although not at that time particularly keen on curry, necessity eventually converted me into a curry fancier. Surprisingly there seemed to be sufficient room in the dining car to seat and serve all the passengers at the same time, the other ranks being treated in the same way in the second class dining car. As far as I could see, our bearers and other third class passengers were expected to buy their own food at the many stations along the line where we halted.

After the meal we drifted back to our compartments along the track and resumed the game of poker which the four of us in my cabin had been playing before we stopped. Cards and reading were the only pastime as there was no scenery worth looking at and the absence of a corridor effectively insulated one from ones friends elsewhere in the train. The platform at every station at which the train stopped, and that was most of them, was thronged with a mixture of food sellers and beggars. We had been firmly warned against buying food from these vendors and the reason was easy to see. Sticky sweetmeats covered with flies and handled by grubby hands were the main delicacies on sale. Even without the warning I would certainly not have been tempted. The fruit, however, did look tempting; mangoes, bananas and several strange varieties unknown to me could be bought for next to nothing. These were not forbidden provided they were well washed in 'pinky parni' (potassium permanganate) before eating. I was impressed when Hukmud Khan produced a small bottle of these crystals which he had been trained to carry everywhere with him. I experimented with my first mango after a brief lesson from Hukmud on how to cut it and deal with the large stone. He used the method of cutting it round the centre and then twisting both ends which, in theory at least, should leave a clean stone in the middle. A more genteel method was to slice longitudinally and then carve round the stone until it could be extracted. The latter method was preferable when wearing white mess kit, and the former in the privacy of one's own bungalow, preferably in the bathroom wearing a towel.

The journey seemed endless. More time was spent at rest than in motion, the train often being diverted into a siding to allow every form of traffic to pass. I doubt whether the average speed could have been more than ten miles an hour – about half that of the *California*.

At last the scenery began to change and the temperature dropped. We all changed into blue uniform which was worn on the Frontier stations for a few months during the cold weather; this was welcome as the evenings and nights were becoming distinctly chilly with no discernible form of heating on the train. The desert gradually gave way to stony, mean-looking agricultural land and we were soon well into the Punjab which was a fairly fertile province, irrigated by the tributaries of the Indus, and lying below the foothills of the Himalayas. As we woke on the fourth morning of the journey, the train crossed the Indus, an impressive fast flowing river about the width of the Thames at Westminster at that particular point. The bridge at Attock marked the border between the Punjab and the North West Frontier Province, and so we were within an hour or two of Peshawar, the capital of the Province and the destination of the train.

To the north the mountains guarding the north west frontier of India began to encroach upon the plain of Peshawar which narrowed towards the Khyber Pass into Afghanistan. The capital stood a few miles from the entrance to this famous Pass and, as the train moved slowly through the suburbs, Peshawar was revealed as a teeming city but with large areas of tree-lined roads and many European buildings. In the warm February sunshine Peshawar looked very attractive after the endless miles of dusty plain. By this time I knew that Kohat was about 40 miles to the south west of Peshawar and that those of us who were going on would do so by road from Peshawar.

It took about an hour to transfer to the six wheeled Crossley three-ton lorries which were awaiting us. Like all military vehicles in India they were painted in sandy yellow camouflage but bore distinguishing RAF roundels. It was a slow two hour journey to Kohat along a well built tarmacadam road, one of the best along the Frontier. Kohat was separated from Peshawar by a range of hills between one and two thousand feet high through which ran the Kohat Pass; one might describe it as a miniature Khyber. I was at first mystified by the habit of the many tribesmen we passed walking in the middle of the road and appearing to give way with reluctance when vehicles approached. Herds of goat and buffalo also kept to the centre of the road and were a constant source of irritation to the drivers. However there was a reason for this behaviour which I subsequently learned. The British Government guaranteed the safety of all travellers provided that they were within three feet of the road. Those who strayed off the road were fair game in the continual blood feuding which was a feature of this tribal territory. Consequently every man carried a rifle and either a bandolier or a belt of ammunition. Many of these weapons were made in the Kohat rifle factory which we passed on our way. The most extraordinary patience and skill was needed to produce quite accurate rifles from old railway lines and any other steel the factory could obtain, using hand tools to bore out the barrels and fashion the breech mechanism.

From the top of the Pass, Kohat came into view, an oasis of green on a dusty plain, not unlike Peshawar but much smaller. A close look revealed the airfield on the outskirts of the town, a square yellowish green patch with all its buildings concentrated on the far side. The airfield looked extremely close to the mountains but that turned out to be an optical illusion as we descended to the plain. Half an hour later our Crossley turned into the gates of the RAF Officers Mess, a low single storey building set in a pleasant garden with a large two storey block of single officers quarters behind it. After almost four weeks of travelling, I had arrived on the Frontier.

CHAPTER 2

FIRST SOLO

After a few days in which to settle in at Kohat and become familiar with the unusual layout and atmosphere of a Frontier station, the time had come for me to start flying again after a break of more than two months since leaving the flat East Anglian countryside behind.

It was ten to six in the morning of the sixth of March 1933 as the 30 cwt Morris truck pulled away from the front of the Officers Mess on its daily run to take the officers to the camp, one and a half miles away. A cold clear dawn was breaking giving promise of a beautiful day. We were coming to the end of the cold weather and, by midday, it would be warm – perhaps 70° – with a hint of the hot weather to come, but we were still in our blue uniform and would remain so for a few more weeks.

The Morris, with its double row of sleepy officers in the back digesting a hasty cup of tea, trundled out of the cantonment through the surrounding barbed wire, down a long straight dusty road with the native village on one side and the aerodrome boundary opposite, and into the main gate of the camp. We dismounted outside Station Headquarters and dispersed to our places of work. For me that was C Flight, 60 Squadron, and today was to be my first acquaintance with the Westland Wapiti. Introduction to a new aeroplane is always an exciting moment for an airman, particularly when as young and inexperienced as I was.

The four aeroplanes which made up the complement of C Flight were all serviceable that morning and were being wheeled out of the hangar and through the wide gates in the barbed wire on to the tarmac apron on the aerodrome outside. The whole of the camp area, but not the aerodrome itself, was heavily wired in, with concrete pill boxes at intervals round the wire and searchlights mounted to floodlight it at night. As the hangars were inside the fence, wide gateways gave access to the aerodrome for both 27 and 60 Squadron. No aeroplanes were ever left outside the wire at night. These precautions were not so much against a threat of armed attack as against the infiltration of thieves and dacoits from the surrounding tribal territory. These perimeter fences dated from 1923 and the famous case of Molly Ellis, a young British girl who was abducted from her parents' bungalow in the middle of Kohat by Afridi tribesmen and taken into the neighbouring Tirah.

It was a cheerful scene in the chilly morning air as the tail skid of each Wapiti was lifted into a wooden trolley, obviously home made from old aeroplane wheels, with a swivelling carriage for the skid mounted between them. One of the airmen steered the tail trolley with a long handle while an assortment of airmen and Flight coolies pushed the aeroplane. Once outside the wire and lined up on the tarmac, the daily inspections were carried out and engines warmed up. As I watched the second Wapiti of C Flight being lined up and lifted out of the tail trolley, I heard a seasoned Corporal yell to one of the coolies:

'Puckaroo that bleeding tail gharry and push the burra sahib's hawajahaz on to the mutti bort jeldi.'

This astonishing order was obviously fully understood by the cheerful Indian who replied 'Achta sahib,' and set off back to the hangar with his tail trolley. With some difficulty I interpreted the order to mean: 'Pick up that bleeding tail trolley and wheel the Commanding Officer's aeroplane out onto the tarmac – as quick as you can.'

I very soon became accustomed to this colourful mixture of Urdu and English, sometimes embellished with a few choice Arabic words if the airman had been one of those unfortunates who had come on from a tour in Iraq. It was simple and to the point and both sides understood each other which was all that mattered.

The Wapiti was a completely new aeroplane to me. I could not recall ever having seen one before as they did not form the equipment of home squadrons, being largely designed as a General Purpose aircraft to fill a multitude of roles overseas. As my Flight Commander, Flight Lieutenant Geoffrey (Pop) Stemp had told me to have a good look over the aeroplane before Flying Officer Bill Coulson took me up for some initial air experience, I walked out on to the tarmac to examine J 9759 which was being serviced by its fitter and rigger. It was a two seat biplane with wings of equal length, not at all unlike the Fairey Gordon, but slightly smaller. The 480 hp Bristol Jupiter was a famous and well proven air cooled, nine cylinder radial engine, driving a very large two bladed propeller. Although liberally adorned with equipment, it had a look of rugged simplicity which inspired a lot of confidence, standing against the background of the forbidding mountain range containing the Kohat Pass a few miles north of the aerodrome. I had already seen enough of the Frontier landscape to realise that it

21

was not as hospitable to the airman as the fenland of Norfolk which I had so recently left.

While I climbed over J 9759, the two airmen explained many of its unusual features with some pride of ownership, obviously praying that this latest and youngest addition to C Flight would treat it with care and respect.

'Very good engine this, Sir, but a bastard to start when it's hot. Please don't stop it if it's needed again very soon,' said the fitter.

Many were the occasions in the future when, on some remote landing ground, my passenger and I were to wear ourselves out winding away at the low geared starting handles while perched precariously on the lower wing. They could indeed be bastards to start when hot. As the propeller was much too large to be swung by hand except by a chain of at least three airmen with a particularly strong one grasping the propeller tip, the only practical alternative to turning the handles was a fearful device called a 'bag and rope'. This consisted of twenty feet of rope with a canvas bag at one end which fitted over the propeller tip. Two or more airmen grasped the rope and, at a given signal, rushed away with it usually collapsing in a heap if the engine fired.

'Very easy to put your foot through the fuselage when you are climbing out and groping for the top step,' said the rigger with feeling as he pointed to a number of new looking fabric patches around the toe holes, of which there were four to climb up into the cockpit. It was essential to start the climb with the correct foot or one reached the cockpit facing the wrong way with a heavy parachute dangling from one's stern, and there was no alternative but to descend and start again.

While I was sitting in the cockpit studying the instruments and getting the feel of the controls, the rigger climbed up and polished the windscreen.

'We can't stop a certain amount of oil getting on to the screen during a long trip,' he said. 'It comes from the rocker box on the top cylinder and is nothing to worry about.'

22

This was a minor snag with most radial engines. We had noticed it in 35 Squadron when converting from the Fairey 111F with its liquid cooled in-line engine to the Gordon with a radial. Even the best maintainance could never prevent some oil from being thrown back along the fuselage.

'How do I use the front gun sight through an oily windscreen?' I asked the airman.

'Oh, that's all right, Sir,' he said, 'we keep a clean piece of rag down there in the map case for you to wipe the glass before firing.' Well, that seemed eminently practical to me. Speeds were not so high that you couldn't reach round the windscreen and wipe it.

The two airmen had finished their inspections and I had spent a profitable half hour, not only in finding out a great deal about the Wapiti from the two airmen who knew it inside out but in getting to know two of the men upon whom one depended so much. Naturally I was not to know it at the time, but in the two and a quarter years I spent in 60 Squadron, I cannot recall a single unpremeditated forced landing away from a landing ground due to an engine or airframe failure. That was a remarkable record and reflected immense credit upon the efficiency of the airman.

My first flight later that morning was as a passenger with Bill Coulson, a Canadian who had joined the RAF on a five year short service commission after which he had ideas of continuing flying as a civilian in Canada. He had been in 60 Squadron for a year or more and was an experienced and most capable pilot with an intimate knowledge of the Frontier. There was no dual control system in the Wapiti in the accepted sense of the term as the rear cockpit had no seat other than a small tip-up flap which the air gunner could use to rest his legs when he became tired of standing in the rotatable Scarfe gun ring which formed the top of his cockpit. There was, however, an emergency 'stick' clipped into the side of the cockpit which could be plugged into the flying controls where they passed through the rear cockpit. In an emergency, such as an injury to

23

the pilot, these controls would allow a competent gunner to steer the aeroplane back to base and, with an auxiliary throttle which was also available perhaps get it down without serious injury. It was customary to allow one's air gunner to fly the Wapiti in this way from time to time, and some of them showed considerable skill and might well have landed safely if faced with a desperate situation.

Like other new pilots, my introduction consisted of standing in the gun ring and looking over the pilot's shoulder while he demonstrated and explained the peculiarities and limitations of the aircraft through the normal means of communication, a mouthpiece on the end of rubber tubing which led into the recipient's earpieces. An air gunner, irritated with his pilot, could 'inadvertently' put his mouthpiece out into the slipstream and almost blow his pilot's head off. As a pilot could retaliate in the same way it was mutually understood that Gosport tubing, as the system was called, should be kept firmly inside the cockpits. It was a rough and ready form of instruction but adequate if taken sensibly and steadily. The characteristics of different types of aircraft were not so dissimilar at that time that they created any great difficulty for the well trained pilot.

As we taxied out on to the hard, dusty aerodrome, which was about 800 yards square, Bill explained that the Wapiti had no pronounced swing on take off – an uncomfortable habit with some types – but that the tail should not be raised too high or the tips of the sixteen foot propeller might touch any uneven piece of ground. As we lifted off in some 300 yards, Bill shouted, 'Keep her down after take off as she gains speed slowly owing to the drag caused by bomb racks and other things hanging below the wings.'

My first look at North West India from the air was fascinating. We climbed away to the north into a brilliant cloudless sky with a hard clear light which is seldom seen in England and which made the mountains appear much closer than in fact they were. Ahead lay the range of hills over which the Kohat Pass snaked and finally ran out into a wide arid plain, with the

Frontier road running as straight as a ribbon towards Peshawar which appeared as a smudge in the distance 30 miles away. Behind us, the Kohat cantonment showed up strongly as a green oasis in the otherwise drab landscape. In a country where roads, railways and rivers – traditional aids to aerial navigation – were few, the distinct outline of mountain ranges and the green oases of cantonments provided excellent alternatives.

We crossed the Kohat Pass, cruising now at 110 mph at 3,000 feet, and Bill Coulson waved his hand to the left, to the west, where a particularly savage and inhospitable area of mountains and deep gorges was coming into view.

'That is the Tirah, the home of the Afridis and the most unfriendly and inaccessible part of the Frontier. That is where Mollie Ellis was taken when she was kidnapped ten years ago. Keep out of the Tirah during your first few trips and stick to the plain, either towards Peshawar or to the south of Kohat.' As we approached Peshawar, which I was later surprised to learn had a native population of more than a million, Bill pointed out the Khyber Pass, a narrow defile which ran up into the mountains to the north west of the city containing both a road and a railway. At the top of the defile I could see that they both ended abruptly at a point which defined the frontier with Afghanistan. Flying beyond the frontier, marked along its length by infrequent white stone markers, known as the Durand Line, was forbidden except in emergency. With the exception of a few places, the border followed a line of mountain ranges, and was therefore fairly easy to identify from the air.

At this point my attention was drawn to another Wapiti catching up with us on the starboard side. I tapped Coulson on the shoulder and as the stranger drew alongside and a cheerful red face grinned at us from behind tinted goggles, Bill said, '20 Squadron, it looks like Holly.'

Squadron Leader Hollinghurst was the Commanding Officer of 20 Squadron, stationed at Peshawar. As he slipped into formation with us, his arm came over the side of his cockpit and he started to 'zog.' Zogging was a useful – indeed the only – form of communication between two pilots and consisted of a form of Morse Code. A long downward sweep of the arm with fist clenched indicated a dash, and a short downward sweep from the elbow, a dot. As Holly, if indeed it was he, zogged away, I translated the message and jotted it down on my knee pad.

WHY ARE YOU POLLUTING OUR AIR?

Bill Coulson thought for a moment and then zogged back,

IS THAT WHY YOUR AEROPLANE IS SO DIRTY?

Our visitor raised his goggles, made a suitable gesture and peeled away in a downward dive towards Peshawar aerodrome which by then was below us.

'Yes,' said Bill, 'that was Holly; I should have added Sir to my message. Before we leave Peshawar, look at the bombing range which is just north of the city. We use it occasionally and you should avoid flying over it unless you can see clearly that there are no markers laid out indicating that it is in use. There's no chance of being hit but its a bit disconcerting for a bomb aimer if an aircraft flies below him when he has started his bombing run.'

We continued in a wide sweep around the Peshawar plain to the east passing over Nowshera, a garrison town 25 miles east of Peshawar from where we could see Risalpur, our sister bomber station and the home of the two Hawker Hart squadrons, Nos 11 and 39. From this position I could clearly see the foothills of the Himalayas to the north with just a hint of gigantic snow capped peaks in the background. Many of the highest peaks, and among them Mount Everest, were within 250 miles of Risalpur and were an awe inspiring sight when seen from the air on a clear day.

Bill Coulson had climbed gently to 5,000 feet as he wished to show me the stalling characteristics of the Wapiti on the way home. The official handbook gave the stalling speed as 56 mph, but the external equipment which had been added raised it to about 60. With engine throttled back and speed allowed to fall off slowly, the stall was nothing more than a gentle sink with no tendency to drop a wing or to spin. Bill demonstrated these manoeuvres and also pointed out that, although the Wapiti was strong enough for limited aerobatics, they were never carried out as they upset the rigging and the bomb sight which was housed below a sliding panel in the floor of the rear cockpit. Accurate bomb aiming was difficult enough in a perfectly rigged aeroplane and any manoeuvre which might strain the aircraft was heavily frowned upon.

We recrossed the Kohat Pass and dropped down to 1,000 feet to join the circuit, the surface wind on this occasion being from the west which necessitated an approach over the village and the main road bordering the aerodrome.

'I find 70 a good approach speed,' said Bill, as we turned down wind and glided down the far side of the camp.

'You can reduce it a little on the final approach, but if you get below 65 the nose heaviness will tend to make her drop onto her wheels before you can get the tail down. Turn in with a little height to spare; she sideslips very steadily and you can slip off any surplus height during the last 200 feet or so.'

Even though the wind was light and steady and the temperature had not yet risen high enough to cause bumpiness, I was impressed with the steadiness of the turn in and final approach: the Wapiti might have been on rails and as Bill landed smoothly, I could see he had the stick right back in his stomach. Even so, the tail only just came down in time for a three point landing.

'Use the rudder coarsely to keep her straight, particularly if you have had to land out of wind; with no brakes and a fairly deep fuselage, she will weathercock into wind very readily if you give her half a chance.'

With these final words, we taxied in and I went through the drill for switching off before climbing out and walking back to the Flight office with Bill.

'That's about all I can show you,' he said, 'and as you have flown a Gordon, you should find it quite straightforward. Have a go after breakfast. W has been kept for you at 9.30.'

In addition to their official numbers, the four aeroplanes of C Flight were lettered W, X, Y and Z on the engine cowling and were also identified by blue wheel discs and propeller bosses. All 60 Squadron's aeroplanes carried two wide black bands around the fuselage behind the rear cockpit to distinguish them from those of 27 Squadron which had one red band.

It was five minutes to eight and the Officers Mess truck was waiting outside Station Headquarters to take those who wished to go back to breakfast, working routine being from 6 to 8 am and 9 to 1 pm. I would have preferred to have got on with my first solo but, on the other hand, the Wapiti was to be the sixth type I had flown and Bill Coulson had made it seem straightforward. A good breakfast and a few moments of leisure to meditate on the characteristics of the type seemed an excellent preparation, particularly as the weather was perfect and likely to remain so. The Mess garden was full of bananas and mango trees and I followed the custom of picking a ripe mango on the way in to breakfast. What a delicious fruit it was, picked straight from the tree and eaten within ten minutes. I have never tasted mangoes to touch those from the Kohat garden.

After breakfast Pop Stemp quizzed me briefly on the various speeds, temperatures and pressures, told me to look round the area for half an hour and then do about three landings as W was wanted again at 10.45. At least he had the confidence that it would still be serviceable at 10.45.

Six ballast weights had been fitted when I walked out to join the fitter and rigger who were waiting to start me up. Owing to its nose heaviness, the Wapiti was seldom flown solo without lead ballast weights which were clipped onto a steel bar pushed through the rear of the fuselage to simulate the weight of a passenger. They were fitted to the ends of the bar where it protruded through the fabric and could be put on or taken off in a couple of minutes.

The engine being cold started easily, much to my relief, as I had visions of exhausted, sweating airmen grinding away at the handles and quietly cursing the new boy in the cockpit for misusing the priming pump. All was well and I set off with a cheerful wave of encouragement from the fitter. The Wapiti taxied much like a Gordon, needing very coarse use of the rudder but not much throttle as the aerodrome was so hard that the tail skid slid over the surface with less braking effect than on a soft grassy English aerodrome. Taxy very slowly and don't be afaid to keep an airman holding the wing tip for as long as necessary was my first piece of advice to myself.

After turning into wind alongside the main road, watched by half a dozen small Indian boys sitting on the fence, W moved forward with very little throttle opening, the tail came up quickly and she took to the air cleanly in 250 yards with no sign of a swing. At 1,000 feet and well clear of the circuit I tried all the controls and found that she responded readily, the ailerons being rather heavy but positive and the elevator control light and sensitive to the tail trimming wheel. I spent the next half hour pottering round over the flat country to the south of Kohat, climbing, gliding, carrying out steep turns, stalling and generally getting the feel of the aeroplane.

It was good to be back at the controls again and I could tell at once that I was going to enjoy the Wapiti. Not particularly handsome to look at, perhaps, but it was solid and dependable and gave me a great feeling of confidence from the start. The emergency landing ground at Lachi, 30 miles south of Kohat, appeared under my left wing and I glided down to look at it more closely. Situated alongside the main road to Bannu, which I was unashamedly following, Lachi was typical of landing grounds dotted about the Frontier region. It looked incredibly small and was, in fact, little more than 400 yards square with a surface of hard packed sand and gravel, or 'mutti', to give it its local name. 400 yards was the minimum length for an emergency landing ground, or ELG as they were usually called. Many were longer but none shorter and, although adequate for the Wapiti, each had its own individual characteristics, needing great care and often considerable skill in using them. Small though Lachi appeared I could see that the approaches were completely flat and totally unobstructed which was some consolation. This was confirmed when another Wapiti landed there as I was circling above. As I watched this with interest, a spurt of sand erupted from the tail of the aeroplane some 50 yards in from the boundary and it stopped within 200 yards. If he could do it, so would I in due course, but meanwhile it was time to return to Kohat and make my own first landing.

I completed a circuit of the aerodrome to check the wind speed and direction from the windsock and then I closed the throttle and started my cross wind leg of the approach with the tail trimmer wound back sufficiently to give me a slight forward pressure on the stick when gliding at 70. As I had noticed when Bill Coulson was flying, it was extremely steady in the glide, indicating that it had not been his skill so much as the inherent stability of the aeroplane. I turned in, perhaps a little late, as there was no need to side slip and crossed the road at 50 feet. The view over the nose with the propeller lazily turning over was excellent, and I rounded out at what I judged to be 2 feet at 65 mph. Although I eased the stick gently back, being afraid of ballooning if I brought it back too smartly, it was not enough to prevent W from sinking on to her wheels with the tail still up. Perfectly safe, but not a text book landing and a very good demonstration to me of the nose heaviness. Two more circuits and landings produced better results but I had still not achieved the three point arrival. Nevertheless I felt the critics on the tarmac, and there were always plenty of those, would not have found too much to chuckle about.

'Well done, Sir,' said my rigger as I climbed out after switching off, 'three landings and you walked away from all of them. They must have been good ones.'

The least I could say in reply was, 'She's so beautifully rigged that she landed herself.'

Pop Stemp seemed satisfied and doubtless slightly relieved

that the newest recruit to his Flight, which boasted only four aeroplanes and five pilots, had at least taken the first step without disaster. He suggested that it would be quite in order for me to stand him a Murree beer in the Mess at lunchtime, a suggestion which, as one o'clock came round, appeared to have been overhead by every other officer in the squadron. I didn't feel that my performance equated to a golfer who has just holed out in one and is expected to treat everybody in the clubhouse, but nevertheless I was more than happy to subscribe to the old adage – 'any reason is a good reason for a party.'

CHAPTER 3

CARDS SHOULD ALWAYS BE DROPPED

After settling in and surmounting the important hurdle of getting airborne in the Wapiti, it was time to tackle some of my social duties which were an important and necessary part of life in our small Kohat community. The first of these, which was punctiliously observed by every junior officer, was to call upon the married officers, certain civilians and the Regiments which made up the Kohat Brigade.

In my luggage reposed two small white cardboard boxes, each containing fifty visiting cards printed for me before leaving home by Messrs Gale and Polden of Aldershot from my own engraved copper plate and identifying me as 'Mr D J P Lee, Royal Air Force.' My rank would not appear on my cards until I became a Flight Lieutenant – a distant milestone for a Pilot Officer in 1933. These small scraps of pasteboard, each one separated from the next by a thin sheet of tissue paper, would be an essential part of my social equipment for the next five years or so. It was important that they should be engraved: printed cards, which could easily be identified by their smooth surface, were regarded as a form of economy which no officer was expected to practise. A strict form of etiquette was required within about a month of arriving at Kohat or any of the other Frontier stations, and no officer was considered entirely acceptable if he failed to observe the custom of calling.

The Mess Secretary maintained a well thumbed list of local dignitaries, messes and families in the cantonment, with advice as to their importance in the social hierarchy. From this list and with plenty of irreverent advice from friends, you compiled the shortest list which seemed to satisfy the social requirements. It could usually be divided into three parts. In the first and most important section came those with whom you would be closely associated, namely the Station Commander, Squadron and Flight Commanders, and the RAF married officers. No time should be lost in showing them that you were a well bred and good mannered officer! Into the second, but hardly less impor- tant category, came various civil dignitaries such as the Chief of Police, magistrates, etc. Lastly it was incumbent upon you to call on other officers messes which in the case of Kohat, were those of British and Indian Army units. This personal list might con- tain twenty or thirty calls and would clearly occupy a consider- able amount of time.

You were now ready to play the 'calling' game, the rules for which were strict and well understood both by those who 'called' and those who were 'called upon'. In the first place the timing of your call was important. You did not arrive so early in the afternoon that the recipients of your call were still enjoying their siesta on their charpoys nor so late that they were about to change for cocktails or dinner. No earlier than half past four and no later than half past five was an acceptable bracket which obviously restricted the number of calls you could achieve in one sortie. Correct dress was as important as correct timing. It was not acceptable to drop your cards in tennis shorts on your way to play in a game at the Club at five o'clock, nor was it good enough to appear in a dinner jacket very late in the 'calling' bracket at, say, a quarter to six, in the hope of a few quick drinks before going on to a dinner engagement. The right and proper dress was a lounge suit (which could of course be a tropical one during the hot weather) collar and tie and a 'Bombay Bowler'.

Ready for the first 'calling' session, suitable transport had to be selected. Very few impecunious junior officers possessed cars and it was usual to go round on a bicycle. If no bicycle was available, it was possible to hire a 'tonga'* from the cab rank which was always sleeping outside the mess gates. It was certainly not wise to go calling on foot. Distances were considerable and it might be necessary to walk two miles in the dust and heat. A bicycle was quite the most convenient transport and, moreover, it was less obtrusive than the jingling harness and bell of a tonga – an important factor in the game to be played.

You approached the first bungalow on an itinerary which had been carefully drawn up to cover as many residences as possible in the short time available. Attached to the gatepost of every bungalow was a small square box with the owner's name and NOT AT HOME neatly painted on the front and a slot for visiting cards in the top. In theory this box was for use when the residents were away, but in practice it was always used unless the resident appeared and intercepted the caller before he had deposited his cards in the box and departed. That was a rare occurrence as the married officers did not wish to have to entertain individual callers almost every afternoon and those calling would have taken months to complete their list if continually invited in. The game was, therefore, to slip the cards into the box

* A horse drawn trap widely used in India as a taxi.

as unobtrusively as possible without, of course, being furtive, taking no notice if a head should be glimpsed peering round a curtain inside the bungalow. The resident, fully understanding the game, was endeavouring to keep in the background and to avoid embarrassing the caller. If, however, as you approached you saw the resident in his garden, dressed in his pyjamas and rubbing the sleep from his eyes, you passed quietly on without dropping your cards, giving the impression that you had not intended to stop in any case. He was clearly in no state to entertain you – which courtesy would have required him to do had you stopped – and his wife was probably even less prepared. Mess intelligence might have told you that certain people were away on holiday. This was an opportunity not to be missed and you hastened to drop your cards in their boxes at once, even doing so on your way to work or to tennis in this instance as there was no possibility of interception. This was a perfectly acceptable procedure.

After completing the calls in the top section of your list, and dropping two cards each time (one for the husband and one for his wife) the game was played in reverse and the husband would return your call. This consisted of placing one of his cards in your letter rack in the mess, and in addition, he usually returned your two cards, knowing full well how valuable they were. A little work with an india rubber and some breadcrumbs made them fit to use again and, in this way, it was quite possible to make a hundred cards last a full five year tour. This part of the game was completed when you subsequently returned the husband's card so that he could make further use of it.

The next section of the calling list containing civilians and important government dignitaries presented no great problems except that they were usually very scattered and necessitated a good deal of hard pedalling. Some possessed visitors books to be signed, others had the usual NOT AT HOME box. Even if these calls were returned, which was not obligatory, your own cards were not and had to be 'written off'.

Calling upon other officers' messes required a different procedure but one which was equally formal and strictly observed. It was clearly inappropriate for a mess to have a NOT AT HOME box screwed to the gate post and it was, therefore, impossible to get away with an unobtrusive approach and hasty departure, hoping that your activities had passed unseen. It was necessary to cycle – or take a tonga as a silent approach no longer mattered – to the entrance to the mess and to enter the hall in search of the visitors book which was usually kept on a small table with a silver salver for cards. In a mess such as that belonging to Skinner's Horse this search might take some time as the hall was bound to be littered with piles of drums, elephant's feet probably holding polo sticks and gigantic trophies which had been 'liberated' during past campaigns and incidents, such as the Boxer Rebellion, in which the regiment had taken part. When you eventually found the visitors book, you signed it and left two cards on the salver. These had to be inscribed in handwriting in the top left hand corner, one for 'The Commanding Officer' and the other for 'PMC and Officers'. These cards would not be returned, but as they had been defaced they were in any case valueless for further use. It was most unlikely that you would be interrupted during the two or three minutes spent in the hall. What usually happened was that a subaltern rushed through on his way to the polo ground grabbing a polo stick from an elephant's foot as he went and was somewhat embarrassed to find a smartly dressed visitor signing the book. He was in duty bound to pause and at least welcome you, apologise for the fact that the bar was not yet open and hope that you would attend a future mess function. You thanked him and hoped that you were not detaining him from his engagement and took your leave. Honour was satisfied and with expressions of mutual good will, you mounted your bicycle or your tonga and went on your way.

There were one or two tactical ploys which were worth adopting when calling on other messes. It was no bad thing to arrive towards the end of the stipulated period at, say, half past five and to be accompanied by another officer who was also paying his duty call. Two advantages might accrue if you were lucky.

The timing was very close to the normal bar opening time and the presence of two visitors might justify some slight advancement of that time. This in turn could develop into a small party which could be greatly to the advantage of inter Service relations. This game, like that of calling on the married families, was also played in reverse, somewhat to the disadvantage of the Royal Air Force. Newly arrived regimental officers would call upon us singly or in pairs and would be suitably entertained if caught in the act. As Kohat boasted a Brigade Headquarters and at least five regiments of cavalry, infantry and supporting arms, there were far more subalterns to call upon our one mess than there were RAF officers to descend upon the Army. As, in addition, we had an excellent reputation for hospitality, the 'mess guest' charge on our mess bills at the end of the month could be substantial.

I started my round of calling one cool and pleasant afternoon in the company of Bob Carter, who had come out with me in the *California*. Our second-hand bicycles had cost us £1 each and were the obvious vehicles to use on this occasion. All went well and we dropped our cards in six NOT AT HOME boxes, all belonging to RAF officers. There was still time for one more call and we decided to pay our respects to Hodson's Horse, one of the two Indian Cavalry Regiments stationed in Kohat. Their mess was almost next door to the Club which we had intended to visit for a cool drink after our exhausting cycle tour. However, this did not materialise as we were caught in the act of signing Hodson's visitors book by a young second lieutenant returning from a hard game of squash. His need was even greater than ours and we were well entertained for half an hour when courtesy dictated that we should leave. That afternoon had cost me fourteen of my valuable cards but I could expect to see twelve of them back again.

Taking advantage of every suitable opportunity I worked my way through my list and completed the essential calls in about a fortnight. It then remained only to wait for invitations to cocktails and dinner to come pouring in. The flood was often slow in starting but I had been advised not to develop an inferiority complex. Suitable invitations would arrive, I was assured, if I were patient. Many factors were involved; the time of year, the generosity of various families and even the information on my visiting card which would be scrutinised most carefully by all the recipients. If, for example, one was fortunate (or unfortunate) enough to have one's card inscribed 'Flight Lieutenant, The Hon George Beauchamp-Cholmondeley-Majoribanks', one's prospect of receiving a quick invitation to dine was infinitely better than if it simply announced one as 'Mr D J P Lee'. An engraved plate with the former inscription would of course have cost at least five times as much as the latter, and would probably have necessitated a large visiting card of a size more appropriate to a lady. I was quite satisfied with my brief inscription and knew that it would eventually produce plenty of invitations, particularly from our own RAF families who were always extremely hospitable to the young bachelors. The first invitation was not long in arriving from a Squadron Leader and his wife who asked a number of the new arrivals to drinks one Saturday evening. Before leaving for the party one of the officers who knew our host and hostess well, said: 'Be very careful what you drink.'

He refused to elaborate on this cryptic remark, but an hour later I fully understood.

The Squadron Leader and his wife were both teetotallers and, furthermore, they knew little or nothing about drinks. Nevertheless they were most hospitable and punctilious about inviting the new boys along to their bungalow. All their drinks were kept in dark cut glass decanters with silver labels round their necks to identify the contents. Whether by design or by the carelessness of the servants, the labels were frequently wrong and as it was impossible to tell what was in each decanter through the dark glass and considered bad form to be seen smelling the contents, some very strange drinks were poured out. I should say that each guest was greeted with the remark: 'We don't know much about drinks, so please help yourself.'

Those in the know had devised ways of disguising the fact

that they were identifying the contents but the unwary, like myself, had to suffer during the first visit.

I poured myself out a generous tipple from the decanters labelled Whisky and topped it up from one labelled water only to find I had taken what I later decided was sherry and gin. That was bad enough, but such concoctions as sherry and soda, whisky and gin and others too terrible to name were quite common. After an uncomfortable half hour I managed to dispose of most of my powerful drink while my hostess was otherwise engaged, but it was difficult to keep a straight face when she told me, a propos of nothing in particular, that she could not understand why she could never make pot plants grow in the house when all her friends did so well with them. They were a charming and warm hearted couple and I believe that some time later, one of the more senior officers plucked up courage to let them into the secret of the dying pot plants. Anyway, the day arrived when bottles took the place of the dark glass decanters. The plants lived happily ever after and no guest ever again took his leave either in an inebriated state or having had nothing but water – and water!

On the same evening that I made my first aquaintance with the 'mixed drinks' party, a few of us decided to go to the cinema after dinner. Kohat boasted a civilian cinema up in the bazaar area, about half a mile from the Mess and outside the cantonment perimeter wire. The evening performance started at 10 pm, a very convenient time for all the officers in the Kohat garrison, most of whom had to dine in Mess each night. Four of us set off at 9.30 and decided to walk as it was a beautiful night and there seemed no point in going to the expense of taking a tonga, several of which were waiting expectantly outside the Mess gates. Externally the cinema looked quite normal, a small fairly scruffy building covered with advertisements in both Urdu and English. The first thing that caught my eye as we lined up to pay our one Rupee at the box office was a pile of rifles neatly stacked beside it: not Lee Enfield service rifles, but every conceivable sort of home made, strange looking weapon tied together with wire, pieces of tin and even string.

The mystery was explained as we went up to a low balcony on which the one rupee seats were placed. Below us, the first dozen rows were separated from the rest of the auditorium by a barbed wire entanglement and were filled with a noisy and extremely smelly collection of tribesmen, some of whom had apparently trudged into Kohat from tribal territory to enjoy the silent film. Talkies had not penetrated to Kohat by 1933. The rule of the house was that all weapons had to be left at the door and, as the tribesmen knew that the cinema was a protected place, they were quite happy to abide by this rule. The audience was divided into three distinct sections: officers in a colourful array of mess kits and other burra sahibs and memsahibs in evening dress on the balcony, soldiers, airmen and both British and Indian civilians in the centre and the tribesmen beyond the wire in front. The extraordinary thing to me about this scene was the cheerful friendliness of this ruffianly looking gang. Somehow one expected an anti-British attitude but that was far from the case. Hostility on the Frontier was almost entirely inter-tribal and the main British role was that of maintaining peace amongst the tribes by protecting the weaker, law abiding majority against a minority of powerful lawless tribal leaders. And so those villagers who walked into the cinema regarded the British as their protectors, without whose presence their lives would constantly be in jeopardy. Promptly at ten o'clock the five year old film got under way with much hawking, spitting and chewing of betelnut from the four anna seats. Not surprisingly these conditions discouraged the ladies with the result that, apart from a few stalwart wives, they tended to view the cinema with a good deal of disfavour.

If it was female company one wanted, the centre of Kohat's social life was the Gymkhana Club, a rambling single storey building overlooking the polo ground. Every officer paid a modest monthly subscription to the club which, apart from the facilities for drinking, dining and gossiping, had some well kept mutti tennis courts and a nine hole golf course laid out round the polo ground. The juxtaposition of polo and golf produced interesting hazards for the players of both games. A well hooked drive from the second tee would not infrequently score through the polo goal posts and a hard and inaccurate polo shot would finish on the third green, occasionally followed by a polo pony.

The young ladies of the 'fishing fleet', a term with which I became increasingly disenchanted, naturally tended to meet in the club and here they were less heavily chaperoned than in the *California*. Penelope was the only one to interest me – an interest shared, I may say, by three of my fellow officers. Penny was the niece of a Major in Hodson's Horse. She was twenty, not particularly pretty but cheerful, good company and a splendid tennis player. She certainly was not on the lookout for a husband and accepted the attentions of all of us impartially. When she departed for home in about May, we all saw her off on her way to catch the Frontier Mail at Peshawar and not one of us could boast of having received more favours from her than the others.

Penny came with me one Sunday to the curry tiffin at the Peshawar Club. It was probably my turn to take her out and we set off with four others in a famous old 30/98 Vauxhall owned by Jack Atkins, one of the few car owners in the Mess. The Vauxhall was an open four seater and, with Penny clutching her straw hat in the back seat, Jack set off at his usual cracking pace until the steep hairpin bends of the Kohat Pass produced the usual clouds of steam from the overtaxed engine.

'Not to worry,' said Jack, 'she's at her best when she's hot.'

The top of the Pass had a wide parking place, doubtless designed for the purpose of allowing overheated engines to cool down. Here we stopped, partly to admire the view and partly to let Jack replenish the radiator from the two gallon can of water which he always carried strapped to the running board. It was the first time I had stopped to look at the view and on this gin clear Sunday morning it was worth pausing to take it in. To the

41

south, Kohat lay immediately below, and to the north Peshawar was clearly visible more than twenty miles away across the plain. A six thousand foot wall of mountains to the west guarded the Tirah and, even on that bright morning, it looked threatening and inhospitable.

When the 30/98 had cooled, we set off down the north side of the Pass and now it was the turn of the brakes to overheat.

'Still not to worry,' said Jack, 'I keep another can of water to cool the brakes; let me know if the smell becomes unbearable in the back or if they catch fire.'

They didn't and gradually the smell of overheated brake linings dispersed as we reached level ground and rattled on to Peshawar, scattering goats and tribesmen alike.

The Club car park was nearly full as it always was on Sunday morning; the curry tiffin attracted a large gathering from all the neighbouring outstations, Nowshera, Risalpur, Kohat and Landi Kotal, as well as Peshawar itself. It was a great gathering of friends and we were soon knocking back gin slings, Tom Collins or Murree beer at one of the tables set out on the Club lawn. One of the regimental bands was playing *Ain't Misbehavin'* on the bandstand over by the tennis courts. The arrival of Kiwi Broughton and a contingent from Risalpur almost caused Penny to change her affections when she heard of the astounding superiority of the Hart over the ageing Wapiti and the sympathy with which we poor Kohat chaps were regarded by Risalpur. As a Hart was, at that moment, sitting on our aerodrome at Kohat with an internal coolant leak and awaiting a new engine, we were able to counter that there was little point in having a superior aeroplane if it spent most of its time on the ground. This technical talk only stopped, doubtless to Penny's relief, when tiffin was announced. The Peshawar curry was superb – chicken on this and most other occasions – and it was served by a long line of small boys, each smartly dressed in white with a red fez and each bearing a dish of a different ingredient for the curry. This line of boys wound its way through the dining room from table to table until each plate was heaped with every delicacy from Bombay Duck to peanuts and Mango chutney to pineapple.

Silence fell on the club dining room for twenty minutes. Discussion on Harts versus Wapitis, polo ponies and the last meet of the Peshawar Vale drag hunt ceased, and little was heard beyond the occasional grunt of approval. Back to the table on the lawn we went and ordered black coffee to offset the irresistible desire to sleep. The sun was hot and the light excessively bright but we were forty miles from our charpoys and only Penny seemed unaffected by the curry and the gin. The old Vauxhall rumbled happily back to Kohat, even forgetting to boil on the Pass although Jack had refilled his watering can in anticipation.

'What we all need is a hard game of tennis,' said Penny, as we descended towards the cantonment, 'I have booked a court for 4 o'clock and Margaret will join us.'

Polite but unmistakable groans were heard above the rattle of the engine, and the others looked at me. I knew exactly what they were thinking; I was the duty escort and it was my responsibility to look after Penny. Well, I was fond of tennis and it was obvious that tennis would be a good antidote to Peshawar curry, and so John Pope and I put on a half-hearted show of enthusiasm and played three strenuous sets on the Club courts before winding up the Sunday by taking Penny and Margaret to the cinema to see a film which we afterwards discovered they had both seen before but in quite different surroundings – not separated from the screen by barbed wire and pungent tribesmen.

These first few weeks at Kohat were giving me an unduly rosy picture of life on a Frontier station. The climate was perfect – day after day of warm sunny weather which made flying a joy after the winter rain and bad visibility of East Anglia. Social life was at its peak with every Mess holding its annual ball and most of the sporting competitions taking place between the various units. It was no wonder that the fishing fleet returned home, starry eyed and eloquent over the delights of British

India, before the weather hotted up and the Frontier became a steaming cauldron of discomfort from which all but the toughest wives and, of course, the nursing sisters, fled to the hill stations.

CHAPTER 4

TRIBAL RECONNAISSANCE

The first twenty hours or so in the Wapiti were spent in familiarising myself with its equipment, armament and general flying characteristics. Being the least experienced pilot in C Flight, I was given more than my fair share of flying during my first few weeks, dropping $8\frac{1}{2}$ lb practice bombs on our own range to the south of the aerodrome, firing the guns on the firing range to the east, taking vertical and oblique photographs and practising forced landings either on the aerodrome or on the emergency landing ground at Lachi. Within a month I was ready to take my place as a fully fledged, if not very experienced member of the Flight, capable of undertaking most missions. I liked the Wapiti immensely and developed a warm affection for its robust simplicity and reliability. It had no vices and forgave one's small mistakes, which were not infrequent.

One of the tasks which I was looking forward to with some eagerness was a tribal reconnaissance. For the purpose of showing the flag and ensuring that the tribes remained constantly aware of the presence of British forces, all the Frontier squadrons participated in a regular series of demonstration flights, planned to cover the whole Frontier at frequent intervals.

The Frontier was divided into three areas for the purpose of these flights. A Northern area comprised the region to the north of the Khyber Pass up to the foothills of the Himalayas, inhabited largely by the Mohmand tribes. From the northern periphery of the Peshawar plain the ground rose steadily, intersected by narrow defiles and deep gorges through the territory of the Wali of Swat until the high peaks of the Himalayas marked the boundary of the area. Flying through and beyond those peaks towards Chinese Turkestan, often referred to as the 'Roof of the World', was confined to one or two restricted and dangerous routes such as that which followed the gorge of the river Indus. The routine tribal reconnaissances did not penetrate this high country where many of the peaks exceeded 20,000 feet. It was a desolate and awe inspiring area but, strangely enough, a relatively friendly place as those unfortunate enough to come down in it found to their relief. When Joe Shaw from Risalpur was forced down on one occasion by engine failure due to carburetter icing on his Hart, he landed upside down in six feet of snow and both he and his air gunner escaped injury. He was looked after extremely well by the Wali of Swat personally and eventually made his way back to his station, but his aeroplane was quite inaccessible and was never recovered.

The second or Central area was smaller and lay south west of the Khyber Pass roughly between the rivers Kabul and Kurram. Although less awesome than some parts of the northern area, it was universally mountainous, criss-crossed by deep valleys and dried up water courses. The Tirah, as this region was called, was the home of the Afridis, perhaps the most lawless and hostile of all the Frontier tribes. Their cruelty was legendary and a forced landing in Afridi territory was viewed with the greatest trepidation. However, money works wonders. And there are several recorded instances of airmen being brought in by Afridis to collect the reward of 5,000 rupees offered in the 'ghoolie chit' which every aircrew carried permanently with him as a protection against some of the more unspeakable practices of the tribesmen. A Flight Lieutenant Anderson from Peshawar crashed heavily in a particularly hostile part of the Tirah one morning and broke his leg. The Afridis who dragged him from the wreckage carried him 70 miles on a string charpoy to Peshawar to claim the reward. It was a terrible journey for a man with a fractured leg and no medical treatment, and so impressed were the tribesmen by the courage he displayed that they sent a deputation to Peshawar hospital every week until he recovered to enquire about his progress.

The third reconnaissance region was the Southern area which lay to the south west of Kohat, from the Kurram river down towards Fort Sandeman and Baluchistan. This was Waziristan, the home of the famous Faqir of Ipi, the scourge of the British on that part of the Frontier for more than forty years. Although he was hunted and hounded for all that time by British and Indian troops, and by the RAF, he eventually died peacefully in his cave at a venerable age long after the British had left India and his territory had become part of Pakistan.

Unless some large scale show of force was deemed necessary to put pressure upon a particularly dissident area, the routine tribal reconnaissances were usually flown by a flight of three aircraft. Each route was carefully planned so that tribes and villages with a bad history of trouble making were well covered, the aircraft often descending over them to leave the villagers in no doubt that they were being watched. The more isolated police posts and Frontier Force garrisons were circled by one or more of the aircraft and messages exchanged. Most of the emergency landing grounds in the area were either inspected from the air or visited by one of the flight while the remainder circled above. In short, the RAF presence was made as widely known as possible throughout the reconnaissance area, not only to the tribesmen but to the British forces and police as well. The flights were quite lengthy – three hours or more in duration – and were tiring but extremely interesting.

My first experience of tribal reconnaissance came before the hot weather arrived in earnest: it was a reconnaissance of the southern area in early May, led by the Flight Commander, Pop Stemp, with Bill Coulson and myself flying as Nos 2 and 3 in the formation. It was planned to be a long flight, visiting several landing grounds and police posts on the way round and landing at Miramshah to refuel and have lunch before returning to Kohat. As we were due to take off at 8 o'clock in the morning, breakfast in the Mess would be out of the question and so Hukmud Khan produced tea and biscuits for me at 5.30 and also a flask to carry with me on the flight. As usual it was a bright, clear morning with the Kohat Pass standing out sharply against a deep, almost Mediterranean blue sky. This visibility, as I knew, would not last all day – the hotter weather was causing an increasing amount of heat haze to rise as the day wore on and by the afternoon visibility would have deteriorated considerably. So it was important to carry out these flights early in the day but not before villagers were out and about at their daily work and could see the aeroplanes and hopefully, be suitably impressed by the might of the British Raj.

For an hour before take off we marked up our maps with the route which Pop Stemp had decided upon. It included two areas, one at Datta Khel on the Tochi river, and one near Razmak in the Faqir of Ipi's country which we had been instructed to circle round several times at low altitude as both were current hotbeds of tribal blood feuding. It was decided that the three aircraft would remain together for most of the reconnaissance but when we reached the southern end of the area, I was to break away and land at Drazinda to inspect the landing ground, followed by a communication practice with the Frontier Force post at Alexandra Picquet at the head of the Razmak valley. I was then to make my way to Miramshah, land and rejoin the Flight for refuelling and lunch. Similarly Bill Coulson was detailed to land and inspect Sora Rogha landing ground and then to conduct a communications exercise with a police post in the same area. Pop Stemp had decided to land at Razmak which housed the headquarters of an Indian infantry Brigade, and to acquaint the Brigadier with any information from the two areas which we had been specifically asked to examine.

All three Wapitis had cameras fitted so that photographs of any unusual activity, damage to a landing ground or the construction of a new road could be taken for intelligence or other purposes. This was to be fairly typical of the tasks allotted to tribal reconnaissance flights which, from our point of view, were of immense training value as they combined in one exercise so many of the tasks which the Wapiti could peform. In addition, our guns were to be loaded and we would be carrying a full complement of ammunition. This was a standard procedure on these flights and, although we did not expect to fire our guns, it was not unheard of for a police post to call for supporting fire against marauding tribesmen.

As we came to the end of our briefing, in which our three air gunners had participated and marked up their own maps, Pop Stemp said, 'We'll fly in loose formation: don't come closer than three spans unless I call you in. We are not trying to impress anybody with our formation flying and I want you to be free enough to keep an eye open for anything unusual on the ground.'

We walked out to our aeroplanes and before climbing in I said to Sanderson, who was flying with me as usual, 'When we land at Drazinda, I dare not stop the engine in case we can't start it again. Will you get out and check the petrol stocks and Verey cartridges in the hut while I taxy round the perimeter and have a look at the boundary markings and the windsock. See whether the chowkidar (watchman) is on duty – he should be at that time of day – and ask him whether he has anything to report. Your Urdu is better than mine, anyway.'

'Right, Sir,' said Sanderson, 'I've been to Drazinda once or twice and you may find quite a bit of wind there as the landing ground stands up on an exposed ridge. If the wind is strong, I'll hang on to your wingtip when you taxy up into the narrow neck where it can sometimes be difficult to turn without help.'

'Thanks. That's a good point,' I said, 'What is the surface like?'

'Excellent,' he replied, 'it's quite firm yellow sand and the chowkidar keeps it pretty free from big stones, straying donkeys and goats. I think its one of the best landing grounds we have.'

I had, of course, studied the details of Drazinda in the official handbook but the personal knowledge of Sanderson was not only valuable but comforting as this was to be my first inspection of one of the many landing grounds dotted along the Frontier. No two were alike, varying widely in size, shape, altitude, gradient and surface. Some were perched precariously on hillsides, some on the floor of deep valleys and few, very few, out on the open plain. Where they had been constructed alongside army garrisons or police posts, it was usual to fire a Verey light over the post indicating one's intention to land. This brought out a few soldiers or policemen who ensured that any goalposts or other temporary obstructions were removed and who were ready to receive the aircraft when it landed. On these inhabited landing grounds several of the garrison troops had usually been taught how to operate the winding handles on a Wapiti and so it was reasonably safe to stop the engine. Drazinda was, though, one of the isolated places with no occupants other than a chowkidar, and consequently no facilities or assistance of any kind. It was highly dangerous to enlist the help of most of the chowkidars or any itinerant natives to help with the handle winding. If the engine backfired, as it often did, the sweating, terrified men on the handles could easily fall into the propeller which would probably mean a new propeller, and most certainly a new chowkidar. Even among disciplined troops and policemen, engine starting was not a popular task and all pilots and air gunners had to take the greatest care to see that the wheels were properly chocked and the men correctly positioned at the winding handles, with strict instructions to stand still if smoke and flames belched out after a backfire. Once they had seen that no harm came to them, it was all right, but of course there was always a first time. Although crude and clumsy in the extreme, the bag and rope technique was sometimes safer as at least the human chain was running away from the propeller if it suddenly decided to spin round. I dreaded having to use unskilled labour for engine starting, but at times there was no alternative.

Precisely at 8 o'clock Pop Stemp led the Flight smoothly into the air and we climbed steadily westwards along the Hangu valley with the jagged landscape of the Tirah rising to 10,000 feet and above on our right. Levelling out at 5,000 feet we approached Thal, at which point the tribal reconnaissance officially began. Thal had an emergency landing ground built up on a large escarpment in the centre of the valley and in the bright morning light it looked exactly like an aircraft carrier, with one side dropping steeply down to the Kurram river which was flowing fast at that time of year, carrying the melted snow from the high peaks which marked the frontier beyond the Tirah down through Bannu and out into the plains of the Punjab.

We carried on to the west but as we passed over Thal I looked to my right up the Kurram river which came down through a wide fertile valley, greener than any part of the Frontier I had so far seen. At the head of the valley, almost crouching under snow capped peaks, I could just make out the sandy smudge of Parachinar, one of the most attractive small British outposts. The landing ground was almost 6,000 feet above sea level and, with a formidable gradient of 1 in 16, was regarded as one of the

51

two really difficult landing grounds on the Frontier, the other being Razmak which we were to see later in the flight. We did not go up the Kurram valley which, for reconnaissance purposes, was part of the central area and therefore no concern of ours at the moment.

Leaving the Kurram and turning some 20 degrees to port, Pop Stemp led us towards the valley of the Tochi river, another major watercourse which had its source up in the high peaks of Waziristan and flowed down to join the Kurram as they ran down into the plains. As the Tochi came into view ahead of us, Stemp throttled back slightly and we began to lose height, dropping down to 2,000 feet above the river which lay in a valley about a mile wide at this point. Keeping to the right bank we flew up to Datta Khel, a fortified frontier village with a large police post standing well above it. Although this was some miles short of the Durand Line itself, which was up in the formidable mountain range beyond the village, it marked the turning point for our flight and was also the first of the two areas to which we had to pay particular attention.

The Tochi valley was one of the popular routes taken by dacoits and raiding parties entering British India from Afghanistan and Datta Khel a well known hotbed of intrigue; hence the large and busy police post. As we approached at 2,000 feet, Stemp signalled us to close formation and Bill Coulson and I tucked ourselves in behind his wing tips. At the same time our gunners removed their Lewis guns from the safe stowages inside their cockpits and mounted them in the firing positions on the gun rings. This was always done during a low level demonstration so that tribesmen could clearly see the guns from the ground and understand the threat they represented.

Losing more height, we swung left around the village and the police post at 1,000 feet and flew back up the far side of the river. We repeated the manoeuvre and, on the second occasion, passed low over the village at 500 feet before climbing away up the valley to the east once more. I was interested to see that whereas the village had seemed almost deserted when we first appeared, everybody had rushed out of their huts at the sound of the aeroplanes and on the second run a big throng of upturned faces greeted us, but I couldn't see any waving or friendly greeting. Datta Khel had a bad reputation; it had been the scene of many skirmishes with British and Indian troops over the years and known to be under the domination of marauding bands from across the frontier.

We were now climbing towards the Faqir of Ipi's territory which lay between Datta Khel and Razmak where the frontier was buried among peaks higher than anywhere along its length, grim, terrifying jagged peaks rising to more than 11,000 feet. Somewhere in this awe inspiring tangle of rocks and deep nullahs the crafty old Faqir lived, constantly moving from cave to cave, always one step ahead of the men of Razmak Brigade who pursued him relentlessly, and always with sufficient time and resources to continue with his raids on innocent villagers or British outposts.

The ground beneath us was rising almost as steeply as we could climb and Pop Stemp was leading us across a shoulder between the Tochi and Razmak valleys. With this shoulder running sharply up to our right, I had the uncomfortable impression of being a fly crawling along a rough, jagged wall. By the time we reached the Razmak valley, 7,000 feet was showing on our altimeters although we were little more than 2,000 feet above the ground. Stemp was keeping us in such a position that, if anything went wrong, we could glide down to the valley on the left with some hope of finding somewhere to crash land in reasonably friendly territory. At this point my eye was caught by a flash of light high up on the mountain to my right. Glancing towards the source of the flash, I saw a small puff of white smoke, quickly followed by a second one. Without much doubt we were being fired at and I pointed this out to Sanderson.

'Well, it's quite common in this area but they haven't a hope of hitting us.' he said, 'Occasionally a bullet hole is found after these flights but the old Wapiti can take plenty of those without much damage.'

Nobody else in the formation seemed to have noticed or at any rate been perturbed by this little incident.

Before reaching the British camp at Razmak, we again closed formation, our passengers having left their guns in the firing position for this, our second demonstration over a village which was known to harbour Ipi's followers, and which had given Razmak Brigade a great deal of trouble in recent months. We repeated the Datta Khel performance but this time it was much more difficult to maintain a tight formation. It was 9.30 and the sun was just beginning to make the heat rise from the mass of rocks below us. It would be a great deal rougher by midday but it was quite bad enough even as early as this. To add to the discomfort I was at the bottom of the formation during our left handed turns over the village, and so uncomfortably close to the huts at times. Pop Stemp was nothing if not thorough and made certain that every man, woman and child in the village saw us at close quarters and heard us. Struggling to hold my position I had no time to wonder whether the odd bullet might come our way and how well placed I was to stop it. In view of this situation and the earlier incident, I made a mental note to ask Miramshah to have a particularly close look at the wings and fuselage for bullet holes during our lunchtime break.

Climbing back to 2,000 feet above the floor of the valley and remaining in close formation in order to appear neat and tidy to the garrison, we roared over Razmak camp where Stemp was to return later on. I had no time to study the camp or the landing ground which was usually regarded as the most difficult on the Frontier, suitable for Wapitis but banned for Harts. I made up my mind to study it more closely on my way back to Miramshah when I would be on my own with time to spare.

On down the Razmak valley to Wana which was another big garrison station of the Frontier Force Rifles. Wana too had its own landing ground with which I was to become extremely familiar during the next few months. It was square, dead flat with unobstructed approaches, but it was very small. Its 400 yard sides were the minimum allowed, and although under good conditions quite adequate, it could be very difficult if the weather was bad.

In another ten minutes Drazinda appeared ahead, the southern point of our flight. As we flew over the landing ground, Pop Stemp signalled to me to break away and with an acknowledging wave I banked steeply to the left into a downward spiral. The first thing to do was to circle the landing ground at about 1,000 feet and study it closely. Whereas most of these landing grounds were constructed in the shape of a square or a cross or a single runway, Drazinda was unusual in being shaped like a fat banana curving through an angle of about sixty degrees. Even at its broadest point it was hardly wide enough to land straight across the banana, and so it was necessary to plan ones approach and landing at the tangent to the curve nearest to the wind direction.

I could see no obstructions on the surface, the wind sock was indicating a gentle breeze from the east and the white boundary markers stood out clearly and looked freshly painted.

'The chowkidar is there,' said Sanderson over my shoulder, pointing to a small hut in one corner with a figure in white standing beside it. I selected my line of approach, almost into wind, which would give me a good 600 yard landing run and room to swing up into wind if I needed it. As I descended to 500 feet downwind I could see for the first time that the landing surface sloped slightly towards me. This was all to the good and would give me an uphill landing to shorten my run. A final look at the threshhold for stray goats, donkeys etc, a tug on my safety straps while Sanderson hooked himself securely to the floor, and in we went. A pleasant sandy, gravelly surface with a few ruts where rainwater had obviously run down the slope. We pulled up in less than half the run I had planned with the propeller ticking over and throwing up little spurts of dust as the tips passed over the dry sandy surface.

'I'll taxy over to the hut and you can get out and do your stuff with the chowkidar while I go round the perimeter. Count the fuel drums – there should be forty eight – tap each one to see

55

that it's full and count the Verey cartridges. Finally see that the lock on the hut is in good condition.'

'Right, Sir,' replied Sanderson as we moved towards the hut.

The chowkidar was a little man with a fierce black beard in a dirty white robe and a yellow puggaree (turban). He had an ancient rifle slung over his shoulder and a bandolier of assorted bullets across his chest. His armoury was completed by a six foot staff which he doubtless used for driving off stray goats. Sanderson climbed out and they greeted each other like old friends as they departed towards the hut. I set off slowly round the landing ground; the wind was light and taxying was easy although I wished, as most of us did at times, that the Wapiti had brakes. Everything seemed to be in order except that the windsock was fraying and would need replacing in a month or two. The corner pylons gleamed in the sunshine and looked as though they had been painted by the old man very recently. Sanderson was enjoying a cigarette with him when I completed the circuit, and we left him with a packet of Players and a bar of chocolate which brought forth many toothless grins and salaams as we taxied away.

'No serious problems,' said Sanderson as he strapped himself in again. 'A lot of the cans are only partially full but all forty eight are there and sealed.'

The problem of evaporation, even from sealed drums, was quite serious on all landing grounds, particularly during the hot weather. The Public Works Department (PWD) was responsible for positioning all fuel stocks and changing them over at about six monthly intervals when the aviation fuel went 'off specification' and had to be diluted and down graded for MT use. Even in the period between PWD visits, it was quite likely that as much as one third of the fuel would be lost from evaporation. For that reason small stocks only were held and it was rare for them to be used. We did not turn the stocks over by refuelling our aircraft, partly because it was an arduous chore to fill up a Wapiti by hand from drums, and partly because we were always a little dubious about the quality of this fuel. We preferred to keep it strictly for emergencies.

Whether to take off uphill and into wind, or downhill and downwind was a decision which the pilot often had to make on these small landing grounds. In this case I opted for the former; the slope was gentle and the breeze strong enough to give the Wapiti significant help. And so we took off along our earlier landing run, getting airborne in 300 yards. As I started the gentle climbing turn to the north towards our next destination, out of the corner of my eye I caught sight of the old chowkidar waving goodbye from outside the hut with Sanderson hanging out of his cockpit and waving back.

'That's finished his hard work for the day.' he commented.

The time was 10.35, a little more than two and a half hours after leaving Kohat and I had almost half of my fuel left, plenty to complete my final task and reach Miramshah. We flew back up the Razmak valley and had a leisurely look at the landing ground where Pop Stemp's aeroplane was now standing by the camp entrance. I hoped he would be able to restart his engine; at least there was no shortage of stalwart soldiers to help him at Razmak. From my position over the centre of the valley below the camp the landing ground looked horrifying. It was roughly square in shape with sides of about 500 yards. To that extent it was adequate but it was the slope that appalled me. The whole effect was of a pocket handkerchief which had been pasted onto the lower slopes of a mountain – and what a mountain! It towered up above Razmak which was itself almost 5,000 feet above sea level and the whole effect from 2,000 feet above the ground was, to put it mildly, daunting. Like Parachinar the gradient of the landing surface was about 1 in 16 and, in a Wapiti it was not only mandatory to land uphill whatever the wind strength and direction, but it was impossible to go round again if the final approach was unsatisfactory. A Wapiti did not have sufficient power at that altitude to climb the slope. Consequently, landing at Razmak required great care and not a little skill when coming in to land over the camp and up the slope.

With the mountain rearing up in front of him a pilot had the illusion that he was diving into the ground and it was essential to watch the airspeed indicator closely and to resist the overwhelming temptation to ease back on the stick and stall the aeroplane. It was rumoured that one in four of all those who landed at Razmak had some sort of an accident or incident. This was probably an exaggeration, but the fact that the rumour existed at all indicated the respect in which this horror was held. Only the most experienced pilots landed at Razmak and it was to be many months before I was judged fit to try it.

As we continued down the valley towards Alexandra Picquet, Sanderson tapped me on the shoulder and pointed over to the east.

'Flying Officer Coulson seems to be leaving Sora Rogha,' he shouted in my ear.

In the distance I could see a cloud of dust moving across a sandy square which was Sora Rogha, a garrison post of the South Waziristan Scouts. The dust cloud ceased and a silver speck appeared glinting in the sunlight above the surrounding hills as Bill climbed out of the valley and set course for Miramshah, having completed his inspection of the landing ground.

Alexandra Picquet stood at the northern end of the Razmak valley overlooking the Central Waziristan road, a British built strategic road which ran down the valley parallel to the Frontier. The picquet was perched high above the road on a razor backed ridge, which, at its apex, could not have been more than 200 yards in width. On to this ridge were crammed the few buildings and parade ground which constituted the picquet. An injudiciously kicked football was liable to descend hundreds of feet before it came to rest. This post was reputed to be the highest in the British Empire, a bleak lonely place which spent much of its time wreathed in cloud. Even for the tough Indian sepoys, most of whom were recruited locally, it must have been a desolate spot. The RAF brought a little variety to the policemen by habitually flying past or below the picquet

whenever in the vicinity; a cheery wave was usually recipro-
cated by a sentry and, sometimes, by a football team on the
precipitous fragment of open ground which had to do duty as a
pitch and a parade ground.

I had been instructed to carry out a Popham Panel exercise
with the post on this occasion. It was a very simple but effective
form of communication between ground and air. Each post had
a large square patch of ground outlined by whitewashed stones
in a position close to the buildings which was easily visible from
the air. White canvas strips of various shapes and sizes could be
laid out in this square in accordance with a code contained in a
small handbook held by each post and carried by every pilot
and air gunner. A post was thus able to lay out simple messages
such as: 'I am under attack from the south,' or 'I have two
seriously injured men, send medical help.' Having read the
message the pilot circling above could only reply by writing out
an answer on his knee pad, enclosing it in a message bag which
was a small canvas envelope with a lead weight stitched into it
and a long multi coloured canvas streamer attached. His air
gunner could then drop this as close as possible to the Popham
Panel. Each post was exercised in this way about once a month.
No advance warning was given and the pilot was required to
record the time taken for the garrison to display its first message. Times varied considerably but the average was about
three to four minutes.

Alexandra Picquet may well have been expecting my visit as
they would undoubtedly have seen our three Wapitis flying
down the valley an hour earlier, and known that we were in the
vicinity. I approached in a shallow dive to cross the razor back
from the west and gave my instructions to Sanderson.

'As we pass over the post, fire a white Verey light, but fire it
upwards so that it won't fall into the post still burning. Start
your stop watch and as I circle to the left, see how long they take
to lay out the first message. We'll both take it down and hope to
come to the same conclusion before I reply. Keep yourself
strapped in as it may be extremely bumpy over this ridge.'

'Verey pistol ready, Sir,' replied Sanderson as we swept towards the tiny parade ground at about 500 feet above the ridge which, by this time, was looking quite alarming. With the usual bang in my left ear which never failed to make me jump against my shoulder straps, the white light soared up above us and described a graceful arc towards the post. Even before the Verey light was extinguished I could see small figures dashing out of the post towards the Popham Panel: they had reacted pretty quickly and it looked as though I would not be kept waiting long.

I have never suffered from vertigo but crossing that razor back in a steepish left hand turn and plunging out over the 2,000 foot valley on the other side was a sick-making experience. It didn't help to see, out of the corner of my eye, Sanderson half hanging out of his cockpit on the end of his slender chain to get a better view of the signal square. The sooner we get this somewhat hair raising exercise over, the better, I thought, as I banked round the end of the ridge on my way back to the post.

After two such circuits a message took shape below us, prefixed by the sign which indicated that it was an exercise only. I had my little handbook in my left hand, a pencil in my mouth and was holding the aeroplane in a left hand turn with my right hand. A third hand would have been useful for writing but, like other pilots, I had to manage with two. It was a simple message which Sanderson and I agreed read:

'We are extremely short of water.'

I rocked the wings to indicate that I had got the message and flew off a short distance from that dreadful ridge to consider my answer and to prepare to deliver it. I decided that had the message been genuine, I would have flown straight to Miramshah, collected a canister of water and a supply parachute, returned to Alexandra Picquet with the load on my bomb rack, and endeavoured to get it down within recoverable distance of the post. Consequently the message I gave to Sanderson over my shoulder read:

'Will return with water within two hours.' Two hours was my rough estimate of the time it would take to fly to Miramshah, have the water and parachute prepared, refuel and return.

While I had been writing my message and struggling with the bumps, Sanderson had extracted a message bag from its stowage. He took the message over my shoulder, buttoned it into the bag and rolled it up so that the streamer would fly out as he threw it downwards. We made our way back to the post and again crossed the parade ground in a rather unsteady left hand turn. I could see Sanderson bending over the side with the message bag held up in his right hand. It was his job to decide when to throw it while I concentrated on turning as accurately as I could over the post. His hand moved downwards and the message departed. It was out of my sight but Sanderson could see the streamer going down and, after a short pause, said: 'A good shot – just on the edge of the parade ground. They are going after it – just picking it up.'

'Good,' I said, 'that worked well, but I wouldn't care to do this in bad weather. Now for Miramshah and lunch.'

'Have a peppermint, Sir,' said Sanderson, passing a humbug over my shoulder. 'It steadies the nerves and brings you back to normal. I need one myself when I remember I'm doing this for sixpence a day.'

'Sixpence a day!' I exclaimed as we climbed up into smoother air, 'is that all you get as an air gunner?'

'Yes, I'm a Fitter IIE basically, of course, and the sixpence is the generous bonus I get for my air gunner's duties. However, I wouldn't give it up for anything; I reckon it's worth doing for nothing.'

I pondered on what he had said as we flew north out of the Razmak valley. Our air gunners were selected tradesmen, mostly fitters and riggers who volunteered and were then selected for the additional flying duty. This entitled them to wear the coveted 'flying bullet' on their sleeves and, as Sanderson had said: 'to receive the handsome bonus of sixpence a day.'

61

It was an arduous job for these splendid airmen as, no sooner were they on the ground after a long and perhaps rough flight, than they had to resume their normal tradesmen's duties working on the Wapitis. It was also a great comfort to the pilots to have a skilled technician in the back as air gunner. They could be invaluable in the event of some technical trouble arising on a remote landing ground; an engine that refused to start, a flat tyre or a tear in the fabric. The immense variety of the work we had to undertake in the Frontier squadrons was making me appreciate the qualities of men like Sanderson far more than I had in a squadron at home.

Miramshah came in sight straight ahead and I had to cease my contemplation of the excellence of air gunners with the thought that I could not have undertaken the morning's tasks at Drazinda and Alexandra Picquet, and learned so much about Waziristan at the same time, without the skill and cheerful support of a Sanderson in the back seat. I could hear him whistling happily as he stowed his Lewis gun safely away prior to landing.

This was my first visit to Miramshah, but I was to get to know it very well indeed during the forthcoming months as the two Kohat squadrons maintained in rotation one Flight at Miramshah. Each Flight spent two months there and so the detachment, which we all enjoyed, came round once a year. Basically, Miramshah was a large mud fort and the headquarters of the Tochi Scouts, an efficient irregular force of Indian troops with British officers. They took their name from the Tochi river which ran past Miramshah and up the wide valley to Datta Khel.

The aerodrome was L shaped, its two arms running along two sides of the fort and the aeroplanes were wheeled inside the walls each night. When darkness fell, all gates were closed and the fort was then protected by Tochi sentries in watch towers on top of the walls, each watch tower having a powerful searchlight to floodlight the walls against intruders. As I flew across the fort I could see the signal square outside the airfield gates with the landing T indicating East to West, which was the long arm of the L approached over a narrow, stony road which was the main route to Bannu, the nearest town of any size. The point at which this road passed the airfield boundary was associated with a tragedy some years earlier. A Wapiti flown by a Flying Officer Arnold Wall was coming into land over the road when a small Indian boy threw a stone at it. Unbelievably the stone found its way through the mass of flying wires and struts and hit Arnold in the eye. He managed to land safely despite intense pain but he subsequently lost the sight of his damaged eye. This unhappy incident finished his career as a pilot but he transferred to the Equipment Branch where he started a new career and reached the rank of Group Captain.

This story was fresh in my mind as I side-slipped down and across the road, pulling off one of my better landings in front of the gates of the fort where the airmen of A Flight, 27 Squadron, were waiting to receive me.

'Flying Officer Coulson is here but not the Flight Commander,' said Sanderson over my shoulder as we turned round at the end of the runway. Taxying back alongside the walls gave me a moment to take in the new scene. The fort was straight out of Beau Geste; thick mud walls and crenellated towers at each corner on each of which I could just make out a turbanned head and a rifle barrel.

'We come up here in about five months time, don't we?'

'Yes Sir,' replied Sanderson, 'October and November – it will be cooling off a little by then; this place can be a real stinker in June and July, but the worst will be over before our turn comes.'

I could well believe it. The temperature was already climbing into the eighties as I clambered down from my cockpit. We had been in the air three hours and twenty minutes and I felt hot, weary and extremely thirsty.

Humping my parachute over my shoulder, I walked into the gates of the fort leaving Sanderson and the 27 Squadron airmen to refuel my aeroplane. The short, bow legged figure of Flying

Officer Isherwood came out to meet me. He was a tough and cheery South African, burnt almost black by the sun and he greeted me with one of his usual quips – 'Still bouncing them I see, David.'

Knowing that I had made a very good landing and that he hadn't even seen it, I replied, 'Just testing my tyre pressures. We do it that way instead of kicking the wheels as I believe is your custom.'

Leaving my flying kit in the office, we walked down through the fort to the tiny but comfortable Officers Mess, built to house no more than six officers. I sank two large 'nimbu parnis' (fresh lime and water) in quick succession and was ready for the inevitable curry tiffin. We waited for Pop Stemp who could be heard circling overhead at that moment. Ten minutes later he appeared, very hot and in a bad mood.

'That landing ground at Razmak gets worse and worse,' he said, gratefully downing his first cold drink. 'The ruts made by water pouring down from the mountain were so deep that I thought for a moment that I'd pulled a tyre off. I've asked the Brigadier to put some troops on to levelling out the worst of the ruts: it's not fit for anything but a real emergency.'

It was certainly beginning to get hot at Miramshah in the middle of the day and the shimmering heat haze which is such a feature of the hot weather was already in evidence. After a very good lunch with the four officers of 27 Squadron, Pop, Bill and I would have happily opted for a short siesta, 'charpoy bashing' or 'Egyptian PT', followed by a flight home in the cool of the evening – but that was not to be. Our airmen would be waiting for us at Kohat to inspect the aeroplanes and prepare them for the next day's flying. They would have been up since 5 am and we could hardly indulge ourselves at their expense. And so, by half past one we were off down the hard, dusty aerodrome in formation, climbing away for the forty minutes flight to Kohat.

The whole reconnaissance had taken a little more than four hours and had been for me a fascinating introduction to the routine. In many ways Waziristan was more interesting than the other two areas with a bigger variety of landing grounds to visit and the opportunity to drop in to Miramshah. If it did nothing else it made me appreciate how difficult it was to control the activities of the wily old Faqir of Ipi.

CHAPTER 5

INCIDENTS AND ACCIDENTS

Flying accidents were fortunately infrequent at Kohat, thanks to the reliability of the Wapiti and its rugged engine. It was also easy to fly and provided that outrageous liberties were not taken with it, it would submit to errors of judgement and careless handling with considerable tolerance. Nevertheless accidents did occur from time to time. Three come to mind.

I was returning to the aerodrome one morning just before lunchtime, having had a frustrating hour and a half trying to take photographs of several police posts with intermittent rain and low cloud drifting across my target. Visibility was not very good at Kohat either and so I flew a complete circuit of the aerodrome at about 800 feet to get a clear view of the windsock and check my intended landing run for obstructions. There was a bustle of activity on the eastern edge of the field beside the road running through the village and I could clearly see the red of a firetender and the cross on the roof of an ambulance. Dropping down another 200 feet, it became apparent through the mist that a Wapiti was standing on its nose just inside the boundary fence with its tail pointing almost vertically upwards. As a precaution I flew round again and received a green Verey light from the tarmac which I interpreted as permission to land but obviously to be careful and to keep well away from the accident. I side slipped down and crossed the road between the crashed Wapiti and the far boundary and taxied in.

'Anybody hurt?' I asked as I humped my parachute out of the cockpit and climbed down the steps.

'Only a camel' was the reply followed by an unseemly roar of laughter from the two airmen waiting for me.

It transpired that Flying Officer Richardson of 27 Squadron had been gliding in to land over the road when a long train of camels, tied nose to tail and led by an Indian merchant, was plodding down the road on its way to Bannu. Keeping his eye on the head of the column, Richardson had apparently failed to appreciate its length and, misjudging his height, had hit the last camel in the line which also happened to be the tallest. The undercarriage of the Wapiti took the head off the unfortunate animal and carried it onto the aerodrome where the Wapiti, literally tripped up by the impact, stood on its nose after bouncing heavily on its wheels.

Richardson was a tough, hefty man with a large ginger moustache, a forerunner perhaps of the Battle of Britain fashion. He was alleged to have unstrapped himself and slid to the ground from his elevated cockpit. Walking round the shattered propeller he found the head of the decapitated camel still impaled in the cross bracing wires of his undercarriage, and wearing that expression of haughty disdain which is the prerogative of all camels. Richardson studied it for a few moments and, according to his air gunner, said, 'Grin at me, would you, you bastard.'

Needless to say the owner of the camel was at the station gates within minutes demanding instant compensation, not only for the largest and most valuable animal in his train, but also for the psychological harm done to the others. The incident created considerable embarrassment and was eventually settled for about 500 rupees, a large proportion of which had to be paid by Richardson who was judged to have been extremely careless and lacking in judgement. Somewhat chastened by this episode, we all added on a few feet when crossing the road in future and treated all camels as if they were giraffes.

Not many days later it was my own turn to become involved in an incident which could have had very serious consequences. I had been detailed as the leader of a formation flying exercise, with Flying Officer Hamley and Sgt Gold acting as No 2 and No 3 in the formation. It was usual for all of us in C Flight to get experience in every position and it was my turn to act as leader for an hour or so. My air gunner for the occasion was LAC Sanderson and we walked to our aircraft in time for a take-off at 06.45 hours on a bright, still morning. I was looking forward to this trip as it was much less effort to lead a formation than to follow. The Wapiti tended to wallow about when the air was at all unstable and had insufficient power to catch up quickly when falling behind. Consequently formation flying could be quite hard work.

I taxied to the downwind corner of the aerodrome, having decided upon a diagonal take off to give the maximum run in the light wind conditions. When the other two aircraft were in position beside me and had put their thumbs up, I opened the throttle gently, got the tail up quickly and remained at half throttle until we were all three running steadily in close formation with tails well up. Opening up gently to full throttle we left the ground cleanly two-thirds of the way across the aerodrome.

Just as we crossed the boundary at about thirty feet, to my horror, a black mass of birds rose up in front of us. There must have been dozens of them and it was quite impossible to avoid going straight into them. Because we were in close formation there was no question of turning sharply and the Wapiti certainly had neither the power nor the speed at that moment to pull up and hope to climb over them. A second later and I was in the middle of the flock and I instinctively ducked into the cockpit as a mass of bodies, feathers and blood hurtled into me accompanied by a series of bangs and thuds as the aeroplane ploughed its way through. I froze onto the controls and kept as straight as possible, trying to remember what lay ahead if I had to land or crash. As far as I could recall, the ground ahead was a swampy banana plantation with native huts scattered through it. It was certainly no place in which to pull off a satisfactory forced landing and the chances of hitting an Indian or a child were quite high. While these thoughts flashed through my mind, the crashing and banging ceased as suddenly as it had started and I cautiously raised my head. The windscreen was cracked and covered with blood and feathers; blood seemed to be dripping down from the top of my helmet and running over my goggles which I pushed up with a quick movement of my left hand. I glanced right and left and saw that Hamley and Gold had pulled out of formation and still seemed to be flying normally. At that moment, with intense relief, I realised that my own engine was running at full throttle and the propeller was intact although it might well be damaged. I couldn't see any other damage but there was a ghastly mess over the wings and fuselage.

Easing the throttle back to normal climbing revs, I continued straight on up to 500 feet, gently testing the controls, all of which seemed responsive. By this time Hamley and Gold were moving back towards me again to see how I was faring and to await instructions. I gave them the crossed hands signal to break formation and pointed downwards to indicate that we should land independently on the aerodrome. It looked as if I had been caught in the centre of the flock of birds and they had been relatively fortunate and missed most of them.

'Are you all right, Sanderson?' I called to my air gunner through the Gosport tube.

'Yes, Sir; something hit me on the head as I dived for the bottom of the cockpit and I'm covered with blood but it's not mine.'

I gently started a turn to the left to go round the aerodrome but my next thought was for the undercarriage which could be damaged. I told Sanderson to slide back the bomb aiming panel in the floor of his cockpit and, as far as he could, examine the undercarriage. After a short pause he said, 'It looks undamaged; at least there are no broken wires or struts hanging down and both wheels are there. There's a bloody great bird – and I mean bloody – jammed in the cross bracing wires above the axle.'

That sounded fairly reassuring.

'Right,' I said, 'will you fire a red Verey light towards the tarmac and then see that you are securely chained to the floor and brace yourself when we land.'

I knew that if the undercarriage collapsed as we landed, the Wapiti was likely to cartwheel onto her back and Sanderson would be in greater danger of being flung out than myself.

There was a loud bang in my ear and a red Verey light soared out towards the aerodrome as I cruised at 500 feet towards a downwind position from which to start my approach to land. A moment later a green Verey light came up towards me from the tarmac. From the rapidity with which this reply to my red light came, I suspected that the whole incident had been seen from the tarmac and they were ready for any emergency.

I turned into wind and started a normal approach noting that, although the engine seemed a little rough, the oil pressure and temperature were normal. The roughness was probably due to a damaged propeller. As the boundary fence approached, I was comforted to see out of the corner of my eye that the red fire tender and the ambulance had started to move slowly out on to the grass towards the point where I would touch down. With a final tug at my straps and a call to Sanderson to brace himself, I touched down gently, holding my breath to see what would happen. Nothing. It was a beautiful landing and we came to rest in the middle of the aerodrome. However, I did not intend to tempt fate any further and switched off there and then to allow the undercarriage to be examined before the Wapiti was moved again.

The firetender was alongside before the propeller had stopped and Sanderson and I unstrapped ourselves and climbed out. Our Flight Sergeant, Percy Brown, was waiting and as I turned towards him he exclaimed:

'Good God, Sir, are you hurt?'

'Not a bit,' I replied, not quite realising what a fearful sight I must have presented with my helmet and goggles plastered with blood and feathers,

'This is only kitehawk's blood.'

'Look at this,' shouted one of the airmen from below the aircraft. 'This' turned out to be the bird which had become lodged in the undercarriage cross bracing wires. When it was removed and examined it was found to be a kitehawk with a wing span of 5 feet 8 inches. That was the only complete bird to come back to earth with me, but the poor old Wapiti bore ample evidence of having slaughtered at least half a dozen more, one of which had badly chipped one tip of the propeller – hence the roughness of the engine – another had cracked the windscreen and damaged the front gun sight, while several others had made holes in the fabric in various places.

As soon as the firetender and ambulance crews were satisfied that Sanderson and I were unhurt, they turned their attention to the other two aircraft which were approaching to land. As there had been no red Verey light or other emergency signals from either of them, it looked as if they had escaped damage. They both landed safely and taxied towards the tarmac. Sergeant Gold had in fact hit one bird with his starboard wingtip which had torn the fabric but not damaged the structure.

Hamley had hit nothing and merely sat watching with horror as I ploughed through the flock.

When we were all down the fire tender set off across the aerodrome to investigate the scene of the incident and came back in due course to report that the birds had been feeding on the carcase of a sheep which was lying in the ditch beyond the boundary fence. The mangled remains of about seven large kitehawks were scattered around and the rest of the flock was busy with them. As it was impossible to scare these birds away until they had completed their gruesome meal, the direction for take off and landing was changed to avoid flying close to the flock.

It was common enough to encounter large kitehawks hovering close to the aerodrome, usually at about three or four hundred feet, looking for refuse. This was a regular hazard of all Indian stations but the birds could usually be seen and, in any case, were generally below circuit height. If a bird was encountered, the rule was always to climb above it and never to pass below it. When frightened, these birds had a nasty habit of closing their wings and diving; they had been known to go right through the fabric wing of an aeroplane below them. A flock feeding on the ground, such as I had encountered, was unusual but by no means unknown as records testify. Some years before, a Sergeant Pilot had hit a flock of kitehawks while flying an early version of the Wapiti. In this version the struts between the main planes had ball ends which were held in sockets merely by the tension of the cross bracing wires. One bird hit an inter-plane strut and bent it with the result that the strut fell out, the wings collapsed and both pilot and air gunner were killed in the crash which followed. As a result of that accident a modification to the struts was introduced and they were bolted into position. My Wapiti, of course, had the modification so that even if one of the struts had been bent on impact, it would not have fallen out.

When reflecting on this accident, I realised how lucky I had been that no vital part of my aeroplane had been damaged and, in particular, that the propeller had not been smashed. A successful forced landing in a banana plantation from less than 200 feet would have been an impossibility and a nasty crash must inevitably have resulted. Yes, I had indeed been fortunate.

I was not so fortunate, however, when involved in another accident a few weeks later, and one for which I could not escape the blame. It happened one morning before breakfast after landing from a practice bombing trip. As I taxied in, I was met by two airmen who hung on to the wing tips in the usual way. I expected to be marshalled alongside the other aeroplanes of the Flight which were lined up on one side of the tarmac apron. This was also the intention of the airman on my left wing but, unknown to both of us, the man on the right wing had instructions to swing me round to the right to take the aeroplane up to the next set of aerodrome gates where the Wapiti was needed for some adjustment.

We taxied slowly off the grass on to the hard tarmac surface and I gave a short burst of engine expecting to be pulled round to the left. To my horror, both airmen pulled together with the inevitable result that I carried on straight ahead. As the Wapiti, at that time, was not fitted with brakes, like most aircraft, and with the tail skid now on the smooth tarmac, there was no stopping. Dead ahead, Ralph Jones was running up an engine prior to taxying out and I ploughed straight into him. Our two propellers met with a splintering crash, made all the worse by the fact that Ralph's was turning at full speed. Wood and splinters flew everywhere but fortunately none of the airmen was injured. It was a terrible shock to Ralph whose head was in his cockpit studying his instruments and had not seen me coming.

A very shaken and crestfallen Pilot Officer climbed out of his cockpit and made his way reluctantly to report to Pop Stemp. The whole station had heard the resounding crash on the tarmac which did not make my progress to the Flight office any easier. The upshot was that the Station Commander found me to blame for failing to give clear instructions to the two airmen on my wing tips – a perfectly just finding as a pilot must always be held responsible for the handling of his aeroplane. I was fined the sum of 400 Rupees, which was almost a month's pay, no light punishment for an impecunious young officer. Fortunately the damage to both Wapitis was virtually confined to the propellers and they were flying again within a day or two but, for me, it was a salutary lesson not quickly forgotten.

CHAPTER 6

A WELCOME BREAK
FROM THE HEAT

Frrom early May the temperature climbed rapidly and, by the middle of the month, was regularly exceeding 100° in the shade. The old hands at Kohat said that it would go above 120° during June and might well reach 125° on a few days.

One began to see the wisdom of confining trooping to the cooler months to give us all a chance to become acclimatised gradually to the extreme heat which blanketed the whole of the Frontier for four or five months each year. Fortunately it was a dry heat and the humidity remained low during these very hot months. It always seemed to me that once the temperature reached about 110°, any further rise made very little difference as one lived in a permanent bath of sweat anyway. The age of air conditioning had not arrived but at least we had progressed beyond the punkah as a means of cooling a room. No longer did a small Indian boy sit outside with his toe tied to a string which went through into the room and activated a large matting punkah to stir the air. The boy usually had to be kept awake by loud shouts from inside whenever the punkah stopped moving – which was frequently.

All our rooms had large ceiling fans which revolved lazily with much squeaking and groaning. They were certainly an advance on the punkah but during the hottest periods did little more than keep the same super heated air moving round in circles.

This was the time when the fishing fleet packed its bags and reluctantly went off to Bombay or Karachi on the way home, leaving the bachelors to sweat it out without the cheerful female company which they had enjoyed during the cooler months. The wives also began to drift away, a few on the long journey home to spend a month or two with children who were at boarding school, but the majority to hill stations such as Kashmir, Murree or Nilgiri, to be joined by their husbands for a spell of leave when they could get away from the plains.

A few, but very few indomitable ladies defied the heat and remained with their husbands but it was a dreary existence for them in many ways; there was virtually no social life, tennis and golf were exhausting and Kohat possessed no swimming pool at that time. Even playing cards was never a success. They stuck to one's fingers and then stuck together or were blown away by the overhead fan. I particularly admired Frieda Stemp during this first hot weather. She stayed down at Kohat and made a great effort to keep some sort of normal life going.

My 21st birthday fell during one of the hottest months and it coincided with my first solo flight at night in the Wapiti. After landing, two things were waiting for me at the end of the flarepath as I climbed out and handed my aeroplane over to the next pilot – a large bottle of cold Murree beer and an invitation from Frieda to a party she was giving for me that evening after our night flying had finished. It went on far into the night in the garden of the Stemps' bungalow with several schools of Liar Dice in session. Dice were relatively cool and pleasant to play with in the heat and every evening found several tables in operation on the Mess lawn, each with a large red lamp hanging from a tree some distance from the table to attract the myriads of insects which appeared after dark. These always included a large type of beetle which flew like a helicopter and had a disconcerting habit of closing its wings and dropping like a stone into one's drink.

These evenings were often enlivened by the antics of three little green parrots belonging to Derek Addenbrook. Named Burberry, Poulson and Skone after well known London military outfitters to whom many of us owed money, Derek would bring them out in the cool of the evening, attach a long piece of string to the leg of each and fly them round the garden. One of them, Poulson I think, had learned some quite advanced aerobatics and could sometimes be persuaded to give a highly professional display before landing on a table for his reward of nuts.

Most of the junior officers, impecunious as we were, could afford some leave in the hills during the hot weather, but this was not the case with the young bachelor airmen. Their pay was low, the hill stations were a long way away and quite expensive. A complete hot weather without a break, particularly throughout a five year tour, would have been unendurable, and an imaginative organisation existed to give every airman on the Frontier two months away from the plains every year.

At Lower Topa, situated in the Murree hills above Rawalpindi, the RAF had constructed a Hill Depot. It was more than 7,200 feet above sea level, within five miles of the civilian hill station of Murree, and consisted of a large hutted camp clinging to the hillside among dense pine forests. Every airman from Kohat and the two other Frontier stations, went to the Hill

Depot for two months between the beginning of May and the end of October. At any one time, therefore, one third of each station was away at Lower Topa and the stations on the plains continued to function at reduced capacity, which was quite acceptable unless an emergency arose, whereupon the men could be called back from Lower Topa within about 24 hours. While there, the airmen attended ground training lectures, carried out their annual rifle firing practice, some drill and played a great deal of sport. The routine was deliberately leisurely, confined to mornings only and the men needed little encouragement to relax in the cool mountain air. It did not count as leave and every airmen was fully entitled to take his quota of leave in addition if he could afford to do so. Most, however, were quite prepared to spend their money in enjoying the considerable amenities of Topa and Murree.

It was usual for each party of airmen to be taken to the Hill Depot by a junior officer who commanded that party throughout its stay. One morning in May, Pop Stemp called me into his office and told me that he wished me to take the Kohat party due to go on the 1st of July, adding that I would be back in plenty of time to accompany the Flight to Miramshah in October and November. I was delighted with the news. Having been in India only a few months, I had not saved enough to go to Kashmir on leave and yet I knew that I would need some break from the hot weather. Topa seemed not only the answer to that problem but also the opportunity to get to know many of the NCOs and airmen better. But I confess that it was the prospect of getting out of the blistering heat for a while which appealed to me most.

A cheerful party of about fifty NCOs and airmen congregated outside the guardroom at 5.30 am on the 1st of July. My own Flight Sergeant, Percy Brown, was the senior airman in the party and the three Crossley lorries were soon loaded with our baggage and bed rolls. Each man carried his own rifle and I had my Colt 45 in its holster. We had picnic type rations for the day, plenty of water and each Crossley contained a couple of crates of Murree beer.

'If you will travel in the leading Crossley, Sir, I'll go in the rear one and we'll keep well apart to avoid the dust.' said Brown.

'Do all the drivers know the route?' I asked.

'Two or three have been several times but LAC Jordan hasn't, so we'll keep him in the middle.'

I climbed up beside the driver in the leading vehicle and Hukmud Khan, with a few other bearers from the airmen's barrack blocks, climbed into the back with the airmen who had made themselves comfortable on the piles of bed rolls.

'It's going to be a long day and a hot one,' I thought as we pulled out of the camp gates at 6 o'clock.

'Do you have to drive the whole way by yourself?' I asked Corporal Kelly, knowing that we had something over 160 miles to do and the Crossley was exceedingly heavy.

'No, Sir,' he said, 'there are three other drivers in the party and we can change over at intervals; it's main road all the way and the only really tiring part is the last 30 miles or so from Rawalpindi up to Topa. I haven't counted the hairpins, but there must be a hundred.'

With the sun rising over the mountains to our right, the small convoy ground its way up the Kohat Pass noisily but steadily. The six wheeled Crossleys were rugged vehicles which did wonderful service in every kind of condition from deep sand to steep mountain tracks, but they were heavy and tiring to drive. Numbers of tribesmen driving their goats and oxen down to market in Kohat confronted us round some of the hairpin bends which added to the sweat and toil of the climb but Corporal Kelly took it all in his stride and cheerful waves were exchanged with the Afridis. Although no trouble from hostile tribesmen was expected on this trip which followed the main road to Rawalpindi, as a matter of routine every airman kept his rifle close to him with a magazine loaded. Being in the cab of the leading Crossley, I knew that I presented an obvious target and kept my own pistol loose in its holster. The Afridis who bordered the Frontier road knew full well that any firing at

British troops would meet with instant and heavy retaliation either in the form of a very heavy fine or military action. Consequently the road was reasonably safe, particularly for a convoy such as ours.

Peshawar was reached by 8 o'clock and we drove into the RAF station for breakfast and a top-up with fuel. Nine of 20 Squadron's Wapitis took off in formation as I made my way to the Mess. After watching with a critical eye for a few moments, I was forced to the conclusion that they looked somewhat better than my own squadron, consoling myself with the thought that, being Army Cooperation types, they probably had more practice in formation flying than we did.

An hour later we were again on our way down the long, dusty road which ran in a dead straight line from Peshawar to Rawalpindi, crossing the Indus at Attock at about the half way point. This was a dreary drive as we thundered along at 35 miles an hour enveloped in a permanent dust cloud, scattering herds of sheep, goats and donkeys at intervals and meeting only a few grossly overloaded buses and the odd tanker: private cars were not much in evidence outside the towns and cities. The combined road and railway bridge at Attock was left behind us and we entered the Punjab as the temperature steadily climbed above the 100° mark. Although the Crossleys were covered with canvas tilts with their sides rolled up to get what breeze there was, they were extremely hot and very noisy. It was difficult to find any shade on that bare blistering plain in which to pause for our picnic lunch, beer and other necessities. However, Corporal Kelly had done this trip before and knew a grove of dusty palms and oleanders where we could pull in and obtain at least a little relief from the midday sun. The Murree beer was unpacked from the ice boxes and hastily drunk before it had a chance to warm up; excellent it was too and had it not been for the intense heat and swirling dust, the picnic would have been a pleasant interlude. The anticipation of climbing up into the cool of the Murree hills in a few hours kept spirits high and the troops were more cheerful than I ever remembered seeing them, sharing sandwiches with the small boys who inevitably materialised from nowhere on these occasions.

The sun was beginning to lose its heat as we reached Rawalpindi which was a disappointing city. It had a dirty and neglected look with a fine coating of grey dust over everything. That was typical of most of the Punjab in the hot weather after several months without rain. Even Flashmans, allegedly the best hotel in Pindi was no more than a dreary collection of single storey chalets and bungalows, somewhat on the lines of a typical motel of later years. We had no need to stop and I was not sorry to get on our way towards the hills which could now be seen encroaching upon the plain from the north. A hint of snow on a few misty peaks in the background where Kashmir lay, gave some indication of the immense range which led up, layer upon layer, to Everest, Rakaposhi, Harmosh and other peaks of 29,000 feet and above. We stopped the convoy for a few moments outside Rawalpindi to allow Corporal Kelly and the more experienced drivers to take over from those who had driven since lunchtime. The most difficult part of the journey lay ahead, a climb of some 5,000 feet in about 35 miles which would test the stamina of the drivers and the Crossleys.

For me, and for most of the airmen, that journey was a first time experience never to be forgotten. After a few miles of straight, level surface leading to the foothills, a superbly engineered road of innumerable hairpin bends and short straight sections clung to the hillsides. The vegetation changed rapidly from the dried up scrub of the plain, through birch and larch trees to thick pine forests. More significant to our small party than the changing scenery was the drop in temperature and humidity. It had been, I suppose, about 115° in Rawalpindi but, as the climb started, I could feel the temperature dropping with almost every hairpin bend. The stickiness and lassitude began to drop off every one of us and a vigour which one had hardly felt since reaching India began to grip one. The effect was quite extraordinary; shouts of 'blankets tonight, boys' resounded from the back of the Crossleys and prickly heat began to disappear before one's eyes.

Half way up the climb we stopped to top up the radiators and allow the labouring engines to cool down; none had boiled and Corporal Kelly said that only happened occasionally at the top of the climb when the altitude reduced the boiling point of the water. As almost every Indian bus that we saw on the climb, with the usual mass of human beings festooned over it, seemed to be spouting steam furiously, the performance of the heavily laden Crossleys was splendid. As Kelly pointed out, these buses were by far the greatest hazard on the road; their drivers appeared to have implicit faith in the value of the horn as a means of clearing the road, even of a Crossley.

'We did once have a Crossley over the edge,' said Kelly 'but, by the grace of God, a tree stopped it before it could turn over and nobody was hurt. I wouldn't give way to these chaps when on the outside for anything, and fortunately we are bigger than most of them.'

Higher and higher we climbed accompanied by remarks from the back about the need for greatcoats and hot water bottles, prickly heat by this time having given way to goose pimples. The pine scented air was like a tonic and the occasional smell of a log fire drifted across. It was very hard to believe that such a change could take place in two hours. The road divided before reaching Murree, which was reached by turning off to the right, while we continued along what was in fact the main Rawalpindi to Kashmir road for a further five miles until we came to a notice board reading, 'Royal Air Force Hill Depot – Lower Topa'.

It was surely one of the most unusual RAF stations, resembling more than anything a Canadian lumber camp in the Rockies. Perched on the crest of a heavily wooded hillside, a small flat area had been levelled for a parade ground – cum football pitch and running track. A few married quarters for the small permanent staff were scattered precariously around this space while the main part of the camp consisted of domestic and administrative buildings dotted among the pine trees on the slopes. Apart from an entrance leading to a small MT yard, there were virtually no roads in the camp, all the buildings being joined by steep footpaths. At over 7,000 feet above sea level, even the youngest and fittest puffed and blew for the first week or so when scrambling from one building to another, and several middle aged and portly Warrant Officers found the going quite difficult, particularly on dark nights after a few glasses in the Sergeants Mess.

On arrival, I was presented with a full programme of work and sport for the next two months. Discipline was relaxed, serious work was confined to the mornings and the afternoons were available for organised sport or simply doing nothing but enjoy the wonderful mountain air and scenery. As contingents from all the Frontier stations were there, the old rivalry of the plains could be continued and competition was encouraged, not only on the sports field but in the annual rifle and revolver firing courses and drill. It was altogether a pleasant interlude and perhaps one of the most satisfying aspects of it was to see the yellow, almost jaundiced look of many of the airmen, which was inseparable from the hot weather life on the plains, gradually disappear. Sores, prickly heat and septic mosquito bites disappeared in a few days and appetites returned. I don't know who conceived the idea of a Hill Depot but it was a brilliant one and its value incalculable.

The day usually began with a simple colour hoisting parade with all the contingents present, after which I would march my Kohat party off to one corner of the parade ground for half an hour of arms drill, uniform inspection or even a talk on the programme of work. That was up to me. The Depot contained a comprehensive store of uniform and clothing with a good camp dhersi (tailor) to make alterations and sew on badges, so we took the opportunity to replace and renovate the airmen's uniform, change battered caps and worn out boots. As Sergeant Brown put it, 'We bring up a shabby bunch of exhausted 'erks' and are expected to take back a relatively smart body of airmen.' He advisedly said 'relatively smart' because the quality of the khaki drill issued in India and the conditions under which airmen had to keep it and wear it, made it impossible for even the most meticulous airman to appear smart.

After the short morning's work was over the parade ground was turned over to the footballers, hockey players and athletes for the afternoons. The night life of Murree was then available for those who craved the bright lights, but it consisted of little more than a second rate cinema, various bars and the Murree Club. However, there were plenty of girls, mostly wives or daughters of the men still down on the plains, and Murree gave many of us an opportunity to repay some of their winter hospitality. Muree was certainly not an exciting place and, after a couple of visits, most of us were content with our own Messes and canteens where a few drinks, a game of cards and bed under a blanket constituted a thoroughly satisfactory evening. I had almost forgotten what it was like to have a long night's sleep without a fan clanking over my head. Hukmud Khan, who had many friends among the other servants, found the change as invigorating as I did and bounced in with my early morning tea and a cheerful greeting each morning at 6 o'clock.

Our two months stay sped by rapidly and the return to the plains at the end of August began to loom up. Feelings were mixed; many of the airmen were understandably reluctant to face the sweat and toil again, but I for one, missed my flying and was anxious to get back to it. My small party had done well at Topa, having won a number of the competitions, notably on the rifle range and the athletic track. Each detachment ended with a sports day when the various units competed in track and field events. I had kept up my middle distance running from my days as a cadet and was able to win the half mile event at Topa in 2 mins 4 secs on a rough track, followed by second place in the one mile, being well and truly beaten in that event by my old Cranwell colleague and opponent Bill Brotherhood. Bill was a fine miler and had been the champion of Wales during his last year at home. We ran against each other many times both at home and in India and the results were always the same; I never once beat him in the mile and I don't think he ever beat me in the half mile. He was not quite fast enough over the shorter distance and I lacked the staying power for the longer race.

We met again in the three mile road race which was the concluding event at Topa. This was the most testing competition. The competitors were taken by Crossley to the point at which the road to Murree left the main road, and the race took place along the rough tarmac surface to the finish at the gates of the Depot. At 7,000 feet it was a gruelling race and I am not sure it was particularly good for the heart – I know that mine didn't return to normal for about two days, or so it seemed. Each unit entered a team of six, and so it was a large field that pounded down the road in the cool of the evening. Brotherhood won the event for Risalpur quite comfortably and again my stamina was not up to his, but I managed to finish fourth which helped to put Kohat into second place over-all. The Crossley with our track suits and sweaters followed the race and picked up quite a number of competitors who were being sick by the roadside. This increased my doubts about the wisdom of the event.

And so, with a final night of celebration during which the officers entertained the NCOs to beer, buffet supper and darts, our Hill Depot detachment came to an end. At six o'clock the following morning we set off on the return journey to Kohat, taking our last deep breaths of the pine laden mountain air, cold and invigorating. Within two hours the goose pimples had all disappeared and, some airmen even swore that they had developed prickly heat again by the time we had reached Rawalpindi. It was like driving into an oven as the temperature climbed towards the 100° mark, although in fact it was marginally cooler than it had been two months earlier, and the worst of the hot weather was over. However, two more uncomfortable months still had to be faced, and it was a subdued party that eventually drove into the camp at five o'clock that evening, perhaps thinking longingly of the blankets of Topa which now had to be exchanged for the mosquito nets of Kohat.

CHAPTER 7

MUTT AND JEFF

Back at Kohat there was plenty to do as Pop Stemp, who had taken the opportunity of our absence at the Hill Depot to give Frieda a month's holiday in Kashmir, was due to take the Flight to Miramshah for our annual two months detachment. Before our departure, however, I had certain duties of my own to carry out which helped me to get back into flying practice after my two months absence.

In 1933 there were very few specialist branches in the RAF and a variety of non-flying jobs were shared out among the junior officers who were expected to fit them in with their flying. Many were uninteresting but nevertheless essential but I was fortunate enough to have completed a course on parachute maintenance before leaving home, and this made me an almost automatic choice to run the Parachute Section at Kohat. Not only was it interesting but it also gave me a certain amount of additional flying.

The short course at home had lasted no more than a week but it had taught me how to pack and service the various parachutes then in use and also gave me the chance to carry out one jump. This was a strange and somewhat unnerving experience, far removed from the modern practice of jumping from the door of a transport aircraft.

I took to the air one morning at Henlow standing on a small platform far out on the lower wing of a Vickers Vimy bomber. Facing backwards and in front of one of the inter plane struts, I was pressed against the strut by the slipstream as we bumped over the rough grass and into the air. The old Vimy climbed to about 800 feet and flew round the circuit, turning back to cross the aerodrome into wind. At a signal from the pilot I edged round the strut, hanging on like grim death as the wind tried to tear me off the small platform. Transferring my grip on the strut to my left hand, I grasped the handle of the rip cord with my right and awaited the second signal from the pilot. I felt giddy and slightly sick as the white circle in the centre of the aerodrome came into view below the wing on which I was standing. My pilot's right hand went up and I knew that in a few seconds he would drop it as the signal for me to pull the rip cord. I tightened my grip; his hand fell, and I yanked the rip cord handle hard. For a moment nothing seemed to happen as I clung to the strut, and then with a bang, I was literally torn from the platform as my parachute opened. The next second or so were confused and I remember little until I was floating quietly down towards the white circle. Suddenly my enjoyment of the floating sensation was rudely destroyed by the realisation that the ground was rushing up to meet me. Twisting round to face downwind, I hit the ground with a good thump, allowed

my knees to collapse as instructed, and rolled over. The parachute was slowly collapsing in front of me as there was very
little wind, and no need to operate the quick release to avoid
being dragged over the grass. The Vimy was droning away into
the distance as I rolled up my parachute and trudged off towards the Parachute Section to repack it. This was the final test
and as I repacked the crumpled canopy and twisted rigging
lines, I thought about the jump. It had been well worthwhile
because it proved to me that my parachute would open properly
and would bring me down without injury, but once was enough
and I felt no great desire to repeat the uncomfortable experience. It was said that George Beamish, who at that time was the
heavyweight champion of the RAF and an Irish international
forward, had hung on to the Vimy strut so grimly that before he
was torn from the platform by his parachute, had bent the strut
considerably. The pilot must have been a little disconcerted to
find his aeroplane trying to pivot around George Beamish out
on the wing tip.

My parachute section at Kohat was housed in a long narrow
building containing two linoleum covered tables big enough to
take fully extended parachutes. An area at one end with a very
high ceiling was used to dry the parachutes when suspended
from the roof. Storage racks and a small office completed the
section which was presided over by Sergeant Stonebank with
one airman to maintain all the station's parachutes. In addition
to the pilots and airgunners, there were streamlined supply
dropping containers which had their own parachutes attached
and a number of coarse fabric ones which could be attached to
packing cases or awkwardly shaped loads which would not fit
into a container. All these parachutes had to be hung for 48
hours to dry, be repaired and repacked every two months. In
addition, which is where I came in, all pilots' and airgunners'
parachutes had to be droptested from 1,000 feet once a year. In
retrospect I am sure that this was totally unnecessary and
caused needless wear and tear. However, it has to be remembered that the parachute had only been brought into general use

for all aircrews during the previous ten years and, as in the case with most innovations, its reliability was viewed with some suspicion. Hence the annual test was in the nature of a confidence building exercise. It was my job, in addition to supervising the parachute section, to drop test all the parachutes at Kohat and Miramshah – not an exciting task but one that gave me a little more flying and had its interesting moments.

In order to carry out these tests, two dummies had been made in the station workshops, well before my time. They were made of hard wood, with truncated arms and legs sufficiently long to hold the shoulder and leg straps of the harnesses in place. These torsos were life size and approximated to the weight of a man, about 170 lbs. The weight was made up by fixing lead sheeting to the chest and back and padding it out to give a human shape. Face and hair had been painted on the heads by an unknown artist and they were affectionately known as Mutt and Jeff after the characters in a popular strip cartoon of the day. The effect was quite realistic and I had many amusing incidents with Mutt and Jeff.

The test procedure was to fit each parachute harness to one of the dummies, adjusting the straps until it was a snug fit. The dummy was then loaded onto one of the Wapiti's bomb racks by means of a lug in the small of its back. One end of a short static line was then tied to the rip cord handle, the other end being secured to a convenient part of the bomb rack so that when the dummy fell, the rip cord was pulled out and left hanging on the static line which was still attached to the bomb rack. Mutt and Jeff could fly together, one under each wing, so that two parachutes could be tested at a time.

Failures were extremely rare, and I can recall no case of a failure caused by the parachute itself. My only faulty test occurred shortly after my return from Lower Topa. Choosing a time when there was little activity on the aerodrome, I warned the Duty Pilot of a test, and as I taxied out with Mutt and Jeff grinning below the wings, he put out the signal indicating that parachute dropping was in progress and landing temporarily forbidden. He then stood by with a red Verey cartridge in case anybody failed to see the ground signal. I took off, completed my usual left handed circuit, and approached the aerodrome into wind at 1,000 feet and 90 mph. As I was nearing the circle in the middle of the aerodrome, my air gunner stood up and looked over the side. His job was to pat me on the shoulder as the circle, now hidden from my view, passed directly under us. Flying with my right hand, I bent down and found the bomb release handle with my left. A tap on my shoulder and I gave the release a sharp pull, feeling the Wapiti rise as it lost some 400 lb of weight, indicating that Mutt and Jeff had departed. I started a turn to the left and looked over my shoulder expecting to see both Mutt and Jeff floating serenely down. There was only one of them, but I could see a large puff of dust on the ground some distance away. Either Mutt or Jeff had arrived first but without his parachute.

'What the hell has happened?' I shouted to my passenger who was still hanging over the side. There was a pause –

'It looks as if his parachute is still attached: the rip cord must have snapped.'

That was unlikely as it was made of high tensile steel wire, but clearly something had failed.

I completed another circuit and landed well away from the tender with which Stonebank was collecting the parachutes.

After we had taxied in I inspected my bomb racks and found one rip cord handle hanging correctly on its piece of cord from one of the racks. From the other, a short piece of static line only dangled. It was clear that what had happened was that the static line had been an inch or so too long which had allowed it to blow out in the slipstream and become entangled in a projection from the rack. When the dummy was released, the sharp edge of the projection had cut through the cord before it had pulled out the rip cord and that was why the parachute had never opened: the canopy was undamaged although the pack was battered and torn. Mutt, or it may have been Jeff, was quite unscathed with the usual stupid grin on his stupid face. We did

91

not tell the owner of that parachute about the incident in case he got quite the wrong idea about the reason for the failure.

Shortly after this incident, I was due to go up to Miramshah to drop test the ten or so parachutes of the detached Flight there. It was decided that I would fly up one Monday morning in September with Flying Officer Collings who had to take his aircraft to complete some survey work in Waziristan. Mutt and Jeff were to accompany us on the bomb racks and I would use one of the Miramshah Wapitis to do the drop testing. The weather was most unpromising as Raymond Collings and I studied the forecast that morning. Strong winds and dust storms mingled with torrential rain indicated that we were catching the edge of the SW monsoon which did not usually penetrate as far as the Frontier. We decided to wait for a clearance which came in mid afternoon, and then we set off, Collings flying the aircraft with me in the back and the two dummies grinning under the wings. We took the direct route up the Hangu valley to Thal and thence over the low hills towards Miramshah. However, half way to Thal we ran into a blinding sandstorm in which visibility was reduced to zero and Collings had some difficulty in maintaining contact with the ground. As the high mountains of the Tirah lay to the north, he gradually edged down to the south towards Bannu, hoping to skirt the sandstorm and approach Miramshah from the south east which was fairly flat.

It was no good. The driving dust and sand became thicker and thicker making visual navigation almost impossible and cutting off our retreat to Kohat. We continued south for a while with myself hanging over the side to try to recognise a landmark while Collings flew as low as he dared. Suddenly a railway line loomed out of the haze, running at a fine angle to our course. As I well knew, there was only one railway in that area and it ran south from Bannu towards the Punjab plain. We had therefore passed Bannu and were heading away from it over flat country. I shouted this to Collings and told him to turn round and try to follow the line back to Bannu. We lost it once during the turn but soon picked it up again and, after a few minutes, the bungalows and buildings of Bannu began to flash past under us.

'We'll land at Islam Chowki and let this clear,' said Collings. I thought to myself, 'If we can find Islam Chowki,' which was an emergency landing ground about five miles to the west of Bannu, on the road to Miramshah.

'Steer about 260° from the centre of the town and it should appear in about four minutes,' I called hopefully.

Raymond stood the Wapiti on its wing tip over Bannu station, which must have looked quite spectacular from the platform, and steadied down on 260. I could dimly see a road running with us which simply had to be the Frontier road to Miramshah. I knew that Islam Chowki lay alongside that road and we were bound to see it if we could stick to the road. The sandstorm was worse than ever and, even under my goggles, my eyes were smarting painfully. Suddenly on the left a white concrete marker stone appeared, dimly visible through the murk. I slapped Collings on the shoulder, pointed down and he spotted it. We had no time to search for a windsock but Collings thought that the wind was roughly from the north. He banked sharply round to the left and I lost all touch with the landing ground. How he landed on it I will never know but, after flying south for a couple of minutes he returned on a northerly heading, getting lower and slower until suddenly one of the marker pylons appeared again. He closed the throttle, held off beside it and landed. From the surface, we appeared to be on the landing ground and subsequently we found we were almost in the centre of it. It was a remarkable effort and I was quietly thankful to have been in the back seat and not the front as I doubt whether I could have put the Wapiti down so skilfully.

Our troubles were far from over. As Raymond started to taxy cautiously through the gloom towards the edge of the landing ground, the heavens opened and torrential rain came crashing down as only monsoon rain can. In a moment the landing ground was a sea of water and the Wapiti was up to its axles and beginning to sink into the churned up sand, aided by the additional weight of Mutt and Jeff. There was no alternative but to stop and switch off before the aeroplane stood on its nose; and there we were, marooned in a flood and soaked to the skin. The water was pouring through both cockpits and creating clouds of steam from the hot engine. I dived down into the tail to try to find the cockpit covers before the electrical system was ruined by the water, dragged them out and flung one over Collings head and crept under the other one myself.

In a few moments the downpour eased to steady rain and we peered out. The whole landing ground, which had now become visible, was under a foot of water and we were right in the centre, a few feet from the circle. We could see the chowkidar's hut ahead of us on the perimeter, but no sign of life at all.

'We'd better cover the cockpits and the engine and make for shelter,' said Raymond. 'There's no need to put chocks under the wheels – nothing will move this.'

We struggled with the heavy, sodden cockpit covers and got them tied down securely. The engine tarpaulin was much more difficult, but we eventually got it over the hissing, muttering engine which would give some protection to the plugs and ignition.

'We'll be lucky if that starts up again,' said Raymond, as we tied the last string.

'With a bit of luck, there may be enough heat left in the engine to dry out the moisture under the cover.' I replied.

Raymond pursed his lips doubtfully as we had a last look round. Glancing at Mutt and Jeff, he said, 'Your damned dummies have brought us this bad luck; who ever heard of anybody flying round with those ridiculous things under his wings.'

'Nonsense,' I replied, 'it was their influence that enabled you to pull off such a splendid forced landing.'

Leaving the forlorn Wapiti we struggled through the water to the chowkidar's hut with our parachutes slung over our shoulders. Fortunately the door was unlocked and we staggered in, soaked and exhausted. Raymond pulled a saturated packet of cigarettes out of his overalls and threw them down in disgust.

'Well, what do we do now?'

It was a difficult problem. Less than an hour of daylight remained; there was no telephone on the landing ground; Bannu was five miles away and the Frontier road was not safe after nightfall. I had brought the sodden maps with me and I studied the large scale one of the area.

'Ah, there is a Frontier Constabulary post about three miles up the road towards Miramshah,' I said. 'Perhaps we should make for that, get a police guard for the aeroplane and phone through to Kohat or Miramshah.'

We discussed the various possibilities and decided that we must stick together, and if that meant leaving the Wapiti unguarded, it was less important than our own safety. Anyway, little harm could come to the aeroplane during the night, bogged down as it was in the middle of the landing ground. There were no signs of life around us and it was highly unlikely that anybody had seen us land in the sandstorm. The police post was closer than Bannu and we could probably obtain guards from there and help to unstick the Wapiti. It should also be possible to phone through to Miramshah, report our plight and hope for a rescue party by road.

By this time it was almost dark and we were getting distinctly chilled in our wet clothes. We hid our parachutes in the darkest corner of the hut and wiped and checked our revolvers which were always carried loaded on flights through tribal territory. The rain had almost stopped as we stepped out along the tarmac road. Gradually my eyes became accustomed to the darkness and, although it was initially a pitch black night, it was easy enough to follow the wet shining road which ran in a dead straight line across the stony plain towards the foothills in the west. Not a light was to be seen and the only sounds other than our own footsteps were the scurrying of little animals in the scrub beside the road. At one point a jackal ran across in front of us and the ghastly laugh of a hyena startled both of us.

The silence and darkness seemed to inhibit speech and Raymond and I tramped along at a fair pace without a word, with our right hands comfortably close to our revolvers. There was not a soul or vehicle on that road and it took us just over an hour to reach the top of a slope from which we could see dim lights ahead.

'That must be the police post,' said Raymond, 'What is it called?'

'Saidiq,' I answered.

For some reason we almost spoke in whispers. A quarter moon was rising, the rain had stopped and our clothes had begun to dry. In fact, I was beginning to sweat under my flying overalls and our spirits rose at the prospect of reaching the end of the eerie journey.

On approaching Saidiq, we could make out the crenellated walls of a small fort. Suddenly a searchlight came on, flooding us with light and dazzling us completely. A sharp challenge rang out in Urdu and we halted at once, answering in Urdu and saying who we were.

'Don't move,' warned Raymond, 'wait until they come out to meet us and leave the talking to me.' His Urdu was a good deal better than mine.

There was a moment's pause while the searchlight continued to illuminate us and the sound of a heavy door being opened in the background was heard. A police constable with a rifle levelled at us, accompanied by a havildar (sergeant) approached down the centre of the beam and we remained motionless – one took no liberties with men on watch and ward duties on the Frontier. Raymond explained to the havildar that we were Royal Air Force officers who had been forced by the storm to land at Islam Chowki and our aeroplane was unguarded and stuck in the mud. The havildar saluted smartly, said that he was in command of the post and invited us cordially to come inside. A very cheerful bunch of about twenty policemen surrounded us and listened to our story again while we were stripping off our clothes and donning police shirts, slacks and stockings which they produced for us. It was then that we discovered that their telephone connection with Bannu had been destroyed during the storm and there was no way in which we could inform Kohat or Miramshah of our plight. We had now been missing for some hours and the routine 'overdue' action would have been taken. At dawn Wapitis would start to scour our route for any signs of us. Saidiq had no vehicles, depending upon transport from Bannu when necessary. As the Frontier road was closed during the night, no civilian vehicles would pass the post until the morning. There was nothing to be done until dawn and as we tucked into the policemen's evening meal of goat curry and chapattis, we accepted the inevitable and relaxed.

The havildar, whose name was Gujrat Singh, was clearly delighted at this unusual incident in the dull routine of his post and could not have been more helpful. He promised that the whole of his small force, with the exception of a couple of constables to look after the post, would set off with us at dawn to help salvage the Wapiti and, hopefully, to get airborne again. With this settled, we bedded down for the night on string charpoys in the open air on the roof of the fort where the storm had given way to a warm starry night. It was now so clear that I could just make out the lights of Bannu some nine or ten miles away.

I was aroused at five o'clock as a clear, cool dawn was breaking and dressed again in the sepoy's clothes as mine were in a terrible state. A posse of eighteen very smart policemen was drawn up outside the fort and, led by Gujrat Singh, we set off back down the road at the regulation 120 paces to the minute. Gujrat Singh hoped that a contractor's truck or a civilian bus might pass which he could commandeer to take us part of the way, but we met nothing at all on the one and a quarter hour march to Islam Chowki. For the last mile of that journey we could see the Wapiti standing out against the skyline on the vast featureless plain and, as we approached the hut, the chowkidar who had come on duty for the day emerged with his rifle slung round his shoulder and a worried expression on his face. He gabbled excitedly to the havildar, gesticulating wildly towards the Wapiti. Gujrat Singh looked puzzled and explained to me that the chowkidar dared not approach the Wapiti as it was guarded by devils. This defeated me and Raymond and we looked at each other perplexed – until it suddenly came to me that Mutt and Jeff would still be grinning from their bomb racks and had been more than enough to terrify the chowkidar. I roared with laughter, which was probably a tactless thing to do, and tried to explain, but neither Raymond nor I found it easy to describe the drop testing of parachutes with our limited Urdu and I am sure that those policemen retained the idea that our dummies were some kind of strange psychological weapon that we were taking to the Frontier to drop on the Fakir of Ipi. During the next hour or two I noticed that even the policemen treated Mutt and Jeff with great respect and the old chowkidar would go nowhere near them.

In broad daylight it was clear that the Wapiti had come to rest in a shallow depression which was still full of wet sand and mud into which the wheels had sunk almost to the axles. As time spent in reconnaissance is said to be seldom wasted, we surveyed the landing ground thoroughly and found one long strip somewhat higher and dryer than the rest which extended almost the whole length of the landing ground, probably 400 yards in all. This strip lay into the wind which was very light, and we reckoned that if we could manhandle the Wapiti onto it – and then start the engine – we should be able to take off safely. We could lighten the aeroplane by leaving Mutt and Jeff behind and collect them later when Islam Chowki had dried out completely.

The first thing to do was to remove the dummies but the policemen were none too keen to handle them. However, with Raymond taking the head of each one, two policemen were eventually persuaded to take the weight of the body while I climbed into the cockpit and operated the release. They staggered a bit as the load dropped into their arms, and, for a moment, I thought the dummies were going to fall onto their toes, but all was well and each dummy was carried over to the hut. By this time the superstitious policemen were beginning to appreciate the joke and even the chowkidar was tentatively prodding Jeff with his rifle. Gujrat Singh maintained a dignified silence throughout this part of the operation but his expression seemed almost to say – 'The odd behaviour of barmy British airmen is no concern of mine.'

After the removal of Mutt and Jeff, the wheels had to be freed from the mud and sand. The chowkidar produced spades and in fifteen minutes we had the wheels standing cleanly in a shallow trough with a sloping track leading up out of it. The question now was whether our combined efforts could lift and move the Wapiti forward onto firmer ground. We ranged eight policemen under each of the lower wings and two on each side of the tail. The lower wing of a Wapiti was quite close to the ground and it was possible for the policemen to bend double and press their backs up against the lower surface. Firstly, those on the tail lifted it up to waist height and, at a given word, the men under the wings tried to straighten up together and so lift the Wapiti bodily. At the first heave the weight came off the wheels and the men were able to inch forward, literally carrying the aeroplane on their backs. They sweated and strained and covered about three feet at the first effort which was enough to bring the aeroplane out of its trench, but not clear of the depression.

Raymond and I slipped two planks of wood under the wheels as they came out of the trench and the policemen thankfully lowered their burden to the ground. The planks held and there was no sinkage. It was now after 8 o'clock and the sun was rapidly gaining in strength and drying up the surface. However the depression in which the aeroplane stood was still very wet and would clearly take several hours to dry out. If we could move the Wapiti a further twenty yards it would be on the edge of the firm strip from which we hoped eventually to take off. A rope was tied to the axle and we put four men on to it with four lifting the tail as before and the remaining ten under the lower wings. With a concerted effort the Wapiti was slowly dragged up on to firm ground leaving smaller and shallower furrows as the wheels moved out of the soft sand. The policemen were as delighted as we were as they sat down to recover their breath and Raymond and I walked round and shook them all by the hand.

'Now, will it start?' said Raymond, 'if not, we must get a lift into Bannu and let somebody know where we are as we are now about 16 hours overdue at Miramshah.'

I climbed up and stripped off the engine cover while Raymond removed cockpit covers and took the portable metal chocks out of the rear stowage. The plugs and ignition harness seemed quite dry in spite of the soaking the previous evening. We might be lucky and get the engine started after all. Unfortunately none of the policemen had ever wound the starting handles of a Wapiti and I was reluctant to risk letting an inexperienced man take a turn in case the engine fired and frightened him so much that he fell into the propeller.

'I'll wind and you take first turn in the cockpit,' I said to Raymond as I placed the chocks in front of the wheels and asked Gujrat Singh to move his men well out of the way. Raymond agreed saying, 'If she starts, you'll have to pack things up, say goodbye and thank everybody while I warm her up and test the magnetos. We dare not stop the engine again.'

I braced myself on the wing and started turning the starboard handle. We were lucky; the engine fired with a bang and a billowing cloud of blue smoke from the exhaust which would have been enough to send any policeman through the prop. It did not continue to run but that was a good sign and I knew that the engine was not damp and should start if I persevered, which I did, winding like fury to the amazement of the twenty spectators and with the encouragement of Raymond from the cockpit. Just as I was beginning to tire, she fired again, and after a few coughs and more blue smoke, roared into life. I disengaged the handle and gingerly climbed down backwards from the wing, joining the havildar and his men who were smiling hugely while I puffed and blew after my exertions.

Starting a Wapiti with one handle was not the easiest of exercises, but Raymond knew his own aeroplane well and had produced a perfect mixture for a good start.

After a little rough and uneven running, the engine settled down to a steady beat and sounded perfectly all right to me as I stood watching the wings and wheels vibrating under the power. The throttle was closed and Raymond beckoned from the cockpit. After I had climbed up to his shoulder he shouted, 'Hang on to the tail while I run her up; then take away the chocks and swing me round so that I can taxy up the hard strip. If it's firm enough I'll go to the end and wait for you there.'

Nodding, I climbed down and draped myself over the tail, an uncomfortable job usually done by our Flight coolies. Raymond ran the engine up to full throttle while I clung on grimly, battered by driven sand and small stones. After half a minute of misery, he throttled back and I went round to the front. He gave me a 'thumbs up' and then waved away the chocks. I pulled them out, stowed them in the rear cockpit and went to the port wing to pull him round to taxy down the strip. Off he went slowly, the wheels making very little indentation which showed that it was quite hard enough for a take off.

I explained to Gujrat Singh that we were leaving, thanked him again for all his help and said that we would send his clothes back in a day or two when the dummies were collected. All the policemen saluted smartly and I set off to follow Raymond to the far side of the landing ground where he had turned into wind and was waiting for me.

'It seems fine,' he said as I climbed in behind him. 'Full revs and no mag drop. I think the water did it good.'

Checking that all the policemen had moved out of the way, Raymond opened the throttle and away we went down the firm strip with a few puddles and damp spots still visible on either side. It was a quarter past ten and we had been at Islam Chowki for some eighteen hours; people must be getting pretty worried about us I thought as we left the ground smoothly in less than 300 yards. As soon as it was clear that the engine was not going to fail on take off, Raymond turned steeply round to the right and dived back across the landing ground where we waved farewell to our overnight hosts. Remaining low, we flew up the road and past the police post where again we waved our thanks to the two constables left on duty, one of whom had lent me the shirt I was wearing.

Thirty five minutes later Miramshah came into view and after sideslipping neatly round the corner of the fort, Raymond landed smoothly in front of the gates and taxied onto the small apron. As we climbed down to the ground, weary, unshaven and still dressed as Indian police constables, the Flight Commander ran out to meet us with a look of astonished relief on his face.

'Thank God you're safe; there's a tremendous panic going on as everybody is convinced that the storm forced you into the Tirah and that you are now in Afridi hands. Where the hell have you been?'

We told him briefly and he rushed off to report our safe arrival.

Over a leisurely lunch in the Mess it was decided that a Crossley should set off at dawn the following morning to take back our borrowed clothes, freshly dhobied, and to collect Mutt and Jeff from the landing ground. In addition to asking for official thanks to be sent to the Saidiq police post, Raymond Collings and I selected a large box of tinned food and small luxuries from the Miramshah NAAFI to go to the policemen with a message of gratitude.

CHAPTER 8

WATCH AND WARD

'Well, that just about completes our plans for the move,' said Pop Stemp as he collected up the papers scattered over his desk. It was a few days after my return from the Mutt and Jeff episode, and Pop was due to take the Flight to Miramshah for October and November. Turning to me, he said, 'I want you to take the road convoy up, leaving here as soon as the airmen have seen the four Wapitis off. It should take you about six hours; if you get going by eight o'clock, you will have plenty of time to get to Miramshah and off the roads before dark.'

On this occasion I was quite happy to go up by road as the route ran through Bannu and past Islam Chowki. It would give me the opportunity to pass the time of day with my friends the policemen.

We were due to move on 1st October, my four vehicles being loaded up after work on the previous day. Miramshah was stocked with the basic essentials for operating Wapitis – fuel, bombs, ammunition, pyrotechnics, trestles, tail trolleys, chocks, etc including a spare engine and propeller. One essential item was the 'Flight Lock-up'. Every Flight Sergeant who was worth his salt kept a Flight lock-up consisting of a thousand and one things that 'might come in useful', borrowed, stolen, liberated and acquired in every conceivable way. Almost any job could be carried out by resorting to the lock-up, and it was essential to take it wherever one went. It usually resided in a large and heavily padlocked almirah (cupboard) in the Flight Sergeant's office under his eagle eye; one of his more important preparations for Miramshah was to pack his most valuable and useful items into cases, also heavily padlocked, for travelling. These lock-ups were illegal to the extent that their contents were additional to the official scale of holdings for the Flight and every artifice had to be practised to disguise their presence during annual inspections. Every inspecting officer knew perfectly well that they existed and, during an inspection, such remarks as 'Glad to see that you are not holding more than your entitlement, Flight' would be made, to which the reply would be, 'Thank you, Sir, the entitlement is quite adequate.' Flight Sergeant Brown was no better and no worse than his colleagues and I was glad to see five large, unmarked but locked cases go aboard the Crossley in which he was to travel.

The airmen were up even earlier than usual on the following morning to prepare the four Wapitis for the flight and to see them off before we left by road. I brought Hukmud Khan and my bedroll, suitcase and flying kit, including the parachute, which had been dried and renovated since its wetting at Islam Chowki, down from the Mess and had my breakfast with the

104

airmen after work on the aeroplanes was finished at seven o'clock. Flight Sergeant Brown, Sergeant Ward and some thirty five airmen made up my party – a very cheerful party as the Miramshah detachment was always popular. Being slightly higher than Kohat, Miramshah was a little cooler, particularly at night, the accommodation was quite comfortable, the discipline relaxed and all of us looked forward to two interesting months, returning to Kohat in plenty of time for Christmas. Apart from their annual trip to Lower Topa and any leave they might be able to afford, the airmen had few opportunities to get away from Kohat and led a very restricted life. Only the half dozen air gunners flew regularly and most of these hard working men never saw the Frontier landscape from the air during their whole tour. Consequently the trip to Miramshah was an adventure for most of them and we always tried to make it as interesting as possible.

The convoy made good time to Bannu and we pulled into the Public Works Department depot there in just under three hours. Here we refuelled to avoid any need for the Crossleys to take up precious fuel at Miramshah. The PWD's heavy and often risky task of maintaining fuel stocks often in the most isolated places meant that both the Army and the RAF did all they could to minimise the risks by economising in petrol, guarding PWD fuel convoys, and taking up fuel at their depots whenever practicable.

I had decided that we would eat our packed lunch on the landing ground at Islam Chowki. The airmen had shown great interest and concern when Collings and I had been missing for eighteen hours with Mutt and Jeff. None of them knew Islam Chowki and this seemed a good opportunity to tell them the story at the actual scene of the incident, followed by a call on the Saidiq police post. We pulled into the landing ground at about midday and there was the old chowkidar, sound asleep outside the hut. I think he recognised me, but he certainly remembered Mutt and Jeff when I mentioned them. The PWD had clearly done some work on the surface recently and repaired some of the damage done by the flooding. In particular, they had filled in the holes and ruts made by our wheels.

We ate our rather stale sandwiches in the shade of the hut and washed them down with Murree beer while I explained how the policemen had lifted the Wapiti bodily out of the mud.

'I reckon you were lucky to get her started again – and with only one handle,' said Brown, looking at some of the remaining evidence of the storm. Leaving some chocolate and cigarettes for the chowkidar who had quickly eaten the last of the sandwiches, we moved on up the Frontier road.

Gujrat Singh was still in charge at Saidiq and delighted to see me. He insisted on shaking hands with every one of the thirty five airmen and would, I believe, have made a curry for all of us had I not insisted that we move on. I left with a promise that I would fly over from Miramshah and carry out a Popham Panel exercise with his post one morning during the next two months. Many of the Frontier Constabulary were Sikhs and Gujrat Singh was an example of the fine type of man that this force attracted. Relations with the RAF were excellent, and I felt that our incident at Islam Chowki followed by this visit by my party helped to cement those relations.

Before we left and while the airmen were clustered round on the roof of the fort looking at the view, I had a few words with them.

'Saidiq police post is the point at which the Frontier road runs into North Waziristan and from now on we will be in tribal territory. We are unlikely to meet any trouble but sniping at convoys is not unknown. Will you mount the Lewis guns in the gun ring on top of each cab, with Sanderson, Jones and Watson in charge of them. I want you all to keep your rifles by your side with magazines in but not with one up the spout; safety catches on, please. Is there anything else, Flight?'

'Perhaps the Crossleys should keep a little closer together now,' said Brown, 'say about twenty yards apart.' I agreed with this and we set off on the last thirty odd miles.

A gentle climb through rocky undulating country brought us

out onto a flat, stony plain entirely surrounded by mountains. This was the plain of Dardoni in which the fort of Miramshah and the aerodrome stood. During the 1920s another landing ground had existed, several miles across the plain to the north west of Miramshah. This old isolated aerodrome had been moved under the protection of the Miramshah fort after Dardoni had suffered a number of attacks from bands of dacoits. As we turned into the aerodrome, the four Wapitis of the earlier detachment had just taken off on their way back to Kohat and our own four were lined up on the small concrete apron outside the gates of the fort. Except in an operational emergency, it was forbidden to keep more than about four aeroplanes at Miramshah at any one time. They had to be wheeled inside the fort at night and hangars only existed for an absolute maximum of six at a time. Any left out on the apron had to be provided with a separate armed guard which created something of an embarrassment.

A busy two months lay ahead for the Flight. The hot weather was on the wane and the season of intensive training with the many Army units in Waziristan was beginning. In addition, there was work on a photographic survey of the whole of Waziristan in progress and there would be constant calls for air cooperation of one kind and another from military, police and civilian sources. We could devote any spare time in continuing our bombing training on the small range which lay close to the site of the old Dardoni aerodrome. There were five pilots in the Flight and we looked forward to getting at least sixty hours flying each during the two months detachment.

One of my earliest tasks could well have been my last had fortune not favoured me. It was a bright, clear, sunny morning and I had been given the somewhat unusual job of taking an Army officer as passenger to inspect a number of villages in the mountains about forty miles away. My passenger was engaged with a civil organisation in compiling a book known as the 'Tribal Directory'. This was a form of encyclopaedia which contained the resources, population and other data of every

107

known village in the Frontier region. It was a book of reference much used by military intelligence as well as by the civilian administration of the Frontier Province. Many of the villages were virtually unapproachable by road or on horseback, either because they lay in inaccessible areas or because the inhabitants were known to be hostile. The obvious way to reconnoitre such villages was to fly round them, assess their size and count the houses, haystacks, cultivated areas and note any fortified towers etc. As I was to find out, this could be a tricky business.

After discussing with my passenger, a Captain Kelly, which villages he wished to study, identifying them on the map and planning our route, we took off shortly after 9 o'clock and climbed away to the south west. Oil pressures and temperatures were satisfactory as I flew up the Razmak valley at 3,000 feet, maintaining a good safe height until I was satisfied that all was well with the Wapiti before plunging into the real business of the day. Our villages lay beyond Razmak camp in the foothills of the high mountain range which formed the frontier at this point. It was forbidding country, consisting of a succession of narrow, deep valleys and defiles leading up towards the high peaks, which in some cases topped 12,000 feet. Six villages had to be reconnoitred and the first five were straightforward enough, all of them lying on the lower slopes of the foothills with plenty of space around them in which to manoeuvre. I flew round each one for about five minutes at heights varying between 500 feet and 1,000 feet, while Kelly made copious notes and gave me instructions to 'go a bit lower' or 'round once more' or 'turn steeper' as he hung precariously over the side and studied each village intently. When I was not keeping a beady eye on the sharply rising ground to the west, I could see upturned faces down below and, remembering my earlier experience in this area, it did cross my mind that I was presenting an excellent target to anyone disposed to take a potshot at me. Neither Kelly nor I saw any telltale puffs of smoke during our twisting and turning, and the engine continued to run sweetly.

I turned towards the last village on our list which was

situated some way up one of the defiles leading into the mountains. We identified the miserable collection of huts and hovels and I circled round it to the left at 1,000 feet. The defile was narrow and I felt horribly shut in by its rocky barren sides.

'Lower,' shouted Kelly, pressing his palms downwards over my shoulder, 'and fly up the left hand side of the village.'

I dropped down to five hundred feet and turned to fly up the left side of the defile to enable Kelly to get a good view and perhaps take a photograph with his own camera as the sun was shining down into the defile. Having put the Wapiti into a good position for him, I turned my attention to what lay ahead for my next manoeuvre. My heart almost stopped with the shock of realising that the defile at that low height was narrowing so rapidly that I could not turn round. The Wapiti certainly lacked the power to climb up over the mountains and I seemed to have no alternative but to fly straight into the rapidly rising ground. There was only one way out of the dilemma. I shouted to Kelly to hold tight, simultaneously pushing the throttle wide open and the nose down. I dived to about 200 feet from the floor of the gorge, keeping as far to the left hand side as I dared. The aeroplane responded nobly and I reached 120 mph before pulling the nose up steeply, letting the speed fall to 80 mph before putting on full right rudder and bringing her over in a semi-stalled turn. The nose dropped away vertically and I let her drop like a stone until she had built up enough speed to pull out, now pointing down the defile in the opposite – and safe – direction. Naturally I kept the throttle wide open throughout the manoeuvre and we came out of it back over the village having gained a little height.

'Don't ever ask me to do that again,' I shouted to Kelly as his very pale face peered over my shoulder. 'I hope you got what you wanted because I don't want to go up there again – not at that height, anyway.' He too had obviously had a bit of a fright and put his thumbs up.

Of course it was entirely my fault, not his, but some trick of the bright sunlight and deep shadow in the defile had misled me into thinking that we had more room than was in fact the case. I learned a very sharp lesson. It was a situation in which it was all too easy to find oneself in the Frontier territory and the Wapiti simply did not have the power to rectify one's mistakes. I had unwittingly taken an appalling risk and got away with it. Captain Kelly, who had not of course understood what was happening, was somewhat shaken when I later explained our predicament to him over a cup of coffee. However, he said he had obtained all the information he wanted so we could call it a successful trip.

This was not the only lesson I learned at Miramshah. There were four of us in the Mess, and the other three were keen bridge players – I had never played the game having confined my activities to poker and liar dice. There was little to do in the evenings; no radio of course, no cinema, no billiards and certainly no night life. It was soon made clear to me that if I did not learn to play bridge, the evenings of my three colleagues would be ruined. I was not particularly keen to play but, for the sake of harmony, I clearly had to bow to their wishes. Bridge was the only game allowed by King's Regulations to be played in a mess for money. No cash was permitted to change hands, but a bridge book was kept in which all winnings and losses were entered and then included in mess bills at the end of each month. It would be an exaggeration to say that I paid the mess bills of the other members of the mess for two months, but it certainly felt like it at the time. Night after night I would go down on the wrong side of the bridge book to my own chagrin and the irritation of my partner of the evening. The experience put me off the game to such an extent that I refused to play bridge again for more than thirty years, and then only family bridge with friends who were close enough to ignore a revoke or forgive an injudicious 'double'.

Fortunately for me, bridge was not played every evening, particularly if we had an over-night visitor who had to be suitably entertained. On one such evening John Pope, who had been with me at Cranwell and was in the 27 Squadron

Flight which we had just relieved, was with us for a day and night due to an unserviceable aeroplane which had caused him to drop out of a tribal reconnaissance and land at Miramshah for repairs. He related an extraordinary experience which he had had during the previous month, and of which I had already heard a garbled account. It happened that he had to fly a portly Brigadier from Miramshah to Sora Rogha one morning, leave him there and return alone. Sora Rogha was a small, irregular shaped landing ground, thirty miles south of Miramshah, alongside the headquarters of the South Waziristan Scouts. The landing ground was tricky in that two sides disappeared over precipices. The Scouts' fort was on the third side and the fourth ran uphill steeply into scrub and thorn bushes.

John landed and taxied up to the fort to unload his passenger. He did not wish to stop the engine as he was taking off again immediately and well knew the problems of restarting a hot engine. As it was always difficult for strangers to climb out of the rear cockpit, John undid his straps and climbed down to help the Brigadier. Standing on the ground, with the engine quietly ticking over, he guided his passenger's feet into the footholds as he started his climb down to earth. When halfway down, the Brigadier, searching for a handhold, put his left hand over the rim of the pilot's cockpit to steady himself. The throttle lever was situated under the cockpit combing and the brigadier pushed it open accidently. To John Pope's horror, the engine burst into life with a throaty roar and the Wapiti started to move forward with the Brigadier in tow and John hanging on to his ankle. The Brigadier was much too confused to react to any instructions to close the throttle and a horrifying situation was developing. John yanked at the ankles of his passenger, who came crashing down on top of him, leaving the Wapiti to depart whither it wished. Luckily the throttle had been only partially opened and it trundled off more or less in a straight line and, also luckily, it was pointing towards the side of the landing ground where the ground rose among the thorn bushes.

By the time John had extricated himself from below the winded soldier, the Wapiti was well on its way across the stony surface, gathering speed all the time but keeping fairly straight. Followed by half a dozen Scouts, John dashed after it but it soon became clear that he was losing ground. Any other direction would have been disastrous; the Wapiti would either have plunged over a cliff or crashed into the walls of the fort. As it was, it reached the end of the landing ground and, brushing thorn bushes aside with the propeller, started to climb the slope. After twenty or thirty yards, the slope became too steep, the tail skid dug in and prevented it from running back and it came to rest, roaring away at half throttle and perched some fifty feet above the landing ground. Panting and blowing, John shouted to the soldiers to keep away from the propeller while he struggled on his hands and knees against the slipstream to reach the fuselage. Blasted by small stones and pieces of thorn bush, he fought his way up to the cockpit, closed the throttle and leaned over to turn off the engine switches. There was silence at last as he climbed down and leaned against the fuselage, completely winded.

When he recovered sufficiently to inspect the aeroplane, nothing seemed to have been damaged. Even the propeller was only slightly scratched by thorns and its tips had not touched the ground, which was extraordinary in view of the gradient of the slope. The tyres had not been punctured and the tail skid looked undamaged although it was buried deeply in the sand and preventing the Wapiti from running back. How on earth to get it down onto the landing ground was now John's problem. He could, of course get a message to Miramshah to send a rescue party of airmen by road to extricate it, but he did not wish to do that if the local manpower which, if unskilled, was plentiful, could move it safely.

The Scouts had two British officers at Sora Rogha which eased the problem of communication with the Indian troops and a careful scheme was evolved. Ropes were tied to both sides of the rear fuselage and led away forward under the wings. A dozen men on each of these ropes held the aeroplane against the slope while others lifted the tail skid out of the sand. Holding the tail up, with the propeller turned into a horizontal position to avoid catching the tips on the ground, the Wapiti was allowed to move back down the slope under its own weight with the men on the long ropes controlling it like two tug of war teams. With the two officers shouting instructions, and John Pope having kittens, his aeroplane slowly rolled back down the tracks which it had made on the way up, and a very relieved Pilot Officer saw it once again on level ground. A more thorough inspection revealed no damage, even to the wooden tail skid which must have been subjected to a severe strain.

After allowing the engine to cool down for half an hour, John managed to get it started again with the help of the Scouts, some of whom had been taught to wind up a Wapiti. It ran perfectly and he flew back to Miramshah, rather late and a little wiser. We all learned something from this incident which was – if you have a passenger and do not wish to stop the engine, either make him climb out unaided or have chocks placed in front of the wheels before you leave the cockpit to help him.

John Pope could have been accused of some carelessness over this episode but he was not in fact criticised in any official way. I think that it was fully appreciated by our superiors that flying in and out of these small, rough and difficult landing grounds created problems which often called for resource and initiative from both pilots and air gunners. Rules had to be flexible in such circumstances and we were all expected to display a good sense of airmanship and solve our problems to the best of our ability without fear of subsequent criticism.

In general the weather was excellent during my stay at Miramshah, the haze and heat of the hot months having given way to clear, cooler weather with intermittent rain to lay the dust. I had not been very comfortable during the first few months flying round the Frontier; the Wapiti seemed a fragile and underpowered aeroplane among the gigantic mountain ranges while the landing grounds seemed impossibly small and often hazardous. With experience, however, came confidence and in the better weather at Miramshah I found the scenery becoming less awesome and, in a curious way, the Wapiti more robust. Incidents such as that with Captain Kelly and earlier with Mutt and Jeff had proved to me how tough and reliable the aeroplane was and, as my confidence grew, so did my enjoyment of flying over Waziristan which I found both varied and interesting.

One afternoon LAC Sanderson and I were flying back from Wana, a Brigade headquarters in South Waziristan where I had been arranging an exercise with the soldiers. The cumulus clouds were beginning to build up over the higher mountains, which was usual in the afternoons, giving us a bumpy ride as the Wapiti wallowed in the airpockets below the clouds. As I flew up the Razmak valley and past Alexandra Picquet at 3,000 feet, I could see a solid wall of rain ahead, barring my way to Miramshah. It covered a wide front. I could not get round it to the left because of the high mountains on the Frontier and it appeared to stretch to infinity on the right. As it was probably an isolated storm, I carried on towards it, knowing that there were no high obstacles on my direct route home at that height.

Only when I entered the storm did I realise that it was hail – and no ordinary hail! Hailstones as large as pigeons' eggs crashed down on to the Wapiti, bouncing off the wings and engine cowling in all directions with a noise that I could hear through my helmet above the roar of the engine. I heard a gasp from the back and glanced over my shoulder to see that Sanderson had disappeared onto the floor of his cockpit. A long crack spread over my windscreen as one hailstone hit the centre of the glass panel. I was committed now and the only thing to do was to plough through, hoping that it was a narrow belt. I lowered my seat to the bottom position to protect my head as much as possible and concentrated on keeping straight on instruments. The hail continued to thrash down for two or three minutes and we emerged into bright sunshine as suddenly as we had entered the storm. The engine had not missed a beat although I had been worried about carburetter icing, but there were some tatty looking pieces of fabric visible on the lower wings. I throttled back to 80 mph in case any damage had been caused and then took an interest in Sanderson's welfare. He had come up out of the cockpit with his handkerchief held to one eye below his goggles. The poor chap had taken a hailstone right in the eye when his goggles had been lifted and he had a black eye to show for it for the next week. Ten minutes later I put the Wapiti into a long slow descent to Miramshah.

As Sanderson and I climbed down from our cockpits, the rigger came round the wing tip.

'Christ, Sir, what have you been doing?'

It was not a surprising question. The wings and fuselage looked as if they had been peppered with a twelve bore shot gun. Some of the hailstones had gone clean through the wings, others through the top surface and were still rattling about inside but rapidly melting. A lot of paint had been stripped off and the propeller looked as if it had been scoured with a wire brush. I felt sorry for the rigger as I explained what had happened. He had a lot of work to do but fortunately there was no serious damage. On the following day he told me that there were 164 holes to be patched up, which in days to come would doubtless be described as bullet holes. It was easy to be wise after the event. Had I any idea of the severity of the hailstorm, which was most unusual for this area, I would have turned back and probably landed at Razmak or Sora Rogha until it had passed, saving my rigger an immense amount of work which he nobly completed in two days. It might also have spared Sanderson his black eye.

The visit which I paid to Wana on the day of the hailstorm led to another adventure, but this time totally unconnected with flying. Wana Brigade was planning to send out a column to carry out one of the periodic armed reconnaissances into specific tribal regions which constituted part of the 'watch and ward' duties on the Frontier. As these columns wound their laborious way through defiles and valleys, they received air support throughout from one or other of the squadrons, and it was usually the responsibility of Miramshah to look after columns from Razmak and Wana. To ensure good communication and understanding between the column and aircraft overhead, we nearly always sent a junior officer out with the column as a liaison officer. Pop Stemp asked me to do this duty with the Wana column which was to go out for four days early in November.

With my bedroll, camp kit and a strong pair of boots, but without Hukmud Khan, I reported to Wana Brigade on the evening before the column was due to leave. I attached myself to the Brigade Major on whose staff I would serve during the expedition. I learned with mixed feelings that I would not be expected to march with the infantry, but would be provided with a horse. RAF officers have never been renowned for their horsemanship and mine was on a par with my bridge. However it was all part of the job and a docile but tough hill pony appeared next morning and the column, some 500 strong, set off at dawn to cover about 20 miles a day on a circular tour of nearly 100 miles through some unfriendly country to the south west of Wana. Progress was inevitably slow because all the hilltops en route had to be picketed to avoid ambush and to deter snipers. The Wazirs regarded sniping at troops or aeroplanes much as we regarded grouse shooting except that they observed no close season. Often it was sporting instinct rather than malice which encouraged a tribesman to take pot shots at us. After all he potted at his own people – why shouldn't he pot at us?

During my four days of soldiering with Wana Brigade we were fired upon on several occasions and usually at night. On two such occasions my sleep was rudely interrupted by the screaming of a mule which had been hit by a stray bullet from a sniper on the hillside. This was always followed by the rattle of machine gun fire as the camp sentries replied in the general direction of the sniping. These and other incidents convinced me that the Army positively invited this kind of reaction from the tribes. The long slow column of men, horses and vehicles winding through the valley and raising clouds of dust, must often have seemed a great intrusion to the villagers and an irresistible temptation to the tribesmen whose rifles were their pride and joy. I kept my thoughts to myself – they were somewhat advanced for 1933 – but it certainly seemed to me that the Frontier could have been controlled with a few more squadrons of aeroplanes and half the soldiers for a fraction of the cost.

With the exception of one incident, I enjoyed my few days of soldiering, jogging along on my old pony during the day and advising the Brigade Major on the capabilities of the Wapitis which were above us for most of the daylight hours. I supervised the exchange of messages by Popham Panel and message bag and instructed small groups of soldiers on this form of communication which, although crude, worked well enough. On the third day of the trek the Brigadier asked me to ride over to an outlying picket to supervise a Popham Panel exercise.

'Take my horse,' he said, 'it's stronger and fresher than your old tat' (riding pony). The large gleaming black charger filled me with trepidation as he rolled his hostile eye at me, but I clearly could not refuse what was intended as a generous gesture. I mounted. No sooner had I set off, gingerly testing the controls, than Peter Hamley from our Flight at Miramshah chose that moment to dive across Brigade headquarters to drop a message bag. If I had any control over the black beast, I lost it at that moment. He took the bit between his teeth and bolted. Although taken completely by surprise I managed to stay aboard, but no amount of hauling on the reins had the slightest effect. All I could do was to keep all my pressure on the left rein which he answered by careering in a wide circle of about a quarter of a mile in diameter, thus providing a wonderful spectacle for the troops, all of whom paused in what they were doing and stood up to watch. I lost my topee under the low branch of a tree and, as we sailed out of control over a deep ditch, I lost a stirrup. We completed about three circuits of this improvised race track by which time the troops, both British and Indian, were cheering loudly. This only encouraged the horse which then sailed over a low stone wall as I passed the worried Brigadier for the third time. It had come to an end and, to my amazement, the horse gave up before I did. He stopped suddenly, put his head down and began to eat a thorn bush. I was shaking like a leaf as I slid from his back, taking great care to hang on to the reins. A burst of clapping broke out from the troops as I slowly led the horse back to the Brigadier; nothing on earth would have persuaded me to remount. The Brigadier was good enough to say, 'I'm sorry, I should have told you that he doesn't like aeroplanes – he's had me off before now when you chaps have come a bit low. You did well to stay on.'

This compliment and the applause of the troops did something to restore my shattered morale, but did even more to convince me that flying was a much more satisfactory and safer occupation than soldiering. Needless to say, when my dusty and battered topee was returned to me by a grinning Punjabi soldier, I set out again on my original journey, but this time on my own dependable pony. As I trotted sedately up the valley I wondered whether I could emulate John Pope and get the Wana Brigadier into the back of a Wapiti on some future occasion.

The column ran into no ambushes although one of our accompanying aeroplanes reported a small collection of tribesmen who looked as if they were attempting to conceal themselves on our route. They were quickly flushed out by a picket sent ahead for the purpose. We returned to Wana with negligible casualties, namely, five mules hit by snipers' bullets and one sepoy who had broken his ankle in a fall. The single Pilot Officer, who might well have broken his neck, returned thankfully to Miramshah with nothing more serious than a sore seat.

As December and the end of our stay at Miramshah approached, the weather cooled down to a delightful 70° in the daytime and blankets were needed at night. We were about to change into our blue winter uniform and the best momths in India were beginning. Our draughty cockpits were becoming extremely cold and a high altitude bombing trip at, say, 15,000

118

feet needed all the clothing and boots that one could pile on. But it was worth dressing up. Flying in the cold, clear air with almost unlimited visibility and with snow beginning to form on the higher mountains was exhilarating, the Wapitis seemed to fly better and the results of our various exercises improved.

On 30th November, we all returned to Kohat, repeating the procedure of two months ago with the difference that one of the other officers took the road convoy back while I flew with the rest. Promotion to Flying Officer awaited me which meant at least another 100 rupees a month pay which came in handy to settle some of my bridge debts and to prepare for my first Christmas on the Frontier.

CHAPTER 9

NO FLYING AT
CHRISTMAS

As the preparations for Christmas got under way at Kohat, I allowed myself a little homesickness. Christmas had always been for me a family holiday whereas, out here, long before the luxuries of airmail, radios and television, I might have been on another planet. Any presents, letters and cards for me had had to be posted way back in early November in England, and I had sent off my own Christmas mail at the same time so that the correspondence between my family and myself had crossed somewhere in the Red Sea in early December. Years later when listening to airmen grouse at failing to get their airmail from home in 48 hours in some outlandish place, I would often recall the wait of seven weeks which we had to endure on the Frontier. In 1933 it was quite usual for the more senior officers to have personal copies of the London *Times* delivered by the weekly sea mail and to open a fresh copy at the breakfast table each morning – seven weeks old. On Monday, 1st of December, for example, they would open a copy dated Monday, 15th October and study the events as if they had happened only yesterday.

Christmas had to be observed with all the traditional trimmings at Kohat as elsewhere in the world where airmen served. In spite of the inappropriate climate, turkey and plum pudding, paper decorations, Christmas trees from the Hill Depot and even roasted chestnuts were insisted upon by the troops who showed remarkable initiative in making their billets as much like home as they could contrive. One of the earliest functions, and a most important one which on this occasion took place on the day before Christmas Eve, was the judging of the decorated barrack blocks. All the officers had clubbed together and bought a barrel of Murree draught beer for the airmen in the block which was judged by the Station Commander to have won. There were six rooms entered for the competition and the ingenuity shown by some of the men was astonishing. As nostalgia was always evident at Christmas, it was understandable that 'Ye Olde English Hostellerie' played a conspicuous part and there were two festive old pubs in the competition – 'The Old Bull' – a reference to the tyrannical discipline at Kohat! – and 'The Green Elephant'. 27 Squadron had a green elephant on its badge, and as there was also a well known brand of beer by that name, nothing could have been more appropriate. Another room which I thought was superbly decorated was disguised as the Faqir of Ipi's cave, but this I gathered was not considered a very original idea which had frequently won the competition in the past. After much deliberation and a second tour round, which called for another drink in each barrack block, judgement was given in favour of a 27

Squadron room made up to represent a troopship 'bound for a Blighty shore' – as the old song said. All the airmen were only too familiar with those well known converted cattle ships, the *Dorsetshire* and the *Somersetshire*, and they had made an excellent job of reproducing part of one of them in their barrack room, complete with portholes, ventilators and even a large cardboard lifeboat – with a hole in it! The finishing touch was provided by a ship's siren which some ingenious airmen had managed to rig up using a carbon dioxide cylinder from the workshops. This was the occasion on which I first heard the doubtless exaggerated story that the siren on one of the troopships had been out of action for years. Steaming up Southampton Water one day, a dangerous situation developed, whereupon the officer of the watch instinctively grasped the lanyard of the siren and and gave it a sharp pull. History relates that there was a great rush of steam up the pipe on the funnel and hundreds of cigarettes, silk stockings and other contraband flew out and disappeared towards the Isle of Wight as the officer of the watch inadvertently disclosed the crew's favourite hiding place. With much hooting of the 27 Squadron siren, which certainly worked, the barrel of beer was wheeled in, broached by the Station Commander – and Christmas had begun.

Early that evening I decided to cycle up to the British Military Hospital which was situated by the cinema, and where one of my friends looked as though he might languish over the holiday with a dose of sandfly fever. I peddled hard, hoping to disperse some of the effects of the beer which I could already see was likely to dominate Christmas. Hardly had I sat down by Bill's bedside when the Matron swept starchily in and I was introduced by Bill whose spirits had been so depressed by the fever that he couldn't care less whether he remained in hospital for Christmas or not. The Matron was a senior, imposing and forthright 'Kiwi', the name by which the Queen Alexandra's Imperial Military Nursing Service (QAIMNS) has always been known.

'Ah, Mr Lee,' she said, 'I wonder whether you could do me a small favour while you are up here?'

Before I could answer or even incline my head in assent, she rushed on.

'The Brigadier, who lives just over there (indication of direction obscured by ample bosom) has invited me over for a quick Christmas snort. I am on my own at the moment and as there are no serious cases and only one woman who might give birth shortly, I wonder if you would look after things for me for half an hour – Christmas spirit and all that you know?'

I hardly had time to clear my throat and croak 'certainly Matron' before she had swept out, rustling like a pile of autumn leaves.

'Good God, Bill', I said, 'what do I do now?'

'Well you could do worse than prescribe a small whisky for me; there is some in my locker, and then perhaps you ought to find out where the prospective Mama is and see if she really is quite happy.'

'Are you allowed whisky, Bill?'

'Only when you are here,' he replied, so I poured him out a reasonable dose in his tooth glass and set out to look round my new domain. I found a small women's ward and peered quietly in. Only one bed was occupied – a mountainous lump which seemed to be sleeping soundly. On returning to Bill's bedside and his empty tooth glass, he seemed so much better that one more small dose was prescribed with one for the acting matron as well.

The matron's half hour stretched on to one and a half hours before the pile of autumn leaves was heard sweeping down the passage. I had long since washed out the tooth glasses and given Bill a mouthwash. He was so much better that I prayed that he would not give himself away. I needn't have worried; the matron had a bottle of whisky under her arm and said, as she sailed in: 'I think we might all have a little Christmas drink – one small one won't do Bill any harm and you've been very good to hold the fort for me. – No trouble, I assume?' she said as an afterthought.

Eventually I got away, a little late for dinner in the mess, not only feeling that Bill had been cheered up but also giving me the undoubted right to claim to be the only officer in the GD branch of the Royal Air Force who had ever been matron of a British Military Hospital. Whether or not it would qualify for the Guinness Book of Records, I have never troubled to find out.

Christmas day can only be described as an alcoholic obstacle race during which one endeavoured to surmount as many pitfalls as possible without disaster. It began quietly enough with a pleasant holiday lie-in until 8 o'clock when I wandered through the Mess garden in the bright sunshine, picked myself a banana and went in to breakfast where my Squadron Commander was buried in his *Times* of the 9th November.

'Morning,' he said without looking up, 'Happy Christmas – looks as if we are in for more trouble on the railways.'

Neither of us knew that the 'trouble' had come and gone long before that paper had arrived in Kohat.

'Morning, Sir,' I replied, 'and a Happy Christmas to you.'

He grunted, still without looking up, but others around the table shot glances of displeasure at this unseemly gossip at the breakfast table. It was taking the RAF a long time to get away from some of the old naval traditions, such as silence at breakfast time, I thought to myself as Hukmud Khan swept in from the kitchen with my bacon and eggs.

The airmen's Christmas dinner was always served to them by the officers and senior NCOs, a tradition which the airmen would happily have extended to more occasions than Christmas day if they had had a chance. Before this, however, most of the officers would go down to the barrack blocks to admire the decorations and have a drink with their own airmen. Bill Coulson and I set off together to see the 60 Squadron boys at 11.30, and to surmount the first hurdle in the obstacle race. Our squadron block was the one which had been done up as the 'Old Bull'. One end of the long barrack room had been curtained off and lined with sacking painted to represent old wooden beams with a false ceiling of sacking similarly painted. The well

124

stocked bar, presided over by Corporal 'Taffy' Watkins, our senior air gunner, stood at one end behind a proscenium and was beautifully decorated with the Squadron badge. The whole atmosphere was so realistic that a couple of drinks were more than enough to transport one back into some 'local' in whatever part of England one called home.

For an hour or more 'Taff' Watkins pulled the pints while bigger and bigger lines were shot and many a yarn was exaggerated beyond belief. My 164 holes from hailstones grew to more than 400 but, mercifully, my recent display of horsemanship at Wana did not seem to have filtered through to Kohat, and I certainly had no intention of mentioning it. It was then time to walk over to the airmen's mess for Christmas dinner, the one great opportunity during the year for the airmen to order the officers and the sergeants about, and this they were not slow to do as we bustled about with great plates of turkey and plum pudding with more pints of Murree beer to keep the party going. I produced a very large and powerful Indian cigar for my own air gunner, Sanderson, at the end of the meal, lit it up for him and left him looking a little dubious about it, as well he might on top of about six pints of beer and a huge dinner. He admitted to me later that I had won that particular round. Only after the Station Commander and the Station Warrant Officer had given an appalling rendering of the most popular song on the Frontier – 'There's a troopship just leaving Bombay' – would the airmen allow us to stagger off back to the Mess. It was much too late for any lunch, but most of us had picked up a few snacks during the airmen's dinner and all we wanted was to collapse on our charpoys for an hour or two before our own Christmas dinner that evening.

Christmas Day may have been hard going but Boxing Day will live in my memory for ever. It was traditional for the Officers Mess to play the Sergeants Mess at some off beat sport, such as hockey with a football, on Boxing Day morning. On this occasion the organiser, whoever he was, had excelled himself in ingenuity. The regulation eleven officers, including

125

myself, arrived on the station football pitch to discover to our horror that the match was to be between eleven officers mounted on donkeys and armed with hockey sticks against a similar number of Sergeants on camels, with golf clubs. As an afterthought a football was provided and a referee on a horse, both of which turned out to be quite superfluous.

The camels and the donkeys were lined up at opposite ends of the pitch and we were invited by the referee who, under the disguise of a villainous tribesman, bore some relation to the Station Warrant Officer. It seemed to my simple mind as I approached my donkey that the officers had a tremendous advantage. Far from it. My donkey stood quietly with his head down as I mounted, my feet almost touching the ground on either side, and in no time the officers' team was ready for the fray, awaiting the referee's whistle. At the other end of the pitch, however, our opponents were clearly in trouble; about half had managed to climb onto their camels, three had mounted and had promptly been thrown off and the remainder were unable to make their camels kneel so that they could climb aboard.

After a few moments of confusion the referee decided to start the game, so he dropped the ball and blew his whistle. With a great cheer the officers encouraged their mounts forward. Not one would move, and the long thin line remained motionless. Several of us dismounted and tried to drag our beasts forward but that had no effect and, in spite of the repeated blasts from the referee's whistle, not a single officer got on to the pitch. Our problems were as nothing to those of our opponents. The camel handlers released their animals when the first whistle sounded and the camels, with or without riders, trotted on to the pitch and began to chase each other. It soon became apparent from the actions of some of them that the sexes had become mixed up and that intercourse and not football was about to take place. One Sergeant, who must have been on a particularly desirable female, had literally to throw himself off, to the delight of the spectators, before he was caught 'in situ' by two large male camels.

126

The pandemonium among the camels spread to the donkeys. Three officers bit the dust as their mounts kicked up their heels and charged on to the pitch. It was bad enough to have had my encounter with the Brigadier's charger at Wana. I had no intention of losing my dignity on a donkey in front of the airmen, and so I slipped rapidly to the ground and held my donkey firmly by its reins. The next few moments were utter chaos until the owners of the various animals rushed on to the pitch and sorted them out. By this time the two teams had lost their appetites for the match and, as the spectators had obviously had their money's worth, the match was declared a draw by the referee and we all trooped off to the Sergeants Mess to restore our shattered nerves. As successive pints of beer did their healing work there were vociferous demands to produce the organiser of the match but he had mysteriously disappeared, although I had my own private opinion that it was none other than our referee – the Station Warrant Officer.

Boxing night was the occasion of one of the grandest functions in Kohat's social calendar, the 'PIFFER' Ball. Kohat was the home of several battalions of the Punjab Frontier Force Rifles (PFFR). Their officers, some British and some Indian, shared a common mess and so their annual ball was a large and magnificent affair. As was usual on these occasions an invitation had come to our mess for the President and six other officers. Those of us who wished to attend placed their names on a list below the invitation card and, if the number exceeded six, names would be drawn from a hat. All the messes in Kohat adopted this system which ensured that the bachelors had their fair share of invitations to the various functions in the cantonment.

Christmas had begun to take its toll and there was not so much enthusiasm as one might have expected to dress up in one's finery of mess kit, boiled shirt and white gloves, and grace the ball with one's presence. However, five of us piled into Jack Atkin's old Vauxhall open tourer at 9 o'clock and set off for the PIFFER mess, having primed ourselves suitably

127

before leaving. It was a clear, starry night as the Vauxhall ground its way along the Mall and up the hill to our host's mess which was brilliantly lit and gay with lanterns swinging in the trees. The regimental dance band was belting out *Ain't Misbehavin* as the Vauxhall stopped with its usual loud clank in the car park. Pulling on our white gloves and straightening our bow ties, we trooped in and lined up to meet the Colonel and his wife. The Colonel was pleased to welcome us with the words, 'Ah, here come the Brylcreem boys!'

If this not unusual form of soldierly greeting was intended to draw a suitable response, it failed as on this occasion we were on our best behaviour.

'Good evening, Sir,' said Jack Atkins, 'it is most kind of you to invite us; we are looking forward to a splendid evening.'

As an Indian orderly handed each of us a neat little dance card with a pencil attached by a silken thread, the serious business of a formal Ball began. There were twenty dances on the card with a supper dance and interval in the middle. The idea was to complete the card in such a way that one fulfilled one's duty to the hosts, to leave adequate blank spaces for drinking at the bar with friends, find an attractive companion for supper and have a thoroughly good evening. These were difficult and often conflicting requirements and we bachelors had worked out a form of strategy which I now proceeded to put into effect.

The first and most important need was to obtain an agreeable and attractive companion for the supper dance. Casting my eye rapidly over the Fishing Fleet, I guessed that there was almost one hundred per cent representation at this, Kohat's biggest social function. I spotted Bubbles, a plump, cheerful niece of a cavalry officer; we had met on the tennis court and, attack being the best policy I went over to her.

'I've saved the supper dance for you, Bubbles; you won't disappoint me, will you?'

'Well ——' she said and paused.

'That's grand of you', I said, 'pop it into your programme

128

and let all those handsome cavalry subalterns wait a bit. They won't run away with you around.'

Bubbles capitulated and I was assured of a cheery supper interval.

My next priority was to circulate and book about eight more dances, leaving blanks between some of them for drinking purposes or for cooling off in the garden if my partner was sufficiently accommodating and attractive. I managed to fill seven spaces with young ladies I knew fairly well and turned to the last and trickiest part of the card-filling operation. Courtesy and good manners demanded that I ask my hostess and a number of other senior wives for a dance. Cards were getting well filled up by this time and, with about five dances only to offer on my carefully concealed card, I found that my hostess and other 'matrons' could not accommodate me on their already well filled programmes. Thus, with expressions of mutual regret, I was unavoidably denied a number of duty dances which left me with a few unbooked dances which I reserved for unforeseen circumstances.

With this performance satisfactorily completed, I was able to repair to the bar for a much needed drink, and view the scene before claiming my first partner. No description of a 'PIFFER' Ball would be complete without mention of the splendour of the uniforms. The mess kit of the Frontier Force Rifles was colourful, beige with scarlet facings, but paled into insignificance alongside the uniforms of the various Indian cavalry regiments. Many of these famous regiments with romantic names such as Probyn's Horse, the Hindu Horsemen, Hodson's Horse, the Guides Cavalry and Skinner's Horse were represented at the Ball. The black uniform encrusted with gold braid of Skinner's Horse easily took the prize in my opinion. It was said that this uniform was so heavy and stiff with gold that it would stand up by itself, and it certainly looked as if that was no exaggeration. The simplicity of our blue and gold mess kit was in striking contrast to some of these 'peacocks' but it was smart and functional and none of us envied the cavalry officers their un-comfortable and extremely costly plumage.

White coated bearers wearing the PFFR colours on their belts and turbans padded silently among the throng with trays of drinks and I could not help thinking that, with the Frontier and the wild tribal territory just outside the door, all this mag-nificence might be compared with the Duchess of Richmond's Ball before Waterloo. After two months out in the blue at Miramshah, there was to me a total unreality about this scene.

It was a good evening; the duty dances were politely per-formed, the Fishing Fleet was rushed off its pretty feet, Bubbles was on top of her form at supper, looking rather like a pink and white milkmaid and chattering too much in too high a key and, when not otherwise occupied, I found convivial drinking companions at the bar. As at all the functions on the Frontier, the men greatly outnumbered the ladies and so a quiet glass with a fellow officer posed no problems. Dawn was breaking when our cheerful quintet rattled home to bed in the Vauxhall which Jack drove slowly and with immense con-centration.

That Christmas was memorable not only for the various functions and the quantity of alcohol consumed during them, but also for the driving test which I had to take on the day after Boxing Day. I had bought a motor cycle, a smart 350 cc BSA, for the sum of 400 rupees (£31). It was almost new and just what I needed to keep me mobile until I could save enough from my pittance of a salary to afford a car. For some extraordinary reason, a United Kingdom driving licence was not acceptable in the North West Frontier Province and, not only was it neces-sary to obtain a local licence, but also to take a driving test (many years before one was introduced in the UK.) Conse-quently I had applied to the local police station for a licence and had been told to bring my machine along for a test at 5 pm on 29th December.

I assumed, quite incorrectly, that a test for a motor cycle could only consist of an inspection of the machine and some sort of demonstration on the police parade ground that I was capable of riding it. As I dismounted outside the police station, a very fat and cheerful Sergeant of the Frontier Constabulary came out with his cane under his arm and saluted smartly. He then indicated, to my consternation, that he would climb onto the pillion and that we would go for a ride together. Furthermore, he proposed that I should take him through the bazaar which, at that time of day, would be packed with native shoppers, donkeys, oxen and every other kind of hazard. There was nothing for it but to acquiesce and pray that disaster would not strike. I kicked the BSA into life, wishing that I had blown up the rear tyre harder as the sixteen or seventeen stones of the policeman depressed the rear springs. If one thing is vital for two people on a motor cycle it is that they act and move in unison to preserve the balance. This was the last thing my Sergeant was going to do; he clearly intended to enjoy his trip, wave to all his friends and shout instructions to pedestrians with much use of his cane.

Fortunately I was an experienced motor cyclist and, equally fortunately, we had about half a mile of clear road before reaching the entrance to the bazaar, to give me time to accustom myself to my highly unstable load. At 20 mph on the open piece of road we maintained a fairly steady course, but I clearly could not keep up that speed through the crowded bazaar; 5 mph was a more likely speed and then the problem of balance would become acute. At the entrance to the bazaar the narrow archway was blocked by a bullock cart and I had to stop. My passenger heaved himself off the pillion and cleared the obstruction with much shouting and waving of his cane. We started off through the narrow streets with its open stalls on either side, scattering pedestrians and donkeys with frenzied use of the horn and clutch from me and much bellowing and cane waving from the pillion. How we reached the end without falling off or crashing into a stall I will never know, but eventually we emerged through the archway at the far end unscathed. As I was beginning to congratulate myself on a splendid performance, the Sergeant indicated that we should return through the bazaar. The second passage was even more harrowing than the first. A stray donkey charged across my bows and, thanks only to the fact that our speed was negligible, I was able to stop abruptly and we preserved what little dignity was left. Finally I reached the end, sweating profusely with my Bombay bowler askew, it having been knocked sideways by my passenger's cane during an altercation with another bullock cart.

The short spin back to the police station was a joy compared to the previous quarter of an hour and as he dismounted, my policeman saluted again and said in Urdu, 'Very good, sahib, you are a good driver.'

With expressions of mutual esteem we parted and, as I rode slowly back to the Mess for a much needed sundowner, I thought to myself that surely no motor cyclist could ever have taken a more difficult test. Had I known what was in store for me I could at least have removed the pillion seat before setting off for the police station. On the other hand, had I done that, would the Sergeant have found it impossible to test me and issue a licence? There was no point in contemplating these possibilities. I had passed my test with efficiency if not dignity and I had a good story to tell in the Mess as the Christmas festivities came to an end.

CHAPTER 10

AFTER THE FESTIVITIES CAME THE OPERATIONS

It was rare for the Frontier to be entirely free from trouble for more than a few days at a time. Occasionally active operations on a large scale were necessary, involving several Army brigades and the whole of the RAF from the three Frontier stations. Much more frequently, however, the trouble was localised and called for measures to control and quell disturbances, many of which arose from inter-tribal blood feuds, sniping at British troops on protected roads or kidnapping. These minor infringements required the attention of small bodies of troops and a few aeroplanes only but they were instrumental in keeping British forces in constant practice and on the alert for the larger disturbances. The months between sowing crops and reaping the harvest and between reaping and sowing again were the favourite times of the year for trouble to spread. Time hung heavy on tribal hands when the land did not require full attention, and nothing was more natural than for the more turbulent tribes to use the opportunity to renew old feuds and settle old scores. Three areas in particular could be relied upon to provide most of the activity. The first of these was Mohmand territory to the north of Peshawar and the Khyber Pass, the second the inhospitable and virtually inaccessible Tirah which lay beyond the mountains north of Kohat and, finally, large areas of Waziristan to the south and west of Miramshah.

The Frontier was controlled by a process known as 'peaceful penetration' which involved pushing roads into tribal territory as deeply as possible followed by a guarantee of safe custody for travellers on those roads. Opening up hostile country in this way was a long and slow process, partly because of the suspicion and hostility of the tribes and partly because of the difficult terrain through which the roads had to be driven. Owing to these difficulties and the great expense involved, a limited penetration only of tribal territory had been achieved by 1933 and large areas of Mohmand country, the Tirah and Waziristan, in particular, remained unpenetrated and far from peaceful. Wherever it was possible, rewards, usually in the form of rifles and ammunition, were given to helpful and cooperative tribes whereas heavy fines were levied on offenders. If, as often happened, the imposition of fines was ignored, tribal headmen were warned that their villages, houses or crops would be destroyed by air action. If these warnings were ignored, leaflets were dropped on the offending villages informing the tribesmen that an attack would take place at a particular time and that they should keep well clear of the target areas. These final warnings were invariably heeded with the result that casualties from air attack were negligible and the desired capitulation was usually achieved by the destruction of houses and crops. It was a humane and economical method of control which had been first used in Iraq in the early 1920s and subsequently extended to Aden and India. Although not always popular with the Army as it reduced their opportunities for exciting but often costly operations, this form of control by air was highly successful and greatly disliked by the tribes who could only sit helplessly on the hillsides and watch the destruction of their property.

My first taste of operations came in the Bajaur and Mohmand country to the north west of Peshawar. A pretender to the Afghan throne endeavoured to raise a rebellion against the Amir of Afghanistan with the aid of the Khan of Kotkai and the Khan of Khar. Afghanistan requested the Indian Government to take action against this dissidence with the result that leaflets were dropped over the area demanding acceptance of certain terms. The Khan of Khar accepted, but not so the Khan of Kotkai, and offensive air action against his territory was decided upon.

It was a brilliant, sunny morning in March when I was detailed with LAC Sanderson to carry out a reconnaissance of the village of Kotkai and, if our warning leaflets which had been dropped by Peter Hamley at dawn had been heeded and the village seemed to be empty, identify and bomb the Khan's fortified house which was thought to be easily recognisable. The importance of positive identification was emphasised by Pop Stemp in my briefing before take off as the area contained many villages whose inhabitants were not hostile and who did not support the Khan in his defiance of authority.

My Wapiti was loaded with four 112 lb bombs, each fused for instantaneous detonation on impact, the guns were loaded and a camera for vertical photography installed in its position below the floor of the rear cockpit. We thus had a full war load as I taxied slowly out to the take off position. After turning into wind, I stopped while Sanderson climbed out and removed the safety pins from the four bombs under the wings. A second safety device remained which ensured that each bomb fell well clear of the aeroplane before it became 'live'. If, therefore, a bomb accidentally fell off during a bumpy take off, it would not explode on the aerodrome.

With the safety pins in his pocket, Sanderson climbed back into his cockpit, trained his Lewis gun well away from my head and gave a 'thumbs up' sign over my shoulder. The take off with a full load was considerably longer than when lightly loaded and the Wapiti felt sluggish as we reluctantly left the ground. I climbed slowly in a wide circle round the aerodrome to check that all was well with the engine temperature and pressure and to gain height before crossing the Kohat Pass. I carefully avoided flying over the camp with bombs on but remained in a position to jettison them over our own bombing range if anything went wrong, with some chance of getting back on to the aerodrome subsequently. These were obvious and sensible precautions which we always took with live bombs; their attachment to the aircraft was quite primitive and the release mechanism a somewhat crude arrangement of wires and pulleys which could not always be relied upon.

Setting a course which would take me a few miles to the west of Peshawar and over the entrance to the Khyber Pass, we climbed slowly up to 6,000 feet which I had decided would be our bombing level if all went according to plan. I levelled out at 6,000 feet over the Peshawar plain and carried on past the city. Looking up the Khyber which was bathed in sunshine, the frontier post at Landi Kharna stood out clearly, beyond which the metalled road deteriorated into a dusty track as it ran into Afghanistan and on towards Kabul. The light was so clear that the black and white barrier across the road at the frontier post was clearly visible. Having motored up to Landi Kharna some months earlier I remembered the barrier, supported at either end on a whitewashed stone pillar which had the Union Jack painted on the British side and the flag of Afghanistan on the opposite face, and as I contemplated that frontier post from 6,000 feet, I had an almost irresistible desire, which always affected me, to fly into the forbidden zone – presumably for no other reason than that it was forbidden.

We were soon approaching Mohmand territory and I identified the town of Malakand on the plain ahead. Opposite Malakand we were due to turn onto a westerly course and enter a wide dried up river bed which ran deep into Mohmand country. According to the map, this river bed should lead us, by a series of well defined points, to Kotkai which lay some thirty miles inside the tumbled mass of mountains, ravines, rocky gorges and terraced cultivation which comprised the Khan's domain.

With my map in my left hand and Sanderson leaning over my shoulder clutching his own map against the efforts of the slipstream to tear it out of his grasp, we followed the dry water course, keeping to the south of it so that we could see it clearly on the right side of the Wapiti with the sun at our backs. The points at which more dried up tributaries joined the main river bed coincided accurately with the map and we moved along from one definable point to the next. The village of Kotkai was shown as lying within the angle formed by the main stream and a tributary which curved away to the north. We came up to the junction which was clearly identifiable but – there was no village beside it. Holding the control column between my knees, I pointed out the junction on my map to Sanderson and shouted, 'That's our junction down there, isn't it?'

'Yes,' he shouted back, 'no doubt about it at all, but no village.'

I decided to continue on my course and follow the main river bed for a few miles. Sure enough the various tributaries coincided with the map as before and there was no doubt that we had correctly pinpointed the alleged location of Kotkai.

'We'll go over the ground once more,' I called to Sanderson. 'Will you follow it through your bomb aimer's panel?'

As I flew back to our starting point, I could feel Sanderson getting down onto his stomach in the back with much grunting and a few curses, and then the draught around my feet as he pulled back the sliding panel in the floor of his cockpit so that he could get an uninterrupted view vertically downwards.

Once again I followed the river bed and identified each feature until we reached the mysterious junction. I went into a steep left hand turn and Sanderson shouted, 'There is definitely no village there, but there is one about four miles to the north which looks about the size of Kotkai – will you fly towards it and come down a bit.'

I closed the throttle, turned to the north and glided down. I could then see the village over the nose. It was a long way from the position shown on the map but, as we got lower, it certainly looked to me as if it could be our target. Furthermore, there was a large building with a typical fortified tower in one corner of it.

'I am not going below 2,000 feet; have a close look at that building through the binoculars.' I said through my speaking tube. At 2,000 feet I opened the throttle and turned around the village to give Sanderson a chance to study it.

'There's a blue flag flying from the tower on that building,' he said. 'It must be Kotkai and that must be the Khan's house.'

I could now see it clearly myself and I was sure that Sanderson was right, but I could not possibly take the risk of bombing it on the basis of our own assumption.

'There's no sign of movement or life in the village, which looks as if the leaflets have had their effect and an attack is expected,' called Sanderson in a slightly strangled voice as he hung out of the bottom of his cockpit.

'Nevertheless we can't possibly drop our bombs,' I replied.

I decided to climb back to 6,000 feet for safety's sake in this rugged area while I considered what to do next. I had the uncomfortable feeling that nobody was going to believe me when I returned with my bombs and the news that Kotkai was not where it was supposed to be. Sanderson helped to solve my problem when he said, 'Don't forget we have a camera, Sir; we could take a few pictures.'

For the moment I had forgotten the camera but Sanderson's reminder made the solution obvious.

'We'll take a series of exposures along the main river bed from 6,000 feet, and then take some more on a line running up to the village,' I said. 'That should give the Intelligence boys enough evidence to amend the maps and identify the village positively.'

It would also prove that our navigation was not as bad as some might think, I thought to myself.

I flew back along the main river bed for about ten miles while Sanderson once again stretched himself out on the floor of his cockpit and opened the bomb aimer's sliding panel. We calculated that if I steered a course of 280° from a point directly above the river, we would include all the points of reference we needed on the photographs. I turned eventually and approached our starting point steadying on a heading of 280° at 6,000 feet and an indicated speed of 100 mph. Sanderson guided me over the starting point with a few minor corrections and then said, 'Steady, steady, camera on.' For the next six or seven minutes there was silence as I concentrated on flying accurately while Sanderson watched the camera clicking off the exposures at regular intervals. As we passed over the spot where Kotkai was alleged to be, the camera was switched off and I made a wide turn to the left to approach the same spot again, but on a new heading of 020°, which would take us on over the village we had assumed to be Kotkai. The same procedure was followed, but this time for about four minutes only.

'Camera off,' called out Sanderson, 'we've taken twelve exposures on the first run and five on the second; that should have covered everything we need, Sir, and the camera worked perfectly.'

'Good,' I replied, 'now we take the bombs home which won't please the armourers who have to defuse and unload them.'

By this time we had been in the air almost two and a half hours and I felt quite weary with all the manoeuvring and craning over the side. The inhabitants of Kotkai, who appeared to have evacuated it, must have been sitting in the shelter of the local hillsides watching us with trepidation and waiting for the bombs to fall on their homes, perhaps silently cursing their Khan for his intransigence. As we turned for home, Sanderson said, 'I wonder where Flying Officer Hamley dropped the leaflets: he must have assumed that that village is Kotkai and dropped them over it as it has obviously been evacuated.'

This was a good point and unfortunately Peter Hamley had not landed from his leaflet mission before I took off, having had some minor engine trouble and dropped in to Peshawar.

'It's one thing to drop a load of paper on the assumption that the village is the right target,' I replied, 'but quite another to send down four large bombs. There are at least a dozen similar villages within a ten mile radius and, with these terrible maps, any one of them could be Kotkai. Anyway, we'll soon find out.'

When I had climbed away into smoother air, Sanderson produced the inevitable thermos without which no air gunner ever seemed to fly. With considerable skill he managed to shield a full mug from the slipstream and pass it over my shoulder. Hot, sweet tea straight from the 'char wallah', it was excellent and was followed by a couple of biscuits which also came over my shouder.

'Thank you,' I shouted, 'I'll try to give you a smooth landing with all those bombs underneath. On the way back, will you jot down on your pad every detail you can remember about that village, so that we can amplify the photos when they are printed.'

It was probably the first opportunity he had to sit down on his small tip-up seat since we took off nearly three hours earlier. Standing up in bumpy conditions, tethered to the floor only by a thin wire cable, could be extremely exhausting as well as risky, and many air gunners suffered painful knocks from the many metal projections which surrounded them.

Thirty five minutes later I glided down into a wide circuit around Kohat, once again avoiding flying over the station with bombs on. The landing was reasonably smooth and well away from the tarmac on the far side of the aerodrome, and as I came to rest Sanderson climbed out with the four safety pins and inserted them into the bombs. We were now safe to taxi in towards the tarmac but, before doing so, I told Sanderson to fire a red Verey cartridge into the air which was an indication that we had live bombs aboard. I parked the Wapiti well clear of other aeroplanes and the armourers came out with bomb trolleys to unload our four bombs.

As I expected, my report about Kotkai was greeted with some scepticism but Pop Stemp was clearly impressed by the comprehensive description which Sanderson and I gave, and insisted that further action against the village should be deferred until my photographs had been studied by the experts; it would take 24 hours to process them. Although I was fairly confident that both my navigation and my judgement had been correct, I was less confident that the photographs would come out satisfactorily, and they alone could prove my point. Consequently I spent an uncomfortable 24 hours, which was not improved by plenty of good natured twitting in the Mess that evening which could only be allayed by standing a round or two of drinks.

'You should stick to railway lines,' or 'How much is the Khan paying you?' were a few of the remarks passed in my direction. Peter Hamley kept pretty quiet during these exchanges of pleasantries, but he admitted that he considered the village to be close enough to the point marked on the map to be Kotkai without any doubt. However, as I pointed out, he had merely been scattering leaflets!

On the following morning, as Sanderson and I made our way to the Photographic section to learn the truth, he told me that he also had had to put up with a good deal of ribbing in the canteen the previous evening. Harry Wheeler, our Photographic officer, had assembled the prints of my two straight runs and a glance was enough to show me that at least they had come out satisfactorily and, furthermore, seemed to be a good sequence.

'Well, there they are,' said Harry, 'and as far as I can see at this stage, you're quite right – the village is not where it is shown on the maps. Whether this village (pointing to the one which we had photographed) is Kotkai or not will have to await interpretation by the Intelligence staff at Peshawar.'

We compared the prints inch by inch with the map and there was no doubt that we had identified the point where Kotkai 'should have been' accurately. I heaved a sigh of relief but realised that others more expert would have to confirm it. Pop Stemp came in at that moment and was soon satisfied that I had been right and that he had been equally correct in insisting that further action against Kotkai must be based on an expert interpretation of my pictures.

'Harry, will you arrange for a despatch rider to take these over to Peshawar straight away,' said Stemp, 'and I will ring the Intelligence boys and ask them to examine the photos as soon as they arrive: if that village is Kotkai, we will have to drop more warning leaflets and arrange for another bombing sortie. Well, David,' he said, turning to me, 'you can claim a few drinks back in the Mess tonight and as you seem to be the only person who knows where Kotkai really is, you had better tackle the job again.'

Later that day the news came through that the controversial village had been positively identified as Kotkai and I was particularly pleased to hear that one of the Political Agents in Peshawar had confirmed that the blue flag spotted by Sanderson was that of the Khan of Kotkai and that the building from which it was flying was undoubtedly his house. And so the mystery was cleared up. The maps were amended and Sanderson and I were able to hold our heads up again.

Before a second raid could be mounted, however, there was a new development. The Khan of Kotkai, doubtless impressed by the leaflets and the presence of the aeroplane overhead at the prescribed hour with four large bombs under the wings, had sent an emissary into Peshawar by fast camel, and capitulated, accepting the Government's terms. Thus my first operation was something of an anti-climax, but the Mohmand campaign continued for some months and I had plenty of other opportunities to take part in this unusual type of warfare.

A strange episode occurred in October, 1934 when I went with my Flight to Miramshah for a second two months detachment in that small, isolated Frontier fort, but this time as a relatively experienced pilot with a Flying Officer's stripe on my shoulders and more than three hundred hours on Wapitis under my belt. The pattern of life had changed little during the twelve months since we were last there but two of my three colleagues in the Officers Mess were different and, to my great relief, were not ardent bridge players: poker and liar dice were more in their line and that suited me. None of us were too worried about the exact adherence to King's Regulations in this Beau Geste environment, about as far from civilisation as it was possible to get.

One weekend in late October the Frontier was quiet, and as we had no commitments, Pop Stemp decided to go back to Kohat to see his wife who was unwell at that time. We also needed some spare parts for the Wapitis and so he flew off early on Saturday morning leaving me in charge at Miramshah for what promised to be a peaceful and rather dull weekend.

On Sunday morning I played tennis with one of the sergeants and two airmen, gave them a couple of beers on the verandah of our Mess, had the inevitable Sunday curry lunch and then retired to have my siesta and rest my poor feet after the suffering they had endured on our terrible concrete court. It was still very hot in the middle of the day and I fell asleep at once under the soporific effects of tennis, beer and curry.

At about 3.30 I was awakened by Hukmud Khan shaking me with a message to ring Major Ambrose immediately. Major Ambrose commanded the Tochi Scouts whose headquarters were here at Miramshah and who occupied the other half of the fort. Hastily pulling on my trousers, I padded along the verandah and called Major Ambrose, rubbing the sleep out of my eyes as I waited for him to reply.

'Could you come over to see me?' he said. 'We have a gasht

(column) which is in trouble to the north of Datta Khel. I've just had a pigeon message saying that they have been ambushed.'

'A pigeon message!' I exclaimed.

'Yes,' he replied, 'come over and I will explain – it's pretty urgent.'

'Before I come over, is this likely to require some action because if so I would like to have an aeroplane prepared to save time?'

'Yes,' he said after a moment's thought, 'that would be a wise precaution.'

I rang off and instructed Hukmud Khan to fetch Flight Sergeant Brown at once. Percy Brown appeared within five minutes and, briefly explaining the situation, I asked him to have my aeroplane wheeled out onto the tarmac and to instruct Corporal Jones, our senior air gunner, to put in a full load of ammunition for both guns and a good supply of Verey cartridges. As we had less than three hours of daylight remaining, I also asked for the Wapiti's lights to be thoroughly checked and the emergency landing flares for the aerodrome to be prepared.

'Be ready to start within thirty minutes, please, Flight,' I called after Brown as he left.

In order to reach the Tochi Scout's quarters, one had to climb over a mud wall which separated two portions of the fort by means of a rickety ladder – a route which created a few problems on a dark night after a guest night in the Tochi Mess, but which was no problem this afternoon. Within ten minutes of his telephone call, I was with Major Ambrose whom I found pacing up and down with a worried look on his face.

'Thank you for coming over so quickly,' he said, 'I don't like the look of this situation and I'm not sure whether you can do anything to help.'

He explained that a 'gasht' of thirty scouts, accompanied by Mr Packman, had set out the previous day for a routine reconnaissance of a mountainous region north of the Tochi river in the Datta Khel area. Mr Packman was the British Political Agent responsible for this part of Waziristan: he lived at Miramshah and used the Tochi Scouts to escort him on his journeys around his territory. He was a well known and courageous man who had one of the most dangerous areas of the Frontier to supervise. We knew him well and frequently flew him on various missions.

Ambrose went on to say that the small party had penetrated a narrow defile leading up into the mountains on the north side of the Tochi river valley about twenty five miles from Miramshah. Their purpose was to investigate a village in this defile which was thought to be under the influence of the Faqir of Ipi, and to harbour some of his followers. Packman wished to interview the village headman who had ignored several orders to come to Miramshah.

'Within a few miles of the village they ran into sniper fire from both sides of the defile and had to go to ground among the rocks,' said Ambrose. 'This happened about four hours ago and Packman sent us a message by pigeon – wireless communication being useless owing to the blanketing effect of the mountains. All our 'gashts' carry a basket of pigeons for this very purpose. One Scout has been killed and two slightly injured. They will probably be pinned down under cover until darkness.'

He handed me a crumpled piece of paper which he had been holding throughout our conversation.

'Here is the message.'

It had been written on a sheet torn from a Field Service Pocket Book and read:

HELD UP BY SNIPER FIRE AT (here followed a Map reference). ONE SCOUT KILLED. TWO SCOUTS SLIGHTLY INJURED. P.A. SAFE. AIR DEMON-STRATION OVER VILLAGE MIGHT HELP BUT EXPECT TO BE ABLE TO MOVE AFTER DARK. T.O.O. 1146.

So we knew that the message had been despatched at 11.46 am. Looking at my watch the time was 3.50 pm. The pigeon had obviously wasted no time and flown straight back to its loft at Miramshah. I was impressed by the efficiency of this simple method of communication, having no idea that it was still used seriously.

Major Ambrose and I studied a large scale map of the area of the ambush and I was perturbed to see that it lay on the side of one of those extremely narrow defiles running up to the Frontier mountain range which it seemed to be my fate to explore.

'Can you get up there, and if so, what can you do?' asked the Major.

I thought it over for a moment or two and studied the height of the peaks in the vicinity – about 9,000 feet.

'Yes, I think I could get over that position low enough to read a Popham Panel message if they display one and always provided there is enough light down in the valley. Depending on the situation I find, I can create a bit of a nuisance around that village and hope it may act as a deterrent to further sniping.'

Major Ambrose nodded his agreement and said:

'Don't take any risks; its nasty country but I would like any up to date news you can get about the conditions of the party. Above all, don't fire unless you get specific authority from Packie.'

As I climbed back over the wall, I glanced at my watch – it was 4.20 pm with a little less than two hours of daylight left, and considerably less where the Tochi 'gasht' had been forced to take cover. There was no time to lose as I hurried up to the aerodrome where Corporal Jones was waiting for me. I climbed into my overalls and briefly explained the situation to him and he confirmed that our Wapiti was loaded up and ready.

'Get the airmen to start it and warm it up while we pin-point our destination on our maps: this will be new territory for both of us.'

While we were walking out to the aeroplane, which was being run up by Sergeant Ward, I told Flight Sergeant Brown to have the paraffin flares laid out and lit for a night landing if we had not returned by dusk.

It was 4.48 pm as I opened the throttle and took off in a dense cloud of dust which was drifting over the fort as I turned and climbed westwards towards the Tochi river. Ten minutes later we were flying up the wide stony river bed which, at that time of year, had a mere trickle of water running down the centre of it. I flew at a height of 3,000 feet while Jones and I followed the map carefully to ensure that we identified the entrance to the defile in which the 'gasht' was trapped accurately. As I had found elsewhere, the many defiles which led up to the high mountain range that marked the Frontier along much of its length, were often difficult to distinguish one from another, particularly as our maps were not always trustworthy as regards detail. In this instance, however, we had no difficulty in finding the narrow valley we sought.

It was an unprepossessing sight as I turned towards it. A mile wide at the entrance, it narrowed gradually to a width of a few hundred yards before the ground rose precipitously to an eventual peak which our maps showed as 9,300 feet, and which marked the Frontier at that point. It was about ten miles from the entrance to the far end of the valley beyond which a Wapiti flying low would have either to turn back or fly straight into the mountain. The floor of the defile was already in deep shadow and it was quite clear that I would have no more than half an hour of usable daylight in which to find and try to help the Tochi party.

The map reference 897426 which Major Ambrose had given as the position of the party lay on the right side of the valley as we ascended it. Being on the east slope, it should have some benefit from the last rays of the setting sun. I therefore flew up the left side to give ourselves the best possible view of the right hand slopes over the sides of the cockpits with the sun behind us. Corporal Jones had his binoculars slung round his neck and scanned the slope intently. No signs of life were visible in the lower part of the valley, but suddenly, from a point half way up, a white Verey light curled upwards towards us. Jones tapped my shoulder but I had already seen it.

'There they are,' he shouted, 'and they are exactly on the pinpoint we were given, so they haven't moved and are probably still pinned down.'

I banked sharply towards the source of the Verey light so the party would realise that they had been spotted. Jones continued to study the position through his glasses.

'I can see something white being waved and I think that a Popham Panel is being laid out,' he said.

Well, we had found them: now the problem was what to do about it. I told Jones that I would fly a little further up the valley, turn and fly back slowly over the party if he would get down and open the bomb aimer's panel in the floor and see what he could as I flew over them as low as I dared. The defile was narrowing rapidly as I turned and the spectacle of the sheer mountain towering above us was forbidding. I allowed the Wapiti to sink to about 800 feet as I returned to the party. I could see nothing of them from vertically above but Jones had an excellent view.

'Yes,' he said, 'their Panel is displayed and I'll read it as we go over.' There was a pause. 'Two white strips, two circles and an arrow.'

While he was checking the meaning of this configuration of the markers in his code book, I circled out into the middle of the valley and then spotted the village, or collection of thatched hovels which lay some 1,000 yards below, and to the west of the party. From my knowledge of the Popham Panel code, I was pretty certain what the message said, but I waited for Jones to verify it from his book. Appearing over my shoulder, he said:

'It means – BEING FIRED ON FROM DIRECTION OF ARROW – the arrow is pointing directly towards that village.' He waved his glove in the direction of the collection of hovels.

This message created a very difficult problem. Had the Tochi Scout's arrow indicated that fire was coming from a sniper's hideout in the mountains, I would have been justified

148

in strafing the position with my guns which were fully loaded. I could not, however, strafe a village without warning and without authority. Many innocent women and children would probably be killed and injured and the chances of hitting the snipers were remote. Mr Packman, who was with the party down below, could give me that authority but it was most unlikely that he would do so under the present circumstances in which there were good prospects for the party to escape from their uncomfortable predicament when darkness fell in about half an hour. It was well known that the tribesmen disliked night operations, particularly when up against the Tochi Scouts.

I decided that all I could do was to try to deter the snipers by creating as much panic and dislocation in the village as possible. With my mind made up, I told Jones to acknowledge that we had read and understood the Popham Panel message, using his Aldis lamp.

'When you have done that,' I continued, 'get down to your bombing panel again with at least half a dozen Verey cartridges – mixed colours preferably. I am going to fly across the village low and fast from the head of the valley, and I want you to fire cartridges vertically downwards into the village. Try to get off two cartridges on each run. From low altitude they should be still burning when they hit the ground, or better still, a thatched roof. At worst they will bounce about and scare the natives; at best they might cause a fire.'

'Right, Sir, ready when you are,' said Jones as he climbed down to the floor of his cockpit again, 'I brought two verey pistols and can fire two cartridges at a time.'

'Good thinking' I replied, 'don't set fire to yourself or me.'

By the time Jones was flat on his stomach over the open floor panel, I had returned to the position at the head of the defile where we had previously turned. Heading back in the direction of the Tochi river, I dived towards the village with the throttle well open. The Wapiti reached 120 mph as I crossed the village at 300 feet. I felt the double concussion as Jones fired his two Verey lights.

'Beautiful,' he called out in a muffled voice from under the floor, 'they are both bouncing about all over the High Street; one red, one green.

It was now 5.35 pm by the cockpit clock and the floor of the valley was almost dark although it was still quite light above the mountains. There is virtually no twilight period in India. As the troops expressed it 'night fell like a bag of soot'. With the mountains silhouetted against the fast disappearing daylight, I reckoned that I could do one more run across the village, and told Jones to repeat his previous performance. I turned on all the lights on the Wapiti to add a touch of colour to the occasion and dived once more upon the village. Thud, thud; two more cartridges were fired through the floor.

'Even more beautiful', called Jones, 'and there's quite a lot of smoke coming up from one of the huts. I think we may have set fire to something.'

'We'll go round once more, but higher this time, and I want you to signal to the Tochis that we have to return home now, and good luck.'

I flew slowly back across the Tochi party and could hear the Aldis lamp chattering away behind me as Jones spelt out his message. As I completed a final turn in the centre of the valley, a green Verey light came up from the Tochi party and curled towards us in the gathering darkness. As it was a green light, I took this, perhaps optimistically, to mean that all was well with them. Only time would tell whether my efforts had helped to save the party from further molestation.

It was a great relief to climb away towards the Tochi river again. I was sweating profusely although it was quite cold by this time. The darker it became, the more those mountain sides seemed to press in on the Wapiti, and the inadequacy of it's power to climb over them tended to dominate my thoughts. It was now completely dark and I adjusted my cockpit lights to illuminate my main instruments. Back at 3,000 feet there was a little light reflected across the mountains from the sun which had long since disappeared below the horizon into Afghanistan. I picked up the Tochi river and turned eastwards towards Miramshah.

Corporal Jones and I were silent as we flew back towards our mud fort on the dusty plain, busy with our own thoughts and doubtless wondering if we had done anything to help the beleaguered party on the hostile mountainside. We would know in the morning, but I was heartened by the memory of the green Verey light which I sincerely hoped had meant that the sniping had ceased. Our Jupiter engine was running sweetly and it was a beautiful cool starlit night now that we were safely away from the mountains. The winking lights of Miramshah began to appear far ahead and I changed course slightly, eased back to half throttle and began to descend towards them. When we got closer I could see the long line of paraffin flares flickering down the centre of the east to west arm of the aerodrome. I had not landed at Miramshah at night before as we only used it for night flying in emergencies, but it presented no particular problems. Arriving over the fort at 1,000 feet I flashed my downward recognition lamp with the Morse code key in my cockpit. I flashed Z which was the letter on the side of my Wapiti and immediately received an answering green light from an aldis lamp alongside the first flare. My acknowledgement was to leave my recognition light on and commence a steady left hand descending turn round the fort. I lined up the smoky flares as I turned in to land and touched down with a gentle crunch and a rattle on the stony surface. I turned round beyond the last flare and taxied slowly back to the gates of the fort. The time was 6.40 but I felt that I had been in the air for much more than two hours as I climbed out of the Wapiti. I walked to the office, dumped my parachute in a chair and lit my pipe.

The first thing to do was to phone Major Ambrose. He had remained in his headquarters in case further news came in, but he would have heard me coming in to land and would be waiting impatiently for my call. I briefly told him what had happened and said that I would come over as soon as I had made a few arrangements in the Flight. I decided it would be wise to have an aeroplane loaded up and ready to take off at dawn if it should be needed. Back to my room for a quick wash and change of shirt and slacks and I was once again climbing the ladder over the wall to the other part of the fort.

Major Ambrose was an accomplished pianist and had brought to Miramshah what must have been the only grand piano in Waziristan. I found him playing softly and in a much more relaxed mood than when I had left him earlier. He was almost effusive in his thanks and pressed a large whisky into my hands as we sat down in front of his map to run over the details again. He seemed optimistic – more optimistic than I felt about the probable effects on the village of my somewhat unorthodox tactics, but I said nothing to discourage him as he was a very worried man. No more pigeon messages had arrived and were unlikely to do so before daylight, by which time he hoped that the 'gasht' would have extricated itself to a position from which wireless messages could be received. Ambrose then told me that he proposed to send out a strong relieving party before dawn which would motor up the Datta Khel road to the point at which the defile debouched upon the Tochi river. The relieving party would then continue on foot up the defile until they came upon the gasht. He fully expected, however, that the latter would have made its way to the river under the cover of darkness and would await the relief which they would be expecting. Ambrose then asked me if I would take off at dawn and cover the relieving party from the moment it entered the defile if that proved necessary.

In case the gasht was still pinned down on the mountainside, I agreed to have a supply dropping container on my bomb racks, loaded with ammunition, medical supplies and additional supplies of food and water, to drop as close to the Scouts' position as I could manage. This was a precautionary measure which we both hoped would be unnecessary. I stayed to dinner in the Tochi Mess with Ambrose and four other Tochi officers who were at the fort at the time. We had great admiration, not only for this regiment, but for the other irregular Scout regiments on the Frontier, notably the South Waziristan Scouts and the Kurram Militia. They all had a reputation for extreme toughness and endurance: anybody who had ever been out on a gasht with them knew that their boast of being able to cover 30 miles a day 'in a straight line' was not an idle one. Shortly after dinner and a little Chopin from Ambrose, I climbed back over the wall to my own quarters, telling my host that I would take off at 5.30 am, and asking him to let me know by then if he had any more news. The moon was rising and as I stood on top of our dividing wall hyenas started to laugh in the Muslim cemetery which lay alongside the walls of the fort. Although I was well accustomed to this sound which always arose when jackals and hyenas were scavenging in the graveyard in the moonlight, it was a hideous noise which never failed to send a chill down my spine.

Hukmud Khan called me at 4.30 am having prepared tea and toast for me in the Mess, and I walked up to the Flight Office as Z was being pushed out of the fort gates onto the aerodrome. The first signs of dawn breaking could be seen where the mountains to the east were silhouetted against a pale sky. It was cool and still and gave promise of being a fine day with hardly a cloud in the sky. Corporal Jones came out to meet me, already dressed in his flying kit and said:

'Good morning, Sir, Major Ambrose has just rung and would like you to call him before taking off.' He added, 'I think he has had a message from the gasht.'

Indeed he had and it was good news. The party had extricated itself from its hiding place after dark and made its way down to the Tochi river, carrying the body of the Scout who had been killed and also the two wounded soldiers on litters. Once clear of the mountains, the party had managed to get a wireless message through to Miramshah indicating that they would await a relieving party on the Datta Khel road.

After giving me this information, Ambrose added: 'The relieving party had left before the message reached me and some morphia is urgently needed for the wounded. I have sent a medical orderly out and I expect he has morphia with him, but in case more is needed, will you take a small package and drop it to them – it's on its way over to you now.'

As no other supplies were needed, I had the supply container, which had been loaded with ammunition, food and water, removed from the bomb racks, by which time the small packet of morphia had arrived.

'That will go into a message bag,' I said to Jones. This was a small canvas bag with a long tail of red and yellow streamers attached to it which we used for dropping messages in the field. The long, brightly coloured tail not only slowed the descent of the bag but made it more easily seen on the ground. Corporal Jones wrapped up the morphia securely and tucked it inside his overalls as we walked out to the aeroplane. The fitter was in the cockpit running up the engine with one of the coolies draped over the tail plane in a cloud of dust and small stones.

'I expect to be back in less than an hour,' I said to him as he climbed down, leaving the engine ticking over steadily.

I took off and climbed away towards the Tochi river for the second time in twelve hours, knowing this time that the gasht was safe and that I would have little to do beyond dropping the morphia and generally checking that all was well. I levelled out at about 1,000 feet on this occasion and flew up the Datta Khel road. Opposite the entrance to the defile which had been the scene of yesterday's drama, a collection of military vehicles was parked beside the road, the red cross on the roof of an ambulance standing out particularly clearly. I could tell from the number of troops scattered round the vehicles that the two parties had already met up.

'Get ready to drop the message bag – use the ambulance as your aiming point,' I called to Jones. A large gloved thumb appeared over my shoulder to indicate that he had heard, and I banked round to carry out a straight run over the Scouts. Reducing our speed to 85 mph I descended to 500 feet on the approach and flew directly over the ambulance. Out of the corner of my eye I could see Jones hanging over the side of his cockpit with his hand holding the rolled up message bag raised to throw it downwards. Again the thumb appeared over my shoulder and we climbed back to 1,000 feet, beginning to circle round and await any developments.

'They've picked up the message bag, Sir,' called Jones, 'and now they look as though they are unrolling their Popham Panel.'

In a few moments a message began to be displayed on a bare patch of ground beside the vehicles. Both Jones and I took our code books out of the pockets in which they were permanently stowed in each cockpit although both of us knew most of the messages by heart. The simple message 'Go home' appeared. I took no offence at such apparently peremptory dismissal. The Popham code was extremely limited and this was the only way the Tochi could say 'many thanks for all your help; we are fine and there is nothing more you can do for us.'

'Right', I said to Jones, 'before going home to breakfast we'll take a look at that village in the defile to see whether any damage is visible; it will also remind the villagers that we are still about and interested in them. I'll keep above 1,000 feet as they may well snipe at us.'

Had I been able to see in the gloom of the previous evening how narrow the defile was on the upper reaches, I would undoubtedly have been worried. The bright light of dawn made the sides look very close indeed. We turned steeply over the village and peered down on the collection of huts and hovels. I could see very little, but Jones, who had the binoculars, said; 'One hut looks as if it has been burned out, and a second one has a blackened straw roof; those are probably the result of our work. Can we have another go at them, Sir?'

'No, of course we can't,' I said, 'but fire a 'red' into the air over the village just to remind them that there are plenty more where last night's came from!'

With the usual bang in my right ear, a red Verey light curled up above us and fell towards the village, extinguishing itself before it reached the ground.

155

Well, that's that little episode over, I thought to myself as I flew down the centre of the defile. The two parties of Scouts had left their meeting point and I could see the clouds of dust from their vehicles about five miles ahead. I descended to 500 feet and waved as we flew past them on our way back to Miramshah, ready for a good breakfast.

My first task after breakfast was to write up my report on the incident while the details were fresh in my mind. Hardly had I started when Pop Stemp walked in on his return from his weekend in Kohat.

'You've been having a busy weekend, they tell me.'

'Yes,' I replied, 'it was rather a sudden emergency.'

I went on to describe the whole episode fully, and he listened without interrupting.

'Good,' he said when I had finished, 'it sounds as if you helped them out of a sticky situation. I think I will go over and see Ambrose, and Packman if he has arrived, and get their report before we let Group know what has been going on.'

The outcome had it's amusing aspects. When Group Headquarters at Peshawar received the news, their initial reaction was to be critical of me for 'conducting active operations without authority'. This was perhaps understandable as they felt their own authority undermined. However, when Mr Packman sent in his report and paid a handsome tribute to the RAF at Miramshah for coming to his assistance promptly and successfully, criticism was difficult to sustain. Pop Stemp received a copy of the report as well as a personal note from Mr Packman, and Major Ambrose was good enough to write to me.

CHAPTER 11

EARTHQUAKE

I awoke with a start. Something had crashed to the ground in my bedroom. As I slowly came to, I began to realise that the bed and indeed the whole room was shaking. There was another crash and some sort of instinct made me roll off and under my charpoy. By the time I was fully awake the vibration had stopped and I rolled out from under the bed and groped for the light switch. Both my lampshade and the ceiling fan were swinging about and one glance showed me that the clock and most of the ornaments had fallen off the mantelpiece. What had woken me up was undoubtedly a silver plated practice bomb which I kept as a souvenir and which had crashed to the floor. I became aware of voices on the verandah and pushed open my wire screen door to see what was happening. Lights were on in most of the other rooms in our bachelor officers block and I could see people congregating on the lawn in front of the block.

'Come on out,' somebody shouted. 'It's an earthquake'.

That was enough for me and, although I had never heard of an earthquake in Kohat, I hastily threw on my dressing gown and padded down the stairs in my slippers. Just as I joined the others on the lawn, another tremor ran through the ground and we all sat down on the grass, well clear of the building. It was most peculiar to feel the earth moving about below one's backside: those who were still standing up, sat down hastily as the movement continued for perhaps half a minute. When the shaking subsided, I glanced at my watch; it showed two minutes past three o'clock. Nobody spoke for a moment or two as, like myself, the others had never experienced an earth tremor before. It was an eerie and faintly threatening experience as we all gazed fearfully at our tall, two storied block of quarters which looked solid enough. The silence was broken by somebody saying:

'I think the centre must be quite a long way away, but someone's probably bought a nasty packet. We'll hear about it in the morning I expect.'

We stayed outside speculating on the whereabouts of the epicentre for a further quarter of an hour and, as there were no more tremors, drifted slowly back to bed. My ornaments remained safely on the floor for the rest of the night.

At breakfast next morning there was plenty of discussion about the night's events until the Station Adjutant came into the dining room holding what looked like a telegram in his hand. He called for our attention and said:

'The earthquake last night was a severe one, and it destroyed a large part of Quetta.'

There was a shocked silence at the breakfast table. Quetta was, among other things, a large RAF station, not unlike

Kohat, with a Wing Headquarters and two squadrons of Wapitis. Naturally enough, our first thought was for the safety of our colleagues and friends.

'I only know,' continued the Adjutant, 'that a great deal of damage has been done and there are many RAF casualties. We have received an emergency call for doctors and nurses. The Station Commander wants you all to report to your Flights at once while the form our help will take is being considered.'

With that the Adjutant departed and a buzz of conversation broke out as we hastily finished breakfast and piled into the vehicle waiting for us outside.

It was almost 400 miles to Quetta, not far short of the full range of a Wapiti, but it was decided to send all the serviceable aeroplanes on the station. We managed to assemble nineteen from the two squadrons. We were to take no air gunners as the rear cockpits were to be occupied by doctors, nurses and medical orderlies from the British Military Hospital and sources who could be spared and gathered together in time. There was a feverish bustle of activity as the aeroplanes were wheeled out, stripped of unnecessary gear, filled to the brim for the long flight and warmed up by the airmen. The Kohat Wapitis were to fly in formations of three or four aeroplanes, each formation separated from the next by fifteen minutes in order to stagger our arrival at Quetta where landing conditions might be extremely difficult.

My passenger was an Army medical sergeant and, when he reported for the flight, Corporal Jones fitted him out with flying kit and explained the cockpit of the Wapiti to him. He had only flown once before and was clearly regarding the forthcoming trip as a tremendous event. I felt he was not going to be disappointed!

My own formation of three took off at 10.30, and led by Pop Stemp, started the long flight over Waziristan and Baluchistan to Quetta. We flew in loose formation at the Wapiti's most economical cruising speed which should enable us to reach our destination without running out of fuel. Miramshah and certain emergency landing grounds lay along our route and could be used for refuelling but we were all anxious to avoid such diversions as we naturally wished to reach Quetta as soon as possible with our medical passengers. The flight was uneventful but, as the temperature rose rapidly in the middle of the day, it became very bumpy over the mountains and we wallowed and weaved all over the sky.

Approaching the end of the trip, a huge cloud of yellow dust came into sight ahead of us. It rose many thousands of feet above the height at which we were flying and extended for miles on either side. It looked like a sandstorm but, quite obviously, was an after-effect of the earthquake. Pop Stemp signalled us to close the formation up to ensure that we stayed together as the visibility deteriorated in the dust. I had not been to Quetta but Pop was familiar enough with it and knew exactly where the aerodrome lay. Visibility got worse and worse as we tucked in beside him and he led us down to 500 feet and into the middle of the dust cloud. After a few moments in the murk, he suddenly banked to the left and, as I followed, the visibility lifted slightly and the markings of the aerodrome could be dimly seen below. We slowly flew round the perimeter and it was apparent that a huge crack or fissure had split the landing area in two. Some hastily laid canvas strips indicated two landing areas, one on either side of this crack which was itself marked by white crosses. By this time Pop Stemp had decided where to land and again signalled to us – this time to go into line astern behind him and follow him in to land. He chose the area to the right of the fissure and sideslipped in to touch down in the centre of it. Peter Hamley landed to the right of him and I followed some way behind and to his left. The surface was very rough and uneven and the Wapitis rocked and swayed from side to side as they slowed down.

'Are you all right?' I called to my passenger whom I had told to sit down on the little folding seat during the landing.

'Yes,' he replied, 'I feel a bit queasy but that will soon pass. What an appalling mess!'

It certainly was; and as we began to taxy slowly towards the tarmac it soon became clear that the station had suffered immense damage. Hangars were still standing but the other buildings appeared to be heaps of rubble with clouds of the choking dust still floating upwards. An airman with a bandage round his head came limping out to meet me as I turned into line with about a dozen other aeroplanes which had arrived before us. While undoing my straps, I looked around; every airman in sight had some part of his body bandaged and, in fact, I don't think I saw a single airman without some injury during our brief stay.

I helped my passenger to climb down from the rear cockpit: he was visibly shaken by what he had already seen. Turning to the airman who had met us, I said:

'You must have had a terrible time.'

'Yes, Sir,' he replied, 'it was pretty grim. All the barrack blocks collapsed on top of us and a lot of chaps are still being dug out. A good many have been killed. I am one of the lucky ones,' touching his bandaged head.

The Wapitis of 60 Squadron were parked together and their pilots had congregated in a group on the tarmac. It appeared that our Squadron Commander had gone off to see how best we could help, and in the meantime we were to refuel our own aeroplanes and prepare them for the return flight. I said good-bye to the medical sergeant who had flown with me as he and his colleagues were taken off to help with the injured. It was fortunate that the petrol supply had not been affected by the earthquake as all the visiting aircraft had come considerable distances – from the three Frontier stations, from Ambala and Lahore – and consequently needed considerable quantities of fuel. I counted more than forty aircraft which had responded to the call for help and it would have been extremely awkward if no fuel had been available to fill them up. Quetta had quite enough problems of its own without being cluttered up with a mass of empty aeroplanes. There was considerable risk of earth tremors and our job was to bring all the aid we could, stay for the shortest possible time and leave with any casualties who were fit to be taken to more comfortable reception areas.

While we were waiting for our Squadron Commander to return, Hamley and I walked into the camp where rescue operations were in full swing. We were appalled by the devastation. Although we did not know it at the time, one officer and fifty two bachelor NCOs and airmen were killed: this high figure, which was one in five of the single airmen, was mainly due to the design of the barrack rooms in which they had been sleeping. These were one storey buildings of brick construction roofed with single flat slabs of concrete. The earthquake caused the brick walls to collapse, allowing the slab roofs to fall onto the sleeping airmen. Almost any man who managed to escape with his life sustained some injury from the falling masonry. The hangars, although still standing, were a shambles. The Wapitis of the two squadrons had charged about, crashing into one another on the twisting, heaving floors. Only three aeroplanes of about twenty four in the hangars were undamaged and many were beyond repair.

I learned from a Quetta officer, who was taking a breather from digging out communications equipment from the rubble of the Signals section, that the centre of the earthquake had been confined to an extremely narrow belt. Quetta, he explained, was divided by the Durrane Nullah. To the north of this nullah or valley, lay the cantonment largely occupied by the 1st Indian Division and the Army Staff College. To the south of it lay the native city and the RAF station. The effects were so restricted that the Army in the cantonment did not even realise until the morning that any damage had been caused. As soon as the news got round however, the RAF and the city were inundated with help to dig out the dead and injured.

We made our way back through the choking dust to our aeroplanes, feeling very shocked and upset by what we had seen and heard. The packets of sandwiches and flasks of tea and coffee which we had brought with us were very welcome as, understandably, Quetta was quite unable to offer us anything.

While we were finishing off our picnic meal, a line of ambulances and private cars came slowly on to the tarmac. These contained our passengers for the return flight, the less seriously injured families of officers and airmen who were considered fit enough to fly out, and so do something to alleviate Quetta's frantic medical problems.

Although the Wapiti was designed to carry two people only, where a mother and child needed to be evacuated together, we decided to stretch a point and take them both in the same aeroplane, one lying on the floor of the rear cockpit and the other sitting on the small collapsible seat. In view of their injuries it was not possible in all cases to fit parachute harness onto them and so, in the unlikely event of an emergency, the pilot would have to stay with his aeroplane and endeavour to bring it down safely. I had one passenger only, the wife of a Warrant Officer Johnson, with a broken arm which had been splinted and put into a sling. Her husband, who was himself bandaged round the leg and limping painfully, was worried about his wife's safety, and I did my best to set his mind at rest, assuring him that I would see that his wife was well looked after at Kohat. Johnson and I managed to get a parachute harness on to his wife with some difficulty. I was anxious that she should wear it, not because she might have to jump, but because the harness contained the metal ring by which an air gunner was fastened to the floor of the cockpit, there being no belt or safety straps. As I knew it would be rough over the mountains, although I didn't mention that to the Johnsons, I wanted Mrs Johnson to be as secure as possible. She was clearly in some pain and looked pale and very unhappy at leaving her injured husband in the shambles, but she settled herself down on the uncomfortable little seat and waved her one good arm cheerfully enough. When I had climbed into my cockpit I showed her how to speak to me through the rubber mouthpiece of the speaking tube and then said, 'I think the most uncomfortable part of this trip will be taking off from here. The ground is very rough and uneven after the earthquake. Hold your injured arm

163

so that you don't knock it on some projection or other while we are taking off. I'll do my best not to bump you about too much.'

We had agreed to fly back in the same loose formation as during the outward flight. If any of the passengers became seriously ill, the pilot of that aeroplane would go into Miramshah, but only as a last resort because the medical facilities there were primitive and it was only a further forty minutes flying to Kohat. The other two Wapitis in our formation had children with their mothers and we were more concerned about how the children would react to this flight than the adults.

I taxied out slowly, leaving a disconsolate Warrant Officer waving to his wife doubtless wondering when he would see her again. The surface seemed uniformly rough and I could see no way of finding a smooth take off run. I turned into wind and waited while the other two took off. Twisting my head round, I could just see Mrs Johnson: she looked all right and I smiled reassuringly at her before lowering my goggles and opening the throttle. The take off was not as rough as I had feared and, being fairly lightly loaded, we left the ground within about 200 yards and climbed into the cloud of dust which still hung above the city. As I turned over the shattered station I had my first look at the native city. There was nothing but one vast sea of rubble, without a building standing that I could identify. Everywhere tiny figures were digging furiously adding to the choking clouds of dust mixed with smoke from many fires which were still burning over a wide area. The smell of dust and smoke even penetrated the cockpit and I was more than ready to turn for home and take Mrs Johnson out of the tragic atmosphere. Five minutes later I emerged from the dust cloud into clear air and blue sky at 3,000 feet. The others were well ahead and I accelerated a little to catch them up as we all set course for Kohat.

It was 4.30 pm by the cockpit clock and that meant that we would not reach Kohat until well after dark. That was no bad thing as the cooling evening air would give smoother conditions for our passengers. Already it was calmer than our morning flight and Mrs Johnson said cheerfully that she was quite comfortable and enjoying what was in fact her first flight. We flew well to the east of the direct track from Quetta to Kohat to avoid some of the mountainous areas of Waziristan, in the hope of giving our passengers a smoother ride. The sun began to sink below the mountains on the Frontier and we were in that brief moment of twilight as we flew over the town of Dera Ismail Khan. Pop Stemp switched on his navigation lights and also his big white downward recognition light so that Hamley and I could see him clearly. I closed in a little and flew behind and slightly below him so that he was silhouetted sharply against the darkening sky.

A new moon was rising over the Punjab as the lights of Bannu came into view to our left, and my mind drifted back to that night a year ago when I had trudged up the lonely Frontier road from Islam Chowki to the police post after Collings and I had forcelanded with 'Mutt and Jeff'. This was certainly a much better night. Over my shoulder I could see a warm glow coming from the rear cockpit where Mrs Johnson had switched on the small spotlight which I had shown her before we took off.

'About thirty minutes to go and it will be quite smooth from now on. Are you in any pain?'

'No, thank you, my arm is quite comfortable and I'm as warm as toast. It's a wonderful night. I'll be almost sorry when it's over.'

Fifteen minutes later pinpoints of light began to appear ahead and I knew they must be Kohat – there were no other populated areas for miles around. We began a gradual descent from our cruising height of 5,000 feet. The three of us flew together over the centre of the aerodrome where the paraffin flares were laid out in a smoking, flickering line from east to west. Hamley and I received the signal to break away and land independently. I turned out onto a wide circuit while the other two went in to land in turn. It gave me a moment to explain the layout of Kohat to my passenger. Our turn to land came and I flashed my aircraft letter Z and received the green signal to land from the head of the flarepath.

'Now for your first landing,' I called to Mrs Johnson, 'We'll make it a good one.'

Two minutes later we were bumping gently along the line of flares whose acrid smoke came into the cockpit and reminded me of that recent Quetta smell. Friendly hands were soon helping Mrs Johnson out of the back seat. She was tired and a little distressed, but she had stood a trying journey so well and given me no cause to worry. In that respect I was lucky as some of the children in other aircraft had been frightened and sick, and had given their pilots a lot of anxiety. All the passengers were taken off to the British Military Hospital for a medical check and a meal before being allocated to their hosts for the duration of their stay with us. I was glad to hear that Mrs Johnson had found old friends in one of our own Warrant Officers and his wife who were anxious to look after her until the future was sorted out. All was well when I called to see how she was faring a few days later and she then confided to me that she had been terrified of the thought of a journey of almost 400 miles in an open cockpit in a flimsy contraption over the mountainous Frontier area but, from the moment she dared look out over the side, she had gained confidence and eventually been captivated by the grandeur of the mountains and the sunset and twinkling lights below.

'Mind you,' she concluded, 'the back of your head and the occasional kind word through my earphones were what reassured me more than anything else. Nevertheless, I'm quite glad my husband is in a ground trade.'

The Quetta earthquake was, as in the case of many major disasters, a nine days wonder. It hit the headlines in the English newspapers for a brief moment and was forgotten. It was six or seven weeks before we saw an English newspaper with an account of the disaster and, by that time, the impact of it had receded even in our minds. In the meantime, the details of

Quetta's tragedy were slow to filter through to us, which was understandable in the circumstances. The RAF casualties were as I have already mentioned; they were terrible enough, but might have been even greater had not a large number of the airmen been sleeping on the verandahs of their barracks because of the heat. Most of those escaped with superficial injuries when the roofs caved in. The native city was the worst hit area of all. The total number of casualties was never precisely known but at least 30,000 were taken from the ruins before rescue operations had to be suspended after about four days when the danger of infection reached such a level that the city had to be sealed up for twelve months. The RAF station was uninhabitable and was evacuated, one of the two squadrons being moved down to Karachi and the other to Rawalpindi where it was accommodated for many months on the Chaklala aerodrome. So badly had the aeroplanes been damaged in the hangars that only sixteen of the original total of twenty seven could be made sufficiently airworthy to fly out to their new destinations.

One happy outcome as far as I was concerned was that Warrant Officer Johnson was posted to fill a vacancy at Kohat and was reunited with his wife in one of our married quarters.

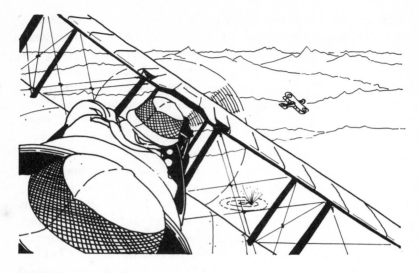

CHAPTER 12

A BOMB, A THERMOS FLASK AND A TOPEE

After a second Christmas at Kohat, similar in all respects to the first, with the sole exception that camels were not used for our Boxing Day match, I knew that in all probability I would be transferred with other junior officers to Risalpur. We would change places with others from Risalpur who had come out from home with me in the *California*. Five years was judged too long to leave a pilot on one station and one type of aeroplane. As Risalpur was the home of two squadrons of the more modern Hawker Hart bomber, it made good sense to give most of us a spell on each station.

Before my exact fate was known, however, one more thoroughly satisfying and enjoyable experience awaited me in the old Wapiti which had carried me so well and forgiven my many mistakes for more than two years. Every winter all the bomber squadrons in India competed for the Ellington Bombing Trophy. It was an impressive piece of silver presented by Air Chief Marshal Sir Edward Ellington and the competition was regarded as the culmination of our year's training. Each squadron entered three crews, one to carry out high level bombing from 12,000 feet, one medium level bombing from 6,000 feet and the third for dive bombing. 60 Squadron had come through the preliminary rounds very well and the final was held over the Peshawar bombing range, which was neutral ground for all the squadrons, on 21st February, 1935.

Whereas high and medium level bombing were exercises in which the air gunner dropped the bombs from his aiming position flat on the floor of the rear cockpit, dive bombing was entirely a pilot's exercise in which the air gunner played no part other than that of an interested and usually enthusiastic spectator. Consequently when I found myself selected to represent the squadron in the dive bombing, I knew that I was on my own. Corporal Wood, who was to be my passenger, and I spent many hours during the days prior to 21st February, adjusting the bomb release mechanism on Z, which had for some time been my own aeroplane and whose peculiarities I knew intimately. The pilot released the bombs by means of a small lever working in a brass quadrant beside his left shin bone. As the lever was connected to the bomb release catches out on the wings by wires and pulleys which tended to stretch and sag in the slipstream, release was not so precise an operation as one would have liked for a competition. However, all the competitors had the same problem and those who spent the time and took trouble over the fine adjustment of their gear were likely to achieve the most precise release. Corporal Wood and I tested each adjustment we made by dropping dummy practice bombs onto a pile of sandbags lying on the tarmac below the wings until eventually I was satisfied that we were getting as accurate a release as was possible. With all the fine adjustment and care in the world, one still needed a fair amount of luck as practice bombs would 'hang up', fail to explode or start to spin uncontrollably for no known reason.

The 21st February was bright and cold with very little wind, perfect conditions for our bombing and, as we were to be the last squadron to compete, and I was to be the last of our three crews, it was uncomfortably apparent that, by the time I took off, I would know precisely what I had to achieve to win the competition. I prayed that I would only need to get a reasonable error of the order of 50 yards to gain the trophy, but my great fear was that some almost unattainable figure of 10 yards or less would confront me. The medium and high level sorties went quite well in the morning and by lunchtime I knew that my total error would have to be something less than 30 yards. Well, that was attainable but uncomfortably low: I had certainly had better results in practice but not consistently so, and I knew that I would need a slice of good luck, accurate aiming, light wind conditions and no delayed, or indeed premature, bomb releases. It was, therefore, with mixed feelings of hope and trepidation that Corporal Wood and I took off at 1.30 pm, to be over the Peshawar range from 2.30 until 3 o'clock, which was the period allotted to me.

It was a perfect winter afternoon as we climbed over the Kohat Pass, with almost unlimited visibility and a light steady wind from the west. Whatever happened I was not going to be able to make the weather an excuse for a poor result. I levelled out at 4,000 feet as we headed over the Peshawar plain, and considered my tactics. The shallow dive bombing which we carried out in these aeroplanes consisted of diving at the target from 4,000 feet to 2,000 feet at an angle of no more than 45° during which the pilot aimed the whole aeroplane as accurately as he could at the 'pin'. It sounds highly inefficient as the pilot had no bomb sight and simply used either his front gunsight or some other fixture, such as the top cylinder of the engine, with which to take aim. This was where experience came in. Each pilot worked out his own method of aiming and releasing the bombs and could eventually evolve a pretty accurate system. It was also essential to know the direction and speed of the wind accurately. When flying downwind the pilot would release his bomb earlier in his pullout than when diving into the wind and, when diving across the wind direction, he would aim slightly to the windward side of his target. So it was customary to find the wind direction and speed of the wind when flying towards the target, and this was where the airgunner played his only part by using his bombsight fixed below the floor of his cockpit to estimate the wind.

As we approached Peshawar we carried out the wind finding procedure which consisted of flying along three different courses while Corporal Wood measured our drift through his bomb sight. With these three measurements, he was able to work out the direction and speed of the wind at that height.

'I make it 8 mph from 278°,' he said through the speaking tube; this confirmed our earlier assessment that the wind was light and fairly steady from the west. We carried eight practice bombs and were allowed to use the first four as 'sighters' to accustom ourselves to the conditions: the last four then counted for the competition.

I kept well away from the bombing range until a few minutes before 2.30 when I turned towards it and looked down at the signals displayed in front of the range marker's hut. He would take sights on my bomb bursts and indicate the error to me by means of white strips laid out in front of his position. As we flew over, the signals indicated the 'all clear' for me to start my bombing runs.

'Right,' I said to myself more than to Corporal Wood, 'we'll do the first competition run down wind, followed by the two cross wind runs and finish with one into wind.' There was no set pattern but the four competition runs had to be carried out from the four quarters of the compass in any order that the pilot chose. He could do what he liked with his four 'sighters'. I decided to carry out my first two 'sighter' runs down wind as I knew from experience that I found those the most difficult, with a personal tendency to release my bomb a fraction too late and overshoot the target.

'Keep absolutely still during the pull out from the dive,' I called to Wood, knowing that even a slight unsteadiness at that point could easily throw one of the small bombs out by as much as ten yards.

We despatched our 'sighters' without any problems. As usual my downwind bombs overshot and all four fell between 25 and 50 yards from the 'pin' which consisted of a white-washed concrete pylon approximately two feet square. Concentric whitewashed circles radiated from it at distances of 25, 50, 75 and 100 yards. The bombs were filled with stannic chloride which gave off a small but dense cloud of white smoke when they burst on impact. A pilot could judge his error fairly accurately from the white smoke, although it drifted so quickly in a strong wind that it was not always easy to judge the exact point of impact. However, the range markers always took two sights on the burst from widely separated positions which were connected by telephone and could plot the exact error within a few moments.

My 'sighters' were not measured and reported but Corporal Wood's assessment of the average was about 40 yards, which was clearly not good enough. As the release mechanism, which had been my chief headache, seemed to be working perfectly, the accuracy and steadiness of my aiming needed improvement. On the whole I concluded that the wind was even less than the 8 mph we had calculated and that I was allowing too much for it. I felt pretty certain that this was so because my 'into wind' bomb had overshot as well as the two 'down wind' bombs.

By this time we were back at 4,000 feet to the west of the range for the first serious run. I closed my throttle, turned the Wapiti steeply to the left and into a dive. The 'pin' came into view over the nose and I adjusted the angle of dive so that it was visible between the rocker boxes of the two top cylinders of the engine – my favourite aiming method. The speed built up – 120 . . . 130 and, finally, 140 mph as we approached 2,000 feet. My left hand dropped down to the release quadrant and I tensioned the small lever between thumb and forefinger, holding the aeroplane steady in its dive with my right hand. At exactly 2,000 feet I eased gently back and lifted the nose above the target as steadily as I could. My passenger was as still as a mouse. When the nose cut the 100 yard circle, I eased the release lever back by one notch on the quadrant and allowed the nose to continue to come up. Transferring my left hand up to the throttle, I opened the engine up and started a climbing turn to the left. The target soon came into view again over my left shoulder and Corporal Wood and I waited, almost breathlessly, for that tell-tale white burst of smoke.

It seemed a long, long wait, but suddenly a wisp of white appeared which rapidly mushroomed into a small cloud. It was just outside the 50 yard circle and an overshoot. It was a disappointing but not disastrous start and I could tell by the fact that Wood made no comment that he too was disappointed.

I positioned myself for the next run – this time across wind from the south which put the wind on my left hand side. As I prepared to start the dive, the range marker put out the error for the first bomb – 57 yards. Down we came as before aiming slightly to the left of the 'pin' to allow for the cross wind. This time the burst came inside the 25 yard circle which redressed the balance a little, but I needed something even better from the last two bombs. The signals showed 22 yards for the second bomb as I turned for my dive from the north, aiming this time to the right of the 'pin.' The wait for the puff of smoke seemed interminable but when it appeared it was well inside the 25 yard circle, and almost half way to the pin. I felt a hollow knocking on the solid top of my flying topee which was Wood's way of signifying his approval. The result came up – 18 yards, and everything depended on the last bomb.

Had I been of the Roman faith I would doubtless have

crossed myself at this point. I contented myself with crossing my fingers as I reached for the release lever for the eighth and last time. The dive was steady and the aim accurate as Z plunged downwards. Up came the nose and away went the last bomb. There was no point in climbing up again and so I banked round the target at 2,000 feet waiting for the smoke to appear. Nothing happened for what seemed like a minute and then – a wisp of white smoke appeared to be coming from the top of the 'pin' itself. The wisp blossomed out into a stream which gave the impression that the 'pin' was smoking like a chimney.

I felt rather than heard Corporal Wood jump up behind me and saw something fly over my head and away.

'You've hit it,' he shouted, thumping me on the top of the head, 'you've actually hit the pin, and my topee and thermos flask have gone down too!' Subject to confirmation, I did, indeed, seem to have scored a bullseye for the first time in my life, and what a time to do it! A moment later the signal was displayed – no error – and I knew that we must have won the trophy. This seemed to justify me in diving down at full throttle past the range marker's hut and waving my thanks to him. He was standing outside with both arms raised in – presumably – congratulations.

On the way back to Kohat, Corporal Wood, minus his topee and flask, calculated that my score was 22 yards which would give 60 Squadron a comfortable win for the second year in succession.

'We were lucky, you know,' I said to Wood as I lifted my goggles and relaxed in the sunshine, 'no hang ups, no dud bombs, almost no wind and no engine trouble.'

By the time I had landed, confirmation of the result had come through by telephone and my score was, indeed, 22 yards. Formal confirmation that we had won the Ellington Trophy was announced by our Group Headquarters on the following day. A few weeks later the Commander-in-Chief, Air Marshal Sir John Steel paid Kohat a visit and presented the trophy to the squadron at a formal parade in one of the hangars.

The successful crews stood in front of the parade and each of us was presented with an inscribed silver medal. Later that day I in turn presented Corporal Wood with a new thermos flask – but he was made to pay for his flying topee.

CHAPTER 13

ON THE MOVE

My expected posting to Risalpur came through officially during March. With three other officers, all of whom had come out to India with me two years earlier, I was ordered to move to 39 Squadron at Risalpur on 1st April – All Fools Day some might say – others with greater respect might say that it was the seventeenth birthday of the Royal Air Force. Whatever associations the date had, it was for me a notable milestone midway through my tour in India. Leaving Kohat would be a wrench. I had settled into a pleasant, comfortable life – plenty of sport, a few not very serious girl friends, good company in the Mess and, above all, plenty of interesting flying. A glance at figures in my flying log book showed that I had completed 450 hours on the Wapiti at Kohat which was a good average figure for two years in an operational squadron. I would leave the Wapiti with a great deal of regret: it had never let me down although sometimes my ineptitude had made some unreasonable demands upon it. It was a tough, rugged and completely reliable aeroplane but I had to admit that the prospect of flying the more modern Hawker Hart was attractive and probably outweighed the many regrets which crowded into my mind as Hukmud Khan and I made our plans to leave.

Hukmud Khan was coming with me. This pleased me immensely as he had looked after me ever since I stepped ashore at Karachi. I was fortunate in that he was a young bachelor without family ties; a Pathan, he came from a remote village which in fact lay closer to Risalpur than Kohat, and so the move suited him well. There was no particular rule about taking one's bearer on posting. Bearers were held on the books of the officers' Mess and their movements with an officer was a matter for negotiation between stations. Hukmud was to remain with me throughout my four years on the Frontier and I was fortunate indeed to have found a bearer so loyal and hard working. Many of my colleagues were not so fortunate and suffered from a variety of dishonest rogues and tricksters. One of Hukmud's last duties at Kohat was to go round and pay my bills to local tradesmen. This was a little ritual which I always left to him because it was an established custom for our servants to obtain a small discount or 'baksheesh' from tradesmen when they paid their officers' bills. We could never have obtained this discount ourselves and it was a perk which we were only too pleased to let our bearers have for themselves.

It was about 70 or 80 miles to Risalpur by road and the move promised to be easy as I had recently given up my motor cycling and saved enough for a car. It was an elderly but sound six cylinder Morris Isis saloon in royal blue – a most unsuitable colour for the heat and dust of India and more appropriate for

Pall Mall in London than the Mall at Kohat. Nevertheless it was roomy and comfortable, ran well and was economical. Hukmud had given it a special polish to ensure that we arrived at Risalpur as smart and presentable as possible. He put on his best clothes for the journey, snowy white pantaloons, a long waisted khaki gaberdine coat and a plain khaki puggaree (turban) with a black cockade. In the face of this finery, I felt compelled to put on my Palm Beach suit, praying that the Morris would not demand some oily attention on the journey.

Piled high with luggage and bedding, we set out in the cool of the morning after breakfast and fifteen minutes later were climbing the lower reaches of the Kohat Pass. At the top I pulled into the small parking area ostensibly to let the Morris cool down, but really I wanted to take a last look at Kohat from this magnificent viewpoint. As it was only 8.30 am, the smoke from cooking fires far below was mingling with the last of the night's mist which was rapidly being dispersed by the sun. Seen from this distance Kohat was surprisingly green, an oasis on the edge of the barren stony plain which stretched as far to the south as I could see. Wapitis were moving like insects on the aerodrome and I watched one climb up towards us and over our heads towards Peshawar. As I sat on the stone wall flanking the parking area, smoking my pipe and looking at the scene below, I noticed that Hukmud had got into conversation with a very old tribesman who had a deeply wrinkled face, the usual brilliant red beard to denote his virility and a rifle slung over his shoulder. He too was resting on his way over the Pass. He salaamed courteously to me as I strolled back to the car and I said good morning to him in Urdu.

'Where is he going?' I asked Hukmud.

'Down to the village below,' he replied, pointing down towards Peshawar. 'He is an Afridi and has been buying ammunition for his rifle in Kohat.'

'Well let's give him a lift; he might protect us,' I said.

Hukmud looked doubtfully at the stack of luggage in the back of the car, but there was a wide front seat with room for three – and a rifle. The old man, whose name was not surprisingly Mohammed, was delighted and salaamed again with a toothless grin. As we climbed in I admired his rifle. A closer inspection of the silver bands which bound the barrel to the stock revealed that one of them had some lettering on it which I soon realised was 'Players Please.' I suspected that it was a rifle made locally in the Kohat Rifle Factory and, although it looked more dangerous for the owner than his victim, I knew that these guns were very effective, as many a Wapiti could bear witness.

We started off down the far side of the Pass and I realised that Hukmud's original doubt had arisen, not so much from the prospect of discomfort in the car but of the smell. However, all the windows were open and we dropped the old boy at a point where a track led off the road to a village at the foot of the Pass. As he climbed out with more deep salaams I gave him two rupees, a gesture which also met with some slight disapproval from Hukmud. I had often noticed how the bearers would frequently assume the authority of their masters and become far more dictatorial and high handed in the treatment of their own people. This was far from the case with Hukmud Khan but even he was not above a little display of arrogance on occasions.

After waving old Mohammed on his way we pressed on across the plain in the morning sunshine towards Peshawar, dodging the herds of goats and bullock carts which thronged the road. I had thought about pausing for lunch at the Peshawar Club but it was much too early as we reached the outskirts of the city and, in any case, I was not too keen to leave the car unattended with all my gear in it. We drove slowly down the Mall which was ablaze with spring flowers and shrubs. The grounds of the Club and the Military Hospital nearby were particularly attractive and I changed my mind and pulled into the Club for a quick Murree beer, leaving the car so that I could keep an eye on it from the bar windows while Hukmud went round to the servant quarters for his own refreshment. As I drank my beer, I watched two pretty girls playing tennis in front of the Club. All girls looked pretty after two years, but these two were unusually good looking and also played good tennis. However, I had been posted to Risalpur – not Peshawar – and there was no point in speculating on the unobtainable.

The 30 miles on to Risalpur were dull, dusty and crowded with native traffic. This was the main road from the Frontier Province into the Punjab and Central India with the North Western railway running beside it. I had the distinct impression of leaving the 'bad lands' and moving into the more civilised areas of India. We came to Nowshera, which was a garrison town astride the road and railway, almost a depot area for the forward stations on the Frontier. Here we turned off the main road as Risalpur lay a few miles to the north facing the foothills of the Himalayas which could just be seen on a very clear day. By this time Hukmud's immaculately polished car was covered in dust and we were both extremely hot and sticky as we had been compelled to keep all the windows closed from Peshawar to keep out the clouds of choking dust.

The cantonment at Risalpur was laid out in a square and, when seen from above, was almost symmetrical with all roads running at right angles to one another; wide, grass bordered roads lined with square bungalows, each in its own garden. The aerodrome and its technical buildings were situated on the north side of the cantonment. Beyond the green foliage of the cantonment and the carefully preserved grass of the aerodrome, Risalpur ran straight back into the dusty, arid bleakness of the Peshawar plain. It was even more of an oasis than Kohat and a remarkable example of British determination to cultivate and beautify the most unpromising stretches of foreign soil.

Being no stranger to Risalpur, I drove straight to the Mess which was situated much closer to the airfield than at Kohat – about three minutes walk which was a great improvement. Being at least 40 miles from tribal territory there was no need to surround the Risalpur cantonment with barbed wire. The Mess lay in a large and shady garden with tennis courts and a swimming pool – another considerable advantage which we had not enjoyed at Kohat. Leaving my car outside the front door, I instructed Hukmud to find out where my quarters were while I strolled over to the swimming pool which was well patronised on this warm April afternoon. There were plenty of old friends about and I was warmly welcomed, with such remarks as: 'Come to fly a decent aeroplane?' After a suitable reply I narrowly escaped being thrown into the pool as an appropriate initiation ceremony. However, respect for my Palm Beach suiting just saved me as Hukmud appeared to take me to our new quarters – No 46 Bungalow.

The bachelors lived in brick built bungalows close to the Mess, each bungalow housing four officers. No 46 was an attractive little house set well back from the road behind a lawn surrounded by jacaranda trees. My quarters consisted of a sitting room, bedroom and bathroom. No running water was laid on and so the bathroom contained a tin bath which the sweeper filled from petrol tins full of hot water, and the inevitable 'thunder box' which the sweeper dealt with at suitable intervals. Used bath water rushed out through a hole in the wall on to the gardens: The hole also provided a convenient entrance for scorpions, tarantulas and the occasional snake. These were to be the hazards of living in a bungalow instead of on the top floor of a block of quarters. No 46 was unique in that one of the previous occupants had decorated the whitewashed walls of the central corridor with the silhouettes of some quite famous occupants of the bungalow. Many of these pictures were at least ten years old and had been carefully preserved with the names clearly visible below each one.

The bungalow was run on a community basis by the four of us, one in each corner of the building. We had our own personal bearers, of course, but we shared a sweeper, a mali (gardener), a dhobi (laundryman) and also, owing to the comparative isolation of the bungalow, a chowkidar (watchman) who prowled round our little domain at night. Provided that one employed a chowkidar one was almost guaranteed freedom from robbery, but if one did not, then an open invitation to theft existed and was constantly accepted, often I suspect by the union of chow-kidars itself. A further advantage of these quarters was that the verandahs which ran right round each building were so wide that a car could be comfortably garaged on them.

One of the features which pleased me when I first inspected No 46 was that the garden was ideal for sleeping outside. This had never been possible at Kohat but it was a great relief during the hottest months when the buildings became super heated during the day and held the heat throughout the night. For the next two years I was to spend most of my nights under a mosquito net in the corner of the lawn. My impression of the climate of Risalpur was that it was hotter and drier than Kohat in the summer months, probably due to its exposed position on the plain. It was at Risalpur that I experienced the highest temperature of 127° in the shade one day in June 1936. It was so hot that, on the following night, I well recall wandering round the garden at midnight with a thermometer in my hand to find the coolest place for my bed, and being unable to find anywhere below 112°, which is unbearably hot for the middle of the night.

The cantonment was unusual in that it had no Officers Club, a strange omission for a brigade of two cavalry regiments and a large RAF station. Nor was there any form of golf course which was a disappointment as I had reduced my handicap to 12 at Kohat and was anxious to continue playing. Nowshera possessed a course, some five miles down the road, and some of us made a habit of driving down for a round before breakfast on holiday mornings; on the first tee at 6 am and back in the Mess for breakfast by 9 o'clock. The lack of a club resulted in our social life revolving round the Mess. Wives and girl friends were free to use the swimming pool, tennis and squash courts throughout the daytime and I soon found that the RAF community as a whole was more closely knit than it had been at Kohat. We bachelors saw much more of the married families, were better able to entertain them and, conversely, received more invitations to their homes which were all closely grouped around the Mess. It didn't take me long to get through the usual charade of dropping my cards on all the right people and getting them duly returned for further use. Having by this time called on at least a hundred people since arriving in India, some of them must have received slightly grubby cards, but it was all part of the social game and well understood.

One of the social misfortunes, and this applied particularly at Risalpur, was that we had little or no opportunity to meet Indians and their families. The British Raj has often been criticised for its insularity and there is undoubtedly some justification for this criticism in cities like Delhi, Lahore, Rawalpindi and Peshawar. The majority of British Service people were, however, located in isolated military garrisons which had been built specifically to house them in strategic positions. Very few, if any, Indians other than tradesmen, shopkeepers and servants lived in these communities. Distances were great and transport sparse with the inevitable result that the military communities were compelled to make their own social life and it was only when on holiday in centres of population that opportunity arose to meet Indian families. The Indian officers in the regiments stationed with us provided most of the very few contacts which I managed to make, and it was a disappointment to me that I had no opportunity to make friends with Indian civilians.

The first day on the new station was occupied with reporting officially to the Adjutant, reading station standing orders and meeting the Station Commander. When those formalities had been completed, I was directed to A Flight, No 39 Squadron where I was destined to spend the remainder of my tour in India. It was commanded by Flight Lieutenant Malcolm Mackay, a hefty fifteen stone Scotsman built on the lines of a front row forward. We were not entirely strangers to one another as I had met him on the sports field during many encounters between Kohat and Risalpur, and he made me very welcome in the squadron hangar which faced directly on to the tarmac apron. It was almost midday and the four Hawker Harts of the Flight had been wheeled into the hangar with the day's flying completed. They looked extremely smart, lined up over their drip trays with red wheels and red spinners on the propellers. I spent the last hour of the morning with one of the sergeants going over the technical details of the aeroplane which was, of course, completely new to me.

The official handbook gave the performance of the Hart as 44 mph faster than the Wapiti, with a top speed of 184 mph, and a correspondingly better rate of climb and range. The engine was an early version of the Rolls Royce Kestrel cooled by ethylene glycol through a radiator which could be wound in and out by hand, situated behind and below the engine. Being liquid cooled, the engine was closely cowled into a streamlined and pointed nose which gave the whole aeroplane a distinctly fast and sporting profile. Unlike the Wapiti, the Hart had wheel brakes operated independently by pedals on the rudder bar and the Sergeant explained to me that this early type of brake, which was pneumatically operated, needed a great deal of maintainance.

'In fact, Sir,' he said, 'our two greatest problems are glycol leaks in the cooling system and the brakes. You'll find that the brakes go out of use just when you need them most, or one will work and the other won't. We do our best but they are quite tricky to maintain.'

I spent a few minutes in the cockpit acquainting myself with the controls and instruments. The cockpit was much smaller than that of the Wapiti and fitted very closely round the shoulders. The controls were as light as a feather and I was intrigued by the compact little control column which was jointed half way down so that, although the whole column moved backwards and forwards to operate the elevators, only the top half moved sideways to control the ailerons. This arrangement neatly solved the problem of trapping one's leg with the column when applying full bank in the narrow cockpit. The only other unusual control to me was a large knurled wheel which wound the radiator in and out. The Kestrel engine was extremely sensitive to the wide range of temperature with which it had to cope in India and the adjustment of the radiator position in conjunction with a temperature gauge was a frequent and vitally important part of the cockpit drill. This completed my introduction to the Hart, other than studying the pilots notes and a technical handbook in my bungalow that evening in preparation for the first flight next morning.

By the time I got back to the bungalow after tiffin – yes, it was curry as usual – Hukmud had unpacked, washed the car and made my new quarters very homely. The charpoy was covered with a counterpane in an appalling shade of puce with a gold fringe, but I could do nothing about it as it had been a present from Hukmud at Christmas.

'Very good, sahib,' he said, looking round with pride, 'better than Kohat.' I had to agree with him; it was indeed most comfortable and his quarters immediately behind were also excellent. I flung myself on my charpoy with a towel round my waist and enjoyed my first afternoon in the new home where the working hours of 6 am to 1 pm were the same as at Kohat.

Next morning, well before breakfast, I walked out on to the tarmac with Flight Lieutenant Shaw, who was a qualified flying instructor and responsible for converting all the new squadron pilots to the Hart. There was no form of dual control, not even an emergency stick which could be plugged into the rear cockpit as in the Wapiti. All that the instructor could do was to take up his pupil in the rear cockpit and demonstrate the characteristics of the aeroplane, answer his questions and draw his attention to any possible dangers or limitations. As soon as the pupil felt confident enough to cope by himself, there was nothing more that the instructor could do but send him off on his own, hide behind the hangar and hope for the best.

As we struggled into our parachutes, Joe Shaw said, 'The Hart is delightful to fly, much lighter and more positive on the controls than the Wapiti, a good deal faster in the air and much more sensitive on the ground. The undercarriage is fairly narrow and stiff and there is a tendency for the Hart to swing on landing if not kept absolutely straight until it has come to rest, particularly if you have had to land out of wind.'

We climbed in and I attached my safety chain to the floor of the rear cockpit and stood up to lean over Shaw's shoulder to get a good view of what was going on in the front.

The first thing you notice is the staccato spit and crackle from the row of stub exhaust pipes along each side of the engine cowling ahead of one. Nobody could accuse the Kestrel of 'ticking over'. Until the throttle was opened it popped, banged and crackled with bursts of blue smoke and flame from the stubs. After thirty minutes in the air and a couple of landings, Joe Shaw had shown me all he could and it was up to me to tame this high spirited, spitting beast. I felt almost like a cadet at Cranwell again as I changed cockpits and watched Shaw walk back to the hangar with a wave of his hand and his parachute draped over his shoulder. The two airmen holding the wing tips grinned in sympathy and one of them clasped his hands in prayer.

I taxied out slowly, testing the brakes at various speeds. It was a strange sensation after flying without brakes and depending on coarse use of the throttle and rudder to steer the aeroplane. The brakes were very effective at low speeds but less so as I taxied faster. Joe Shaw's injunction to use them with great care was obviously important as the narrow undercarriage and high pressure tyres caused the Hart to rock and bounce disconcertingly on the uneven surface. As the throttle was opened to take off, the spitting and crackling changed to an even roar and a slight swing developed which was easily corrected. But as the tail began to rise a pronounced swing to the right started and this required a lot of rudder to correct. The acceleration compared to that of a Wapiti was exhilarating and we were off the ground at 80 mph in no time. I eased back the throttle to climbing revs, the pressure came off my right foot and the tendency to swing disappeared. The lightness of the controls delighted me and there was a taut responsive feel which was quite a new experience. It was more like flying a fighter than a bomber. Before I became too obsessed with the delights of this new aeroplane, I remembered to look at the radiator temperature; it was climbing fast and I had forgotten to wind out the radiator after take off. This was easily put right and I spent a happy half hour getting to know this splendid new aeroplane.

The time arrived to try the first landing. There was a light northerly wind which meant approaching up the road past the Mess and over a line of trees which bordered the aerodrome with a run of about 800 yards over the thin grass surface. Remembering this time to wind in the radiator, I closed the throttle and glided down over the station turning into wind at 85 mph. The engine spat and crackled but I was getting accustomed to this and no longer found it disconcerting. The most satisfying feature was the steadiness and stability of the Hart when gliding. The controls were so light that I found myself 'pump handling' in an effort to find my exact position above the ground. My speed was a shade fast and I finally touched down on the wheels alone which created a certain amount of bounce, but it was safe if not all that tidy. I kept my toes off the brakes for this first landing and used the whole of the available landing run.

'You can do better than that,' I murmured to myself as we came to rest, overcoming a strong desire to call that single landing enough, and taxy in. I carried out two more circuits and landings, each one a little better than the last so that, when I finally taxied in to the tarmac and switched off, I knew that I was going to get immense enjoyment and satisfaction from flying the aeroplane. Joe Shaw strolled out to meet me: he had been watching my performance from his office window.

'Well,' he said, 'no great problems that I could see. The first two approaches were on the fast side but that was a good fault. Be very careful not to touch the brakes if you are running fast with the tail up. These Hart brakes can be temperamental; they never seem to work when you really need them but they will trip you up if you use them carelessly. I find them valuable for stopping at the end of the landing run and for taxying.'

'It's almost lunchtime,' continued Joe, 'we'll go up to the Mess and I shall allow you to buy me a beer to celebrate.'

We did just that.

CHAPTER 14

TO KASHMIR WITH AN MG

So much had been said about the delights of Kashmir that I was determined to go there on holiday before leaving India. It was a remote and romantic country, locked in by mountains with the burning plains of India on one side and the highest and most insurmountable peaks of the Himalayas on the other: a land of beautiful lakes and dense pine forests not unlike Switzerland, but primitive and under-developed. Parts of Kashmir were very popular with British residents in India for holidays and escape from the exhausting heat of the plains during the period May to October. It was not an

189

official hill station on the pattern of Murree, Simla or the Nilgiris. Although it was difficult country to reach by means of the one appalling and dangerous road which clung precariously to the sides of the river Jhelum – with no railway and no airfields, its climate and scenery were so magnificent that, even in the early 1930s, tourism was beginning to be an important element in Kashmir's economy and many were prepared to accept the hazards of the journey for the subsequent rewards.

When I moved from Kohat to Risalpur, I was overdue for a long leave having foregone my entitlement during the previous two years for various reasons, among which lack of funds figured prominently. But now I was ready for a good holiday and as the weather got hotter and hotter at Risalpur, my determination to get away to Kashmir for at least a month increased to the point at which I raised the matter with my Flight Commander, Malcolm Mackay. He was due home at the end of his tour in about September and, as there was some chance that I might take over command of the Flight from him, it was convenient for me to get my holiday in before he departed. But before going on holiday I wanted to change my car for something more sporty than the staid Morris Isis which had done me well for about a year but was desperately unexciting.

The Morris agent in Peshawar was a cheerful rogue named Ghulam Sarwar who was interested in the Isis saloon and had promised to look for a suitable sports car to exchange for it. One day in June he rang up to say that he had exactly what I was looking for – something of an exaggeration as I was not quite sure what I wanted myself. 'Would I come over and look at it?' he said. It turned out to be a fetching pale blue MG Magna with an open four seater body. It was in beautiful conditon, only two years old which made it a 1933 model and reputedly belonged to a wealthy young Indian prince. With a ground clearance of less than four inches, it was even more unsuitable for India than my sedate dark blue saloon, but I fell for it at first sight. A short run showed that the six cylinder engine was smooth and sweet and I clinched the deal on the spot, paying the equivalent of £160 for the MG and getting £130 for the Isis. I was happy and, as he obviously had a customer for the Isis, so was Ghulam Sarwar. Furthermore he told me that he would be happy to take the MG back at the end of my tour and give me a credit note against a new car at home, which is in fact what eventually happened. What a treat it was to have an open car after the stifling heat of the saloon which had become unbearable at times during the hot weather. The little MG was a delight to drive and during the run back to Risalpur from Peshawar I made up my mind to take it up to Kashmir on holiday with me, a decision which future events were to reveal as unwise but exhilarating. One snag only came to light during the short initial drive along the Peshawar–Nowshera road. The MG was so close to the ground that even bullock carts and camels were above me, and I collected all the dust and sand from those as well as from all the other traffic. It was clearly going to be necessary to wear goggles, at least during the hot and dusty months, but it would be a small price to pay.

A few eyebrows were raised when I applied for leave of about six weeks so soon after arriving on the station, but it was due to me and no objections were actually voiced. The holiday was to be divided into two parts, the first three weeks to be spent with two other officers on a houseboat on the Nagin Bagh, a small lake outside Srinagar, the capital, and the remainder of the leave playing golf at Gulmarg, high in the mountains thirty miles from the capital. There was no shortage of 'old hands' to brief me on Kashmir and all thought I was mad to take my new MG. The usual means of getting to Srinagar was to take a train to Rawalpindi and then to hire a large American taxi and to share the cost of the journey up to Kashmir with two or three other travellers. Alternatively, if short of funds, a seat in an overcrowded and ancient bus would ensure a cheap but hair raising drive.

'If you don't knock your sump to pieces on the rocks, you'll be pushed over the "khud" side by a bus,' was the gist of the views expressed on my determination to drive up by myself

191

with, of course, Hukmud Khan. Well, I didn't fancy a hair raising ride crammed into an ancient bus, nor did I see why I should spend money on an expensive taxi when I owned a perfectly good, if somewhat unsuitable car myself.

My leave was due to start on the 3rd July and by 6.30 that morning Hukmud and I were shaking the dust of Risalpur from our Dunlops. Hukmud, who took even greater pride in the MG than he had in the Morris, had arranged for two sets of white washable linen seat covers to be run up by the local 'dhersi'. He had fitted them the previous day. The little car was heavily loaded with my bedroll, luggage and golf clubs and Hukmud's battered tin box and his bedding wrapped up in his prayer mat, without which as a good Muslim he never moved far. We had an unspoken agreement on the subject of his prayers, facing Mecca five times or so a day. If we were travelling, I would stop from time to time, ostensibly for a rest and a pipe. He would seize these opportunities to unroll his prayer mat and quietly walk away for a short distance to complete his devotions. Five minutes later he would return, rolling up his mat, and off we would go without a word being spoken on the subject.

By 7 o'clock we had left Nowshera behind and joined the main trunk road to Rawalpindi. Even at that early hour the heat of the sun could be felt and we could expect a temperature of 110° by early afternoon but by that time I hoped to be starting the long climb up towards Murree and the Hill Depot at Topa, where I intended to spend the night with friends in one of the RAF married quarters. The MG ran smoothly, but high speed was out of the question. We were on one of the best roads in Northern India but even so, the tarmac surface had plenty of deep potholes, any of which could have spelt disaster for my low slung and heavily loaded suspension. The usual traffic of bullock carts, herds of 'shoats' (a cross between a sheep and a goat), ancient buses and itinerant tribesmen in the middle of the road, not to mention stray dogs which rushed out in every village, abounded, and made progress interesting but slow. However, I had six weeks of holiday in front of me and was quite happy to take things as I found them.

Rawalpindi was sweltering and I decided to stand myself a good lunch at Flashmans which was a well known hotel consisting of a collection of single storey buildings set in beautifully tended gardens under waving palm trees. It was not easy to find a shady spot for the car, an essential need if the metal work was not to be untouchable after lunch. I found a spot under a palm tree where Hukmud could keep an eye on our belongings from the servants' quarters. Most of our worldly possessions were in the back with only a tonneau cover to protect them from thieving fingers.

I suppose I knew that I was almost bound to meet some friend or other in Flashmans and, sure enough, two Flying Officers from one of the squadrons which had been evacuated from Quetta to Rawalpindi after the earthquake were propping up the bar. We stood each other a few rounds of Murree beer and played poker dice for an hour before I tore myself away for the inevitable curry lunch. The combination of beer, curry and heat made the light unbearably bright as I returned to the MG for the next stage of the journey. The thermometer in the front porch of the hotel showed 108°, and I was thankful to get some air moving over the car again as we took the long straight road towards the foothills to the north. The tarmac shimmered and swam in the heat until the climb started but, after the first half dozen hairpin bends, that exhilarating freshness which I had experienced on the same road two years before began to make itself felt. Rawalpindi is about 1600 feet above sea level and Murree more than 6,000 feet, and so it was a considerable climb. I wondered how the new car would cope with it but there were no serious problems. The water temperature began to approach boiling point at the half way stage and this was a good moment to stop to cool down and to drink in the view, allowing time for Hukmud to offer up a prayer. The scent of the pines was overpowering as it wafted up the precipitous slopes of the valleys below the road. While I sat on the stone parapet the MG was crackling and grumbling to itself as it cooled down and I shivered for the first time for many months – it was a splendid feeling. At intervals of about five minutes a bus would clatter past, grossly overloaded with passengers on the roof and clinging to the outside, swaying wildly on the corners. It was terrifying to watch the drivers of some of these ancient Dodge, Ford and Chevrolet vehicles spinning their steering wheels on the corners, often using a full turn of the wheel to take up the excessive play in the steering. I was driving with the greatest care, particularly when on the outside of a corner where there was often a sheer drop of hundreds of feet on to pine trees, with no guard rails, stone walls or protection at all. Even Hukmud, usually a most phlegmatic soul, was occasionally clutching the side of the car as we met a bus careering round a hairpin bend.

'Allah will protect us,' I said to him after a particularly close shave.

'I have just asked him to do so,' he replied.

We talked away in our strange mixture of Urdu and English – his English getting better all the time and my Urdu improving slowly.

As we continued to climb to 6,000 feet and above, it became apparent that the rarefied air was beginning to affect the MG's carburation and I stopped once to adjust the mixture, a process which became essential on several occasions during the next few weeks when we made large changes of altitude. A more serious problem was that the tendency for the radiator to boil increased with height and I had to watch the temperature continually, making occasional use of the two gallon can of water in the back. I pulled into the Hill Depot at Lower Topa just before 6 o'clock and spent a pleasant evening with Sandy and Linda Heard, old friends from Peshawar. That first cold night under a blanket was wonderful.

My plan was to spend two more days on the journey to Srinagar with the intervening night in a 'Dak bungalow', (a post house for travellers on the road). This was to be leisurely progress but I knew that the road deteriorated badly when it reached Kashmir and I expected to encounter a few hazards and problems which might need time to overcome. The dutiful Hukmud was polishing the Magna, having loaded it up, when I emerged after a breakfast of eggs and bacon with the Heards who were intrigued with the car and clearly dubious about my prospects of getting it to Kashmir.

Lower Topa stands astride a 6,000 foot high ridge and, having ascended one side of it from Rawalpindi, the Kashmir road then plunges down the other side almost to sea level again to a place called Domel where the road crosses the Jhelum river and then starts to climb up again into Kashmir. It was a long, long way down to Domel with even more twists and hairpin bends than on the earlier ascent. But the road still had a tarmac surface, broken here and there by landslides and potholes. From some of the corners, when I could spare a glance, there were incredible views down through the pine forests to the Jhelum, several thousand feet below and in the distance as the mist cleared, glimpses of snow covered peaks could be seen far away to the north. It was wild and rugged country and the area above and beyond the Himalayas was aptly named 'The Roof of the World'.

The miles of downhill driving, usually in third and sometimes in second gear to save the brakes, brought a new problem for the MG – the plugs started to oil up, a not unusual fault with MGs if they could not be periodically cleared with a burst of the throttle. This was not easy to do as there were no straight or level stretches on the descent and the twists and turns were so frequent and sharp that it was difficult to use the throttle at all except by pausing and revving up occasionally. I decided that I would have to clean the plugs at Domel. The surface got worse as we descended and I was very nearly hit by one bus when the driver swung wide on a hairpin bend in order to keep his speed up at the moment that I was avoiding a boulder in the road. The fifty odd passengers cheered loudly, quite oblivious to the fact that they were on the outside of the bend and in a much more dangerous position than the MG.

195

'Allah is still with us,' murmured Hukmud, this time with a slight smile on his face.

Eventually we reached the bottom and ran into Domel, spluttering and misfiring badly from the oiled plugs. The Customs post for entry into Kashmir was just beyond the village and, after filling up with Shell at an ancient pump, I pulled in to one of the bays. Kashmir is a Hindu State, where the cow is, of course, a sacred animal. It is a very serious matter to hit or kill a cow or a bullock on the road, the penalty often being expulsion from the country. In addition, no beef or beef product may be taken into Kashmir and the customs officials always ask whether a traveller is carrying anything like Bovril or Oxo cubes. If found they are immediately confiscated. As we were checked over, I was sorely tempted to pull the Custom official's leg by declaring as an afterthought that I had a pound of bullseyes in the car. This game had already been played elsewhere by one young officer resulting in the confiscation of his sweets by an official who was either puzzled by the bullseyes or getting his own back. I suspect the latter as the culprit was certain, as he glanced round on leaving, that he saw a distinct bulge in the man's cheek. My customs man looked somewhat dour and humourless so I decided not to tempt providence, particularly as my little car was exciting a lot of interest and doubtless a few comments about its unsuitability for the road ahead. I pulled away from the barrier into a parking area to clean the plugs while Hukmud poured us a cool drink from the thermos. The plugs were well and truly oiled and, to save the trouble of cleaning them on the spot, I put in my spare set and we were on our way within twenty minutes. We were now down to 2,000 feet again and the fresh air had given way to stifling heat, perhaps not quite as hot as the plains had been but much too hot for comfort and it was no time to hang about cleaning plugs.

The tarmac road, rough though it had been, had now disappeared altogether and I was faced with an unmetalled surface, full of huge holes and covered with boulders and stones, with choking clouds of dust every time a vehicle passed. Within a few miles I realised why all my friends had been so disparaging: it was going to be a tough journey. Fortunately there was not much traffic, about one bus or large car every mile, but each one left me in a thick cloud of pungent dust, forcing me to come to almost a standstill in case I hit an unseen boulder. I could rarely exceed 25 mph, and my average was no more than 15. The car seemed to take it very well and as the climb was now fairly gentle, the risk of boiling had diminished. The scenery, during the occasional moment when I could see it, was superb. The road clung to the steep sides of the south bank of the Jhelum, several hundred feet above the river and followed its curves and twists closely. The river itself was full and flowing fast, but not in spate as it must have been a few months earlier when the snow was melting on the lower slopes of the mountains. There was however, still a great deal of water coming down from the higher mountains, some of which had a permanent mantle of snow. Occasionally the road descended to river level to cross a tributary, usually by bridge but in one or two cases when the tributary was dry, the road simply picked its way through the stones on the bed. I negotiated two of these crossings successfully but with my heart in my mouth, and Hukmud had to get out to remove a few outsize stones from our path. Only once did the sump touch the ground and I held my breath, but no damage was done.

By 4 o'clock I was exhausted and we had covered only about 50 miles from Domel. Thoughts of a bath and a few 'chota pegs' were becoming increasingly persuasive and there was no point in pressing on to Sringagar where I was not expected until the following day. Somebody had recommended the 'dak' bungalow outside the village of Baramula which lay a few miles ahead and so I made up my mind to spend the night there. By this time we had climbed back to 5,000 feet and the temperature had dropped to a pleasant warmth but, owing to the dust, the air lacked that invigorating freshness of the pine forests of the previous night. Passing through Baramula, narrowly missing two wandering cows and three dogs, I came upon the 'dak' bungalow which was situated above the road up a short, stony track.

The 'dak' bungalow was a unique form of rest house which only India could have devised. That at Baramula was a typical example: it had deep shady verandahs on all four sides and contained four bedrooms and a large central dining room cum sitting room. Each bedroom had a number of charpoys on which the traveller spread his bedroll. As was customary in India, no bedding was ever provided. If one was lucky, one might have a bedroom to oneself, but the charpoys were there to be used and, if there were many travellers on the road, each bedroom might have three or four occupants. Separation of the sexes was the only concession to privacy and, therefore, a man could not share a room with his wife unless the bungalow was virtually empty. Each bedroom had its bathroom with the ubiquitous tin bath filled by the sweeper from petrol tins of boiling water, and a 'thunderbox'. The bungalow was staffed by a 'kitmagar' (major domo), a cook, sweeper, etc. A meal would be provided for all the residents in the dining room and, although total strangers in most cases, they were expected to eat, drink and spend the evening together. Prices were ridiculously low and one rarely had to pay more than five rupees (about 40p) for dinner, bed and 'chota hazrie' (breakfast).

There was only one other car outside as I drove up to the bungalow, belonging to a Police officer on his way down from leave in Kashmir who proved to be a pleasant drinking companion, and who gave me some disquieting news about the state of the remainder of my road to Srinagar. He pursed his lips when he saw my MG and said, 'You'll have a job getting over the river bed at Patan; my Chevrolet had a pretty rough passage and even the buses were reduced to a crawl.'

This was bad news as I was beginning to hope that the worst was over and that the road across the relatively flat vale of Kashmir ahead of me would be an improvement on the Jhelum gorge.

I luxuriated in a tin bath which Hukmud prepared for me, a large whisky and soda reposing on the ledge by the bath. A sense of well being flowed over me as the dust and grime of the road was washed away until I was completely galvanised into action by a huge tarantula appearing on the wall by the side of my bath. Imitating Archimedes, I leapt from the tub and rushed naked into the bedroom to find a suitable weapon. Hukmud, who was undoing my bedroll, rushed in and killed it with a broom handle and the remains were washed out with the bath water. We were accustomed to finding these horrible creatures, which could measure four or five inches across, in our bungalows on the plains but I was surprised to find one in the comparatively cold air at 5,000 feet.

At Baramula, the road runs out onto the western end of the broad and fertile plain on which Srinagar stands. It is a complete contrast to the Jhelum gorge, with highly cultivated fields and poplar trees flanking the road not unlike parts of Northern France. The main difference lay in the roads which were appalling and I began to fear for the springs and shock absorbers as the little car banged and bumped its way along often in third gear, after leaving the rest house the following morning. We negotiated two dried up river beds which lay across the road, with Hukmud walking ahead and removing the worst of the boulders, but when we came to Patan, I realised that the policeman's gloomy predictions were only too true. The river bed here was not only wider than the earlier ones but deeply trenched with outcrops of solid rock and with a fair depth of water flowing down the centre. I left the car at the roadside and Hukmud and I walked out onto the river bed. There was no question of driving across and even a large Dodge bus which I watched had to cross with extreme caution, aided by its passengers. Thirty miles from our destination and completely stuck! I could see no alternative but to leave the car in the village and load our kit onto a bus, or to hire a car. Hukmud, however, was quite undismayed. He explained to me that he would collect a team of coolies from the village and they would carry the MG bodily across. 'Impossible,' I thought – but then I wondered. The Kashmiri coolie, like the sherpa in Nepal, had a reputation for carrying unbelievable loads up the mountain tracks. It was rumoured that a single coolie carried a piano up the four mile track to Gulmarg. I never believed that but it did at least illustrate the strength and endurance of these men from the hill villages. Hukmud's suggestion was worth trying and I sent him off to Patan with instructions to find not only some twenty men but also four long wooden or metal poles to place transversely under the car for lifting it. The last thing I wanted was to find twenty shouting natives grasping the wings, lamps, running boards and any other part that came to hand, and heaving enthusiastically.

Hukmud departed with an air of importance and I started to unload our belongings to lighten the car as much as possible. I then peered under the car to decide where the lifting poles could go without crushing some vital oil pipe. Luckily the MG had a strong rectangular chassis, the side members of which could take the strain of the poles easily. After that inspection, I sat down to await Hukmud's return with, I may say, some trepidation, and watched about five buses and large cars crossing while I smoked my pipe. They all had great difficulty.

Twenty minutes later, a shouting, laughing throng of ruffians came into view, carrying four young pine trees and led by Hukmud. He said that they were mine for eight annas each (4p) and would carry the car and all our luggage across the river bed. Firm leadership was clearly called for as the mob grabbed hold of various parts of the car and proceeded to test their strength. I told Hukmud to take them back a few yards and line them up. Each pole was then brought forward by two men and pushed under the car while I got down on my back and positioned it. Hukmud managed to get three coolies onto each end of the poles and hold them against the underside of the car while I made a final check that nothing was being damaged. So we had twenty-four coolies holding the four poles waiting eagerly for Hukmud to give the Kashmiri equivalent of

'Two-six hup' which he did with a great show of authority. The MG rose up like a feather and I wondered why I had troubled to unload it. Off went the little army to the cheers of a passing bus load. The coolies were steady and sure-footed and the car hardly swayed at all as they tramped solidly through the water and over boulders with much grunting and laughing. In ten minutes the car was safely across and on its wheels once more to my intense relief. My one regret was that my camera was buried somewhere in my luggage. A photograph taken in the middle of the passage would, I'm sure, have been more than welcome to the MG Car Company as an advertisement.

After bringing the luggage across, the coolies lined up for payment; not unexpectedly, their numbers had risen to thirty by this time but Hukmud was alive to this and weeded out the scroungers in no time at all. Twelve rupees were handed over, the equivalent of a days pay for each of them and I had the MG safely across for less than £1. Later on I rewarded Hukmud with five rupees for his initiative: I would certainly never have thought of his idea as a possibility. We left amid cheers and shouts from our improvised porters and roars of laughter from Hukmud who had been asked most seriously when we would be returning to hand out some more easy money. It was a good question because I had to come back eventually by the same route, but that was a problem which could be faced later.

The car seemed to have suffered no damage from its unusual treatment but its once immaculate pale blue paintwork was now thickly coated with dust and grime which had penetrated everything. Even Hukmud's usually spotless white pantaloons were stained and dirty and the white dust covers on the seats were filthy. The last thirty miles into the capital were compara- tively easy, along a dead straight road between poplar trees with fields of vegetables and grain on either side. The road improved as if to herald the approach of the capital and turned into a tarmac surface for the last few miles. It was unbelievably smooth after the previous two days experience and the MG hummed along with hardly a squeak or rattle.

It was mid-afternoon as we entered Srinagar, warm and sunny with a pleasant breeze off the mountains to keep the temperature down to about 75°. The town which was built by the Moghuls is well laid out with gardens and flowers in profusion. The river Jhelum bisects the town and its water is diverted into many canals, ornamental lakes and water gardens. I was much too dirty and tired to stop in the town and was anxious to get on to the houseboat on Nagin Bagh, one of the lakes beyond the town fed by the main river.

Nagin was the smaller of two lakes with houseboats moored round the edge. These large solidly built boats were Victorian in origin having been built when the British first came to Kashmir to escape the fierce heat of Delhi, and found themselves unable to buy land on which to build summer houses. The boats were real Victoriana, ornately carved and furnished, as the Kashmiris were excellent wood carvers. Each boat had two or three bedrooms, a dining room, sitting room and a flat roof for sunbathing. A separate cookboat was moored alongside and the houseboats were usually let complete with a cook and sweeper, leaving the occupants to bring their own bearers or other household staff. There were some fifty or sixty such boats moored around the lake, often separated by only a few yards of water which made for a closely knit little community, particularly as many of the occupants were either stationed together or knew each other down on the plains. Some boats would have complete families in them, some had either unaccompanied wives or wives and their children awaiting the husband for his annual leave; others, like our own, housed a party of bachelors.

The lake had a rough and treacherous tow path running round it which was just about negotiable by a car. Having no idea where my houseboat was moored, I set out cautiously along the track telling Hukmud to keep his eyes open for 'Hamley or Isemonger Sahib'. They were to be my companions for the next three weeks, the boat having been taken by a party of a dozen of us for two months, changing over at intervals according to the leave which each of us had. Half way round the lake Hukmud spied the black beard of Peter Hamley's bearer, and we had arrived.

Neither Peter nor Harry was at home and I had an opportunity to inspect the houseboat which was much larger and more roomy than I had imagined. A large sitting room, extending to the full width of the boat was situated at the forward end, opening onto a small deck in the bows with a staircase leading up to the roof deck. Behind the sitting room was a full width dining room and behind that a central passage with two bedrooms opening off it on each side. Baths and thunderboxes were in the stern. The top deck was covered with coconut matting with a striped awning over half of it with several bamboo chairs and tables scattered about. Our bearers lived in the cookboat which was moored at the stern and connected to the houseboat by a flimsy looking gangway.

I sat down on the top deck with a 'nimboo parni' (fresh lime and water) and studied the scene. Most of the neighbouring boats were silent and appeared unoccupied but this was probably because their occupants were out in the centre of the lake where the bathing boats were moored. The water near the shore and around the houseboats was reedy and fairly dirty, but out in the centre, where the current flowed steadily through the lake, the water was clean if not particularly clear and two large bathing boats were anchored some distance apart. They were adapted houseboats with a flat top deck equipped with high diving boards and spring boards. Below this deck was some accommodation for changing, although most bathers came changed from their boats. The bathing boats were more than three hundred yards from me but I could see that a lot of people were using them and the sound of shouting and laughter floated across the water. Plenty of small craft were moving about the lake. Most of these were 'shikaras' which were an essential adjunct to every houseboat as most of the travelling around Srinagar and the lakes was by water. In this respect Srinagar bore some resemblance to Venice and the shikara was the Kashmiri equivalent of the gondola. They were hired, complete with a boatman, separately from the houseboats but for the same period. They were constantly available throughout the 24 hours: I sometimes wondered when the 'shikara wallah' had any sleep but came to the conclusion that they were all experts in sleeping at their posts during the intervals of paddling their fares from place to place. Their little boats, not unlike gondolas in shape and size, but less extravagantly shaped at front and rear, were extremely comfortable. The passengers reclined on deep cushions under an awning with curtains which could be drawn to conceal any 'goings on' from the interested gaze of onlookers. The boatmen seemed totally disinterested in the behaviour of their clients and would quietly sing Kashmiri love songs in a tuneless and monotonous chant in time with their paddling.

As the sun started to go down Peter and Harry came across from the bathing boats in our own shikara. Like all of them, this one had its name on a headboard; they were usually exotic or erotic and ours was called 'Love came to me on the Gatmal Night'. The Gatmal Night is New Year's Night. But most shikaras carried additionally the advertisement that the boat had 'full spring seats'. Ours was no exception, with the embarrassing result that we floated about in a boat which stated on its headboard – 'Love came to me on the Gatmal Night on full spring seats'.

Harry was astonished that I had not only managed to get the MG to Kashmir, but had even negotiated the towpath and parked it alongside the houseboat. This feat and my arrival called for a celebration and the evening was spent at the Srinagar Club where we dined and danced until the early hours. Like all British clubs in India it was quite formal: dinner jackets and long frocks being the standard dress for dining and dancing every evening, tails and white ties being worn for gala occasions. Nobody was allowed to be in the club in shorts or in short sleeved shirts after sundown. On the plains this was a sensible anti-malaria precaution but it was carried on in Kashmir merely as a social formality, as there were very few if any mosquitos. At 2 am Peter Hamley and I paddled slowly back to Nagin Bagh on our full spring seats, Harry being otherwise occupied in seeing a girlfriend home in her boat. The moon was rising over the Shalimar gardens, picking out the snow covered mountains in the distance and bathing the lake in a soft yellow glow. The only sounds were the monotonous crooning of our boatman and the occasional 'plop' of a jumping fish.

'Not a bad life,' said Peter drowsily, 'and to think they pay us for this!'

The Kashmir lakes were a veritable lotus eater's paradise and the next three weeks were passed in a haze of sunshine, sleep and alcohol with a few mildly amorous adventures thrown in. The daily routine was to swim and laze on the bathing boats all morning, followed by a few rounds of John Collins on some-body's houseboat before a late lunch – almost always a curry. A well deserved sleep until 4 pm followed and then it was time to take a little exercise such as visiting the Shalimar Gardens or the Srinagar bazaar, paddling a canoe round the lake, fishing or simply bathing again. Cocktails with one's many friends and acquaintances followed at 6 o'clock, and anything could happen after that.

The Srinagar bazaar and shops were colourful. Kashmir has always been famous for carpets, wood carving and brasswork. Had I been older, married and less impecunious, I would have invested in some rugs and carpets which, at that time, were wonderful value. I have often regretted that I did not do so but equipping some future home was far from my thoughts and I had more immediate needs. Nevertheless many of my friends took some excellent bargains back to India, or even arranged for them to be shipped back to England, a small favour which the Kashmiris were only too pleased to carry out. During one of these expeditions I watched an old man with a long white beard working on a huge square carpet which I was told he had been making for the past twenty years and had almost lost his sight in the process. Some of the wood carving was equally fine but often ruined by the use of cheap and nasty hinges, locks and catches. I ordered a large cigarette box with the 60 Squadron crest – a macaw's head – on the lid. This crest was beautifully carved for me in three days and all the craftsman had to copy from was the crest on the heading of a sheet of squadron notepaper which I left with him.

Nagin Bagh ran into the larger Dal lake on which were fewer houseboats but a number of islands and floating gardens containing thousands of lotus flowers and almost every other known variety of water plant. One evening I paddled our canoe over to the Shalimar gardens on the Dal lake and wandered among the beautiful beds of flowers laid out, somewhat formally, alongside symmetrical lakes with a variety of fountains playing over the lotus blossoms. Several ornate buildings of typical Indian design gave the gardens the atmosphere of a miniature Taj Mahal but, due to their comparative isolation at the end of the Dal lake, visitors were few and far between which made them a quiet and peaceful spot that has probably been responsible for the air of romance always associated with them.

The Club was the centre of British night life in Srinagar. There was little else to attract us that was even faintly respectable. In consequence our evenings were spent either in the Club or, more frequently, entertaining on our own boat or joining a party on another boat. With a large dining room and the cookboat alongside it, it was possible to provide a full scale dinner for up to a dozen people as all the necessary crockery and cutlery was provided with the boat. Our dinner parties usually continued with liar dice or dancing to my ancient gramophone on the roof. If the party had been sufficiently cheerful, it might finish with a midnight swim from the bathing boats, but it wasn't a particularly popular pastime with the girls as the lake could be quite chilly at night. One of these occasions was the only time in my life I have ever dived from a sixty foot board into pitch blackness.

It was not, however, the only unusual swimming experience of the holiday: a gala ball at the club provided another. It was a full dress occasion which meant climbing into one's white tie and tails. I was asked to join a party of ten as partner for a young, pretty and lonely Army wife who lived on a houseboat about 400 yards from our own. It was a good party and Betty and I got on splendidly together. When the ball finished at 2 am, chivalry demanded that I should take her home in her shikara. Scenting romance, our boatman was unusually slow with his paddling and equally persuasive with his crooning. Neither Betty nor I were in a mood to object to the tardy progress and it was well after 3 am before we reached home – her home. I was persuaded to go in for a final nightcap which took a while longer than necessary. When I dragged myself away, I found that it was almost broad daylight outside and that her shikara had pulled out into the lake and the boatman had fallen asleep. Betty and I debated the situation in whispers. I dared not shout for the boat for fear of waking her neighbours and compromising her. There was nothing for it but to swim home in my evening dress, hoping to make the distance safely and to avoid waking the occupants of other houseboats on the way. Leaving my tail coat, white tie, collar and shoes for Betty to return later, I crept down the ladder and into the water, which was horrible. I struck out quietly for our own boat and then, to my disgust, found a huge patch of weed in the way. I had to plough my way slowly through the dirty, clinging stuff and it took me a good quarter of an hour to reach the houseboat. Filthy and weary I dragged myself up the ladder and surveyed the wreckage of my boiled shirt and best evening trousers. 'This will test Hukmud and the dhobi,' I thought as I stripped and fell into bed wondering whether the night had been worth it.

The three weeks on the houseboat passed rapidly and happily, and remarkably cheaply considering that the three of us spared no expense to enjoy ourselves. The MG had not been used once but I had prepared it for its next trip, a short one of only 30 miles up towards Gulmarg in the mountains above the vale of Kashmir. Peter and Harry were going back to work having finished their holiday and our houseboat was being handed over to three more bachelors. Hukmud and I packed up the car on the morning after our farewell party for all those friends who had comforted us in our loneliness. I was surprised to find from the solicitous enquiries about the state of my 'tails', that the early morning swimming exploit of a few days before had become common knowledge round the lake and I came to the conclusion that my gallant attempt to safeguard Betty's reputation had been a waste of time.

We bumped our way back along the tow path with the lake sparkling in the early morning sunshine and the MG burbling contentedly after its long rest. I was not sorry to be on my way. Three weeks idleness had been enough and the prospect of golf at 10,000 feet above sea level at Gulmarg was attractive. I drove through Srinagar and back along the poplar lined road. Some ten miles from the city a road branched off towards Gulmarg and we began to climb steadily. Once again the engine started to spit back and I paused to adjust the carburetter by the roadside while Hukmud took the opportunity to say his prayers. The vale was a patchwork of neat green fields with the Jhelum winding through them. From my vantage point there was something almost English about this scene as I sat on a front mudguard and smoked St Bruno Flake which tasted so much better in this cool climate. Ahead of us the lower slopes of the pine forest started, dark and dense, hiding any possible view of Gulmarg.

I carried on, up and up, until we reached the line of the trees. Here the road ended at the small village of Ferozpur and it was impossible to take a car any further. A splendid arrangement had been made for the few holidaymakers who arrived in their own cars – and I gathered there were very few who risked that journey from the plains. A long row of lock-up garages had been built in the village by Nedou's Hotel in Gulmarg and these were rented to their guests for a very small charge. The garages were guarded by a chowkidar and were reckoned to be fairly secure. The remainder of the journey, a further four miles up a rough track through the pines, had to be completed on horseback – if that is a correct description of the broken-down but tough mountain ponies which were provided for the trip.

Hukmud sought out the garage chowkidar and I presented my reservation for Nedou's Hotel which gained me the allocation of No 13 garage. While Hukmud unloaded, I made the car as safe as I could by disconnecting the battery, removing the plugs and covering it with a dust sheet which we had brought with us. Being an open car it couldn't be locked but the garage seemed to have a sound padlock and I felt reasonably happy about leaving it for three weeks. As this was going on we were surrounded by a gabbling throng of 'pony wallahs' and an even scruffier collection of coolies who would carry our luggage. This was the kind of situation in which Hukmud was so valuable. He sorted out our needs in no time and, with the two of us mounted and three coolies laden with our luggage, our little party started on the final 1,000 feet through the trees. The rough track wound steeply upwards; the forest thickened and it became darker and colder, reminiscent of the Murree hills but that much colder owing to the extra altitude. Although quite warmly dressed I was shivering long before we reached Gulmarg and Hukmud looked as blue as a swarthy Indian can look.

Our loaded coolies kept up with the ponies at a steady, shambling trot which they could maintain for hours on end. After watching them for a while, I was almost prepared to believe the story of the coolie who carried a piano up this track. An hour's hard climbing took us over the peak of a hill and out of the pine woods. A most beautiful green land-locked valley opened out in front. It appeared to be several miles long but narrow, with wooden buildings scattered over it and towering, snow covered mountains dominating it on all sides. This was Gulmarg, resembling a small corner of Austria in the summer. A little stream sparkled in the sunshine as it meandered back and forth through the valley and I could see the fairways and greens of the three golf courses which accounted for at least fifty per cent of the area of the Gulmarg valley. There were two full length 18 hole courses and a 9 hole course for 'rabbits'.

Our modest caravan plodded down the rough track towards the main collection of wooden buildings. These comprised Nedou's Hotel, the one and only hotel in Gulmarg. A large central wooden building contained the main public rooms and all the guests were housed in wooden bungalows attractively sited amid the pine trees around the main building. All these buildings had open fires and there was a smell of smoke from pinewood fires hanging in the clear cold air. I felt remarkably fit, if slightly saddle sore from the unaccustomed ride as I dismounted in front of Nedou's and walked in to claim my reservation. Half an hour later, Hukmud and I were settling in to one half of a log cabin with an Army officer and his wife from Peshawar occupying the other half. It was sparsely furnished and very basic but at least it had electric light and some extra blankets which I could see were going to be more than welcome. Furthermore a log fire was already burning on the open hearth and a good stock of pine logs lay handy. I had long since changed my standard dress of shorts and khaki shirts for flannels, a blazer and a warm pullover.

The valley at Gulmarg is about 10,000 feet above sea level and its surrounding mountains vary from 12 to 15,000 feet. Even in July it is not all that far below the snowline and one or two of the nearest peaks remain permanently capped with snow. Fortunately the valley is deep and extremely well sheltered, with the result that the almost continual sunshine makes it a warm spot throughout the day with the temperature dropping sharply towards freezing point as soon as the sun dips below the mountains which, owing to their proximity, is usually mid afternoon.

Golf being my main reason for coming up to Gulmarg, I was up early the next morning, loosening up my swing outside the cabin before going down to the hotel for breakfast. Both the hotel and the small golf clubhouse were friendly places. There were many unattached golfers like myself and there was no difficulty in finding partners or opponents. Many adopted the habit of playing a serious singles on the upper championship course in the morning and, if energetic enough, a leisurely foursome on the lower and much easier course during the afternoon. But I had been warned to take it easily initially. Until one has become acclimatised, golf at 10,000 feet can be extremely exhausting, and I discovered this on my first round. Even the slightest climb up to an elevated tee or green, and there were plenty of both, left me panting like an asthmatic old man – and I was a fit twenty three. A few days were sufficient to return my breathing to normal and for the rest of my stay the invigorating air was a wonderful tonic: the prospect of returning to the plains became increasingly unattractive.

The upper course on which the championship of Northern India was sometimes played was an absolute tiger, and totally unlike any course at home. It was mountainous with large outcrops of rock scattered throughout its length, many water hazards from the stream flowing through it, and very narrow but beautifully green fairways between the rocks. In fact rocks took the place of bunkers with the obvious difference that if one hit them, the ball would shoot off at any angle instead of falling dead into sand. Three holes in particular on this course were quite unusual. One, which had the longest and least hazardous fairway from the point of view of rocks, had its own peculiar hazard. The fairway sloped from a pine forest on the right down to the stream on the left, and so it was essential to keep well up the slope and as close to the trees as possible. But the trees were the home of a large colony of apes, several of whom would rush out, retrieve a ball from the fairway and retire chattering into the forest with it. Occasionally one would see them playing about on the green and the flag was continually being removed from the hole. Although the small boys who run ahead to spot your ball did their best, no effective answer to this menace was ever found and the rule was that you placed another ball at the place where your own was last seen with no loss of strokes. Most players were sensible enough to use an old ball on this hole and occasionally an angry and chattering monkey would hurl a ball back onto the fairway, well chewed and quite unusable.

Another hole, the ninth, at the far end of the course had a bar permanently manned by a steward from the hotel, smartly dressed in white with his 'puggaree' and belt in Nedou's colours. Weary golfers could take a glass before embarking on the second nine holes, and it was customary for the individual or pair who were losing at the ninth hole to stand the round of drinks. Naturally, there was a rule that following players were not to be held up while those in front were drinking. Nedou's must have made quite a good profit from this bar during the course of a season.

Perhaps the most difficult and unusual hole was one where the tee was almost vertically below the green. Using something like an eight iron, one struck the ball straight up to a green perched on a ledge on the hillside about 100 feet above the tee. The green, and of course the pin, were totally invisible to the player and there was no guiding pole to mark the whereabouts of the pin. The hole was officially some 130 yards long but I doubt whether the horizontal distance between the tee and the green was more than 30 yards, so steep was the ascent. If the drive hit the hillside below the green, the ball would career down past the tee leaving the player with an even more precipitous shot than his drive. If the ball pitched above the green, it could run back right across the green and still come back past the tee. Many hearts, and doubtless clubs, were broken on this hole and, quite apart from its technical difficulties, the winding goat track from the tee up to the green left most players completely winded and unable to putt accurately. There can have been few, if any, more outrageous holes in the world.

Another Gulmarg phenomenon was the distance that a golf ball travelled at that altitude. I reckoned that a well hit drive carried thirty or forty yards further than at sea level which certainly flattered one when on form. It also accentuated ones errors with the result that a hefty slice which then hit a rock outcrop was probably never seen again. After playing round the polo ground at Kohat for two years, the course seemed excessively difficult and I spent most of my first week playing on the lower course which confined itself to the floor of the valley and was easier and less exhausting. My handicap at the time was 12, and it wasn't long before I was playing down to that and beginning to enjoy this unusual golf immensely. A host of small boys, each neatly dressed in khaki shirt, shorts and a red fez, was available to act as caddies and scouts to run ahead and mark the balls and, if agile enough, defeat the monkeys on the fourteenth. Thus a foursome was a formidable sight as it set out from the clubhouse with four players, four caddies and two scouts. Each of these lads was paid five annas (2½p) for a full round and they clearly regarded this as a good wage. Golf trolleys had not been invented, or were certainly not in use in India in 1935, but I doubt whether a trolley would have been practicable on the upper course with its precipitous slopes and rough going. The answer, if one had to carry one's own clubs would undoubtedly have been a very light bag and the fewest possible clubs.

One afternoon, I was being inveigled into playing tennis, fortunately in a leisurely mixed four. The hotel possessed two or three hard courts out in front of the main entrance and it did not take me long to find out why they were little used. Not only was the game too exhausting for us visitors who were not fully acclimatised to the height, but the balls were very difficult to control and one's usual strokes seemed to result in the ball floating out of the court. It was not a success and I decided firmly to stick to golf.

The Championship of Northern India was played on the upper course during my last week and I had the temerity to put my name down. Failure to survive the first round did not upset me much as my opponent was an immensely tall Sikh Lieutenant from the Guides Cavalry who played off a handicap of two. I think he played even below his handicap on that day and beat me 6 and 5. My defeat would have been even greater had he not had a complete disaster at the vertical hole when his ball twice came back beyond the tee.

With golf all day and dancing and drinking each evening

after dinner in the hotel, the days drifted by pleasantly enough except for one incident half way through my stay. A dog died of rabies and a number of the hotel guests, including myself, were suspected of having had contact with it although I cannot personally recall ever having patted it. Nevertheless, anti-rabies injections were prescribed for all of us and I was certainly not inclined to argue about it, knowing what a terrible thing rabies was. The treatment at that time consisted of fourteen injections in the stomach on fourteen consecutive days. After the first six or so, it took all my courage to report to the clinic for the next morning's dose. So tender was my stomach that the approach of the needle, which was usually fairly blunt, almost sent me climbing up the wall. Fortunately the injections, although unpleasant, had no ill effects.

All good holidays come to an end and after almost six weeks of the delights of Kashmir, I was ready to return to flying, knowing that the worst of the heat would be over on the plains. Also, with my third hot weather over, I felt that I was getting through my tour in India pretty well and could begin to look forward to a posting home. Hukmud Khan, who had had an easy time with the minimum of duties to carry out, had enjoyed his change as much as I had although he probably found Gulmarg too cold for his liking. We allowed three days for the return journey and set off early one bright morning on our ponies with the usual string of coolies carrying our luggage down through the forest. The MG was covered in dust and dirt when I pushed it out of its garage at Ferozpur and, after loading it up, Hukmud insisted on washing it down while I put in a clean set of plugs and some more air in the tyres. She started without difficulty and, after paying off our pony wallahs and coolies and giving the chowkidar a good tip, were soon on our way down to the main road through the vale of Kashmir. I enjoyed my last pipe of St Bruno Flake in the cool.

By lunchtime we were back at the river bed at Putan which had caused so much trouble on the outward journey. I parked the car beside the road and got out to survey the crossing. It looked a little easier than before and I was tempted to drive over. After walking across and inspecting some of the rocks and potholes, however, I decided it would be tempting fate too much; a cracked crankcase would be disastrous. So Hukmud set off to round up a party from the village and the ceremony of carrying the car over the river on poles was repeated. I recognised some of the coolies who greeted me as an old friend and seemed sorry that I didn't do the journey several times a week. While Hukmud paid them, I handed out cigarettes and we finally departed in a cloud of dust amid much cheering and shouting.

It was too early in the day to stop at the Baramula 'dak' bungalow and we spent the night closer to the frontier at Domel which was equally good and just as cheap. From Domel there is an alternative road down to the plains through Abbotabad and I decided to take it, cutting out the Hill Depot at Topa and Rawalpindi. The new route worked out well and I reached Abbotabad in time for lunch at the picturesque little Club. The town – a garrison town in fact – was small but well laid out with masses of dusty palm trees, oleanders and flower beds. Being on the very edge of the foothills rising up from the Punjab plain, it was hot but not unbearably so and greatly preferable to Rawalpindi. The run back to Risalpur was a long one but uneventful and, with a day of my leave to spare, I turned into the drive of 46 bungalow shortly after nine o'clock in the evening.

It had been a splendid holiday and I had certainly fallen in love with Kashmir, and Gulmarg in particular. Seeing much of it from four inches above the ground in the MG had been quite an experience, not one perhaps that I wanted to repeat, but one which had given me a great deal of fun and not a little anxiety at times. My friends and critics were surprised to see me back with the MG undamaged and still running beautifully.

CHAPTER 15

MORE INCIDENTS AND ACCIDENTS

The hot weather of 1935 was very slow to depart after my return from holiday in Kashmir and the tail end of it was punctuated by some unusual and disquieting incidents at Risalpur. The combination of a five year tour with no possibility of any home leave or mid tour break and conditions of extreme heat and often great discomfort in which that tour was served, placed a considerable psychological as well as physical strain upon the young men of both the Army and the RAF. Most of them, and I was a typical example, had no previous experience of the tropics and little idea of how to fit themselves mentally for what was a considerable ordeal. Medical services were developing extremely rapidly but were still only competent within the fairly limited knowledge of the day and India abounded in diseases, from rabies to malaria and typhoid to sandfly fever for which the treatment was rudimentary. It was not surprising, therefore, that some cracked under these conditions and various forms of mental breakdown were not unknown. It was a small proportion but considerably higher than twenty years later. By then tours of duty had been drastically reduced in length, modern comforts such as air conditioning and refrigeration were commonplace, and air travel had made home leave practicable. Medical knowledge had also advanced by leaps and bounds.

One case of complete mental breakdown, which could have had the most tragic consequences, occurred shortly after I had picked up the threads of work again and taken over command of my Flight from Malcolm Mackay. A young Pilot Officer, whose name for the sake of this narrative shall be George Sandford, had shown signs of being intensely withdrawn and uncommunicative, which was unusual in an extrovert community such as ours. He was a 'loner' and not a very happy one at that. The first indication that all was not well with George came on a Monday morning, just before lunch. The last aeroplanes of the morning's programme were returning from their various missions and I was cycling down the path to the Mess, doubtless thinking about an ice cold shandy as I sweated at the pedals. It was very hot indeed with that shimmering haze which always made one feel that one's eyesight was defective.

As I neared the Mess, I idly watched a Hart approaching up the road past the Mess gates to land on the aerodrome which lay just beyond the end of the road. He was obviously too low but I assumed that he would open up his engine to clear the line of trees which bordered the aerodrome on the approach. Not a bit of it. He continued gliding down and I stopped and jumped off my bike when he was less than 100 feet up and several hundred yards from the aerodrome boundary. Making no attempt to use his engine, he actually touched down on the road outside the

Mess gates. The road was straight and wide at that point with flat grass verges and, fortunately, no traffic at that moment. The Hart ran along the road, disappearing from my view, and I waited thunderstruck for the inevitable crash as it could not possibly get through the trees onto the aerodrome. I didn't have to wait long for the splintering crash as the Hart ploughed through the line of trees. Without realising it I had remounted and was pedalling madly back up the Mess path, expecting to find a pall of black smoke and a sea of flame by the road side. By some miracle, the Hart had jumped a small ditch and gone between two trees which had neatly removed the wings, allowing the fuselage to go through and slide onto the aerodrome. The fire tender was even quicker than I was and we both arrived at the scene to find George and his airgunner sitting in a dazed fashion in their cockpits with no wings and no wheels – quite unscathed. The firemen had them out in a trice and doused the hot engine with foam as it lay spluttering angrily to itself on the grass.

'What happened?' said George shakily as we helped him to the ambulance.

'I don't know, I was going to ask you that,' I replied, but he only shook his head in a perplexed way as he was taken off to sick headquarters for a medical check.

I thought about this mysterious crash as I rode slowly back to lunch because I knew I would undoubtedly be called as a witness at any inquiry held. The whole episode was very strange. It could not possibly have been an error of judgement on Sandford's part: nobody could undershoot so grossly with a line of high trees between the aeroplane and the aerodrome. It did not look like an engine failure as the propeller was turning quite normally and the exhaust sounded as healthy as any Hart when throttled back. If he had made any attempt to open the throttle, I would certainly have noticed it as I was no more than fifty yards away when he touched down on the road – a perfectly good landing incidentally. I could make nothing of it nor could anybody else in the Mess when we discussed it over lunch.

It was not long, however, before the reason for the accident became clear. Our doctor could find no physical injury to George Sandford and he was quite unable to give any reason for his strange accident. He was allowed to come back to the Mess with instructions to take things quietly for a few days under medical observation.

After dinner that evening, several of us were sitting round a table in the Mess garden playing liar dice. It had been a blistering day and at long last a cool breeze was beginning to stir the mango trees and the oleanders. We were all in our hot weather Mess kit of trousers, shirt, bow tie and cummerbund, feeling relaxed after the heat of the day and enjoying the night breeze. We had persuaded George Sandford to join in the game but he was quiet and disinterested. We did not discuss the accident and he was clearly not disposed to raise the matter.

It must have been about 11.30 when he suddenly got up, stretched himself and said, 'I think I'll go and shoot the Adjutant.'

I don't think everybody heard what he said but I certainly did, hard to believe though it was. He walked off into the darkness towards the swimming pool and bungalows without any of us reacting to what he had said for a few moments. Suddenly someone – it may have been Peter Hamley – said, 'By God, I believe he means it – we'd better go after him.'

We all got up and set off towards the bungalows and soon caught up with George who was, indeed, making for the quarters of the Adjutant, Bob Randall. Furthermore, as we came up to George we could see something shining in his hand in the semi-darkness – his Webley Service revolver. Ahead, the lights of Randall's bungalow gleamed and the sound of his piano could clearly be heard. He was a good classical pianist and owned one of the few grand pianos in the cantonment. Fortunately for us, George was quite amenable to our suggestion that he came back to the Mess and discussed things quietly. He allowed me to take his revolver and I was appalled to find that it was loaded and with the safety catch 'off'. I fell behind and quickly unloaded it so that George could not see what I was doing. As we approached the Mess, Peter Hamley fell back a pace or two, joined me and whispered, 'I'll fetch Dick Stewart.'

He disappeared quietly in the direction of the doctor's bungalow while the rest of us escorted George back to the table where we had been sitting. He showed no signs of violence or resentment at our interference with his plans: nor did he ask for his gun which I had hidden behind my back and pocketed the ammunition. Instead he started a long rambling diatribe against Bob Randall whom he alleged had turned down a scheme which George said he had put to him earlier in the day.

We encouraged him to tell us about this in order to keep him occupied until the doctor arrived. George wanted to collect all the official files and documents in our central registry, load them on to the bomb racks of the Harts, fly to Delhi in formation and drop the mass of paper on the RAF Headquarters. By the time the details of this great bombing raid had been explained, it was perfectly clear that George's mind was unhinged, and the cause of his strange crash that morning was no longer a mystery. It seemed sensible to tell Stewart of these developments before he arrived, and so I slipped quietly away, not forgetting to take the revolver with me, and walked to meet Stewart and Hamley. Dick Stewart did not seem surprised and said that he had expected some such development although he was appalled when I showed him the revolver.

'We must humour him until we can get him into hospital at Peshawar,' he said. 'If we oppose him he may go completely out of his mind and become violent.'

'I hear you have a great scheme for bombing Delhi, George,' he said as he sat down with a meaningful glance round all of us. 'Tell me more about it.'

It was long past midnight and the situation was very tricky but the doctor handled it splendidly.

'You realise,' he said to George, 'that before we can carry out this raid we must get authority from Group Headquarters at

Peshawar. I think we should all go over there in the morning, explain the plan and get authority to do the job on Wednesday.'

Some of us cottoned on to the fact that the Group Headquarters at Peshawar was very close to the British Military Hospital.

'David,' he continued, looking at me, 'you have a good car; will you take George, Peter and myself over to Peshawar in the morning, and we will waste as little time as possible in getting this plan into action?'

What else could I do but nod assent at this piece of calculated lunacy.

'Well, that's that – now I prescribe a couple of sleeping pills and a good night's rest before we set out at, say, 7 am.'

He took a bottle of white tablets out of his pocket, gave two to Peter and myself, whispering as he did so, 'throw them away,' and gave two to George, saying, 'Take them now George, you need to be really fresh and alert in the morning.'

Walking back to the bungalows, George was engaged in conversation while Stewart drew Peter Hamley and myself back and said quietly:

'Those pills will knock him out in minutes. I intend to spend the rest of the night in his sitting room but, when he is asleep, I want you two to take over the watch while I ring the BMH at Peshawar and arrange for his reception. I expect all hell will break loose when he finds out that we have tricked him and the BMH must be ready for it.'

The night passed as we had planned it. George slept soundly under the influence of his 'knock out' pills and Peter and I took turns to relieve Dick Stewart in the sitting room. He informed the Station Commander and George's Squadron Commander of his intentions as well as alerting the BMH to expect us at 8 o'clock in the morning.

Dick thought there was a faint possibility that the patient might seem quite normal when he awoke and have no knowledge of the night's happenings. But that was not to be. He awoke in exactly the same frame of mind as before and could hardly wait to get on the road to Peshawar.

We set off with George sitting beside me in front and Dick and Peter on the alert behind him for any dangerous behaviour such as attempting to grab my steering wheel. It was a nerve-racking drive – the longest 26 miles I ever remember – but it was without incident. I kept the speed down to 40 as a precaution against any violence and we all did our best to be bright and cheerful as we discussed the details of the forthcoming 'raid'. I drove steadily down the Mall as we entered Peshawar at five minutes past eight and the BMH came in sight on the right hand side. I judged my speed with what little traffic there was so that I could swing straight into the hospital entrance at a fair speed without a pause and with no signals. As we approached, I could sense that Peter and Dick were leaning forward ready to grab George if necessary – and it very nearly was necessary.

As I swung through the gates, George exclaimed, 'This isn't Group; it's the hospital. What goes on?'

Quick as a flash Dick said, 'I want to pick something up that I ordered last night.'

George, who must have sensed that he was not quite normal, was highly suspicious but before he could do anything about it, we had driven under the porch at the main door and two hefty orderlies were waiting for us. As soon as they opened the car door, poor George knew that we had tricked him and became violent and abusive. He struggled with the orderlies but was led away protesting and almost foaming at the mouth. Dick Stewart stayed with him but it was the last that Peter and I ever saw of him. We drove along the Mall to the Club for breakfast feeling very sad and not a little shaken. After breakfast Peter rang the hospital to see whether Dick wished to come back to Risalpur with us, but he decided to stay. George was by then under heavy sedation, having been extremely violent and completely uncontrollable.

George recovered after a few weeks in the BMH sufficiently to be invalided home by hospital ship and he subsequently returned to normal and remained in the RAF for a time, but not to fly. Eventually I believe he retired voluntarily and disappeared

222

into civil life. It was an unhappy incident but it could have had much more tragic consequences. He could have killed both his air gunner and himself in the crash and there is no doubt that he had the wherewithal to kill Bob Randall sitting peacefully at his piano. I suppose he could have turned his gun on any of us who went after him but fortunately none of those things happened.

Sending home snapshots and photographs was about the only means of conveying something of the atmosphere of the Frontier to relatives and friends. Peter Salter was one of the best amateur photographers among us and he was expert enough to indulge in various forms of trick photography. Many an officer sent home pictures of himself carrying his head under his arm, accompanied by such comments as 'the natives are not always friendly!'

Peter's trickery very nearly landed me in trouble on one occasion. He took an excellent picture of me flying a Hart while we were practising formation flying. The number on the tail of my aeroplane was clearly visible which identified me without any doubt. He also had a fine photo of the Khyber Pass and, by superimposing one negative upon the other, he produced a highly realistic picture of me flying up the Khyber Pass – but upside down. Not only was I inverted but appeared to be no more than about 50 feet above the ground with the Jamrud Fort in the background.

I was delighted with my copy of this composite picture but, unfortunately, Peter distributed copies to a few other people and, eventually the Station Commander heard about it and demanded to see it. Nobody thought to tell him that it was a fake, and I was summoned to his office one morning.

'What,' he asked, giving me a piercing look, 'is this dangerous nonsense? I can hardly believe my eyes.'

I wanted to roar with laughter, but suddenly realised from the look in his eye that he was serious.

'Well Sir,' I said, 'it's a fake.'

I didn't want to implicate Peter unless I had to.

'Hmm,' said the Wing Commander, studying the picture

closely for a long time. 'I find it hard to believe that that could be faked: I take a pretty serious view of this, Lee. Who took this picture?'

I was obviously in trouble and clearly I had to get Peter to bail me out.

'It isn't one photo, Sir, it's two, the one superimposed on the other inverted.'

He looked even more disbelieving.

'Flying Officer Salter is an expert at trick photography and he actually took both pictures and produced the faked one from them. Have you not seen any of his other work, Sir?' I said almost in desperation as he still looked grim.

Peering closely at the picture once again, he finally replied, 'I still find it very difficult to believe that this could be faked and yet . . .' a long pause and more close examination . . . . 'I doubt if you could do that in a Hart and get away with it. Ask Salter to come and see me, will you?'

Peter was flying but as soon as he landed I let him know that he had dropped me in the cart and would have to back up my explanation.

'Take that picture of George with his head under his arm to show the old man,' I said.

Off he went and came back half an hour later, laughing his head off.

'All over; you are officially exonerated from blame and the old man wants me to do one of him carrying his head.'

'Best place for it,' commented George quietly from the adjoining office.

Thus the matter ended except that the Station Commander approached me in the Mess that evening and, somewhat lamely, I thought, said: 'I didn't really believe that picture was genuine because I doubt if you are a good enough pilot.'

The hot weather seemed to go on endlessly that year and before it was over, another unfortunate incident occurred which affected me closely and which ended in tragedy. One unbearably humid morning, my Flight was engaged in an air firing programme using the firing range at Peshawar. I flew the first sortie myself, taking off at 6.15 am in Hart K 2129. The Peshawar range was a desolate, stony expanse some miles to the north of the city. A line of six square canvas targets stood on it and a normal exercise consisted of diving towards the targets to enable the pilot to fire his fixed forward firing Vickers guns. After he had used up his ammunition, he would make a series of low level runs along the line of the targets so that his air gunner could fire the Lewis gun over the side at the targets. It was a bright clear morning with all the promise of another blistering day and my exercise was completed satisfactorily when I landed back at Risalpur at 7.15.

The guns were reloaded and it was the turn of James Chandler to take the same aeroplane for the next sortie which was to be a replica of my own. For the story of what happened subsequently we had to rely upon LAC Fitzgerald, who was Chandler's usual air gunner and knew him well. Fitzgerald was also the engine fitter of that particular Hart, which is important in view of what followed. He said that the flight to Peshawar was quite normal and took twelve minutes. Chandler fired his front guns and appeared to get a satisfactory score. It was afterwards confirmed that he obtained 73% hits – quite a good figure. He then started the first run along the line of targets at 200 feet, and Fitzgerald prepared to fire as they came into his sights. He fired one short burst and then, to his amazement, his pilot shouted to him, 'Bale out, bale out at once!'

Fitzgerald had his chest type parachute on but he knew it was extremely dangerous to go over the side at such a low height and that his parachute would not have time to open fully. Being a well disciplined airman, he didn't argue about the order from his pilot but he did say, 'Can you pull up a little to give me more height?'

Apparently Chandler nodded, pulled the nose up into a climb and, at about 800 feet shouted, 'Now jump quickly!'

During that brief pause while climbing, Fitzgerald had time to peer over his pilot's shoulder at the instruments – of his own engine which he knew so well. He asserted afterwards that pressures, temperatures and revolutions were all normal and the Hart seemed to be flying perfectly and obviously answering to the controls. At 800 ft he threw himself out of the cockpit on the side opposite to his Lewis gun. His parachute opened immediately and he landed in the middle of the range. Unfortunately he broke his ankle on the hard, rock strewn surface but he was quite lucky to suffer no worse injury. As he landed, there was a terrific crash as the Hart heeled over and dived into the ground several hundred yards away. Occupied with his own problems, Fitzgerald did not see exactly what happened, but the range safety officer said that the Hart heeled over and dived straight into the ground as soon as the air gunner had baled out. Chandler made no attempt to get out and was killed instantly in the crash.

As soon as the news reached Risalpur, I jumped into another Hart, flew to Peshawar and went to inspect the crash on the range. The aeroplane had not burned but had clearly gone in very hard, probably with the engine on, as it had disintegrated completely. No attempt had been made to land it on the range as would have happened with a normal engine failure. The fact that Chandler had the time and ability to gain height to give his gunner a safer jump, showed that he had control. He was wearing his flying topee and, in any case, sunstroke could be ruled out after little more than half an hours flying at 7.30 in the morning. After looking at the crash, I went to the British Military Hospital and saw Fitzgerald who was comfortable but severely shaken by his experience and flabbergasted by his pilot's behaviour.

The accident was a complete mystery; no technical explanation could be found for it and it began to look like another mental breakdown or brainstorm except that Chandler had been quite composed and had shown every care and consideration for his air gunner's safety.

James Chandler was one of the very few young officers – he was about 23 – who was married, and when his affairs were looked into after his death, it came to light that he was in fairly deep financial trouble, about which his poor wife, Peggy, knew nothing. No marriage allowance was paid to officers until they were thirty years old, unless they achieved what was virtually impossible and became Squadron Leaders. Consequently, officers who married very young could reckon to be badly off for several years unless they were lucky enough to have private incomes. The Chandlers had no such help and had found married life almost beyond their means. Although nothing could ever be proved, I and many of my colleagues came to the conclusion that James, desperately worried about his financial affairs, had deliberately taken this way out of his troubles in a fit of intense mental depression. Everybody at Risalpur was deeply shocked by this incident coming, as it did, so soon after George Sandford's breakdown. They provided a distressing ending to what had been an exceptionally long and trying hot weather.

As we moved into October, the heat gradually died down but, as far as I was concerned, the incidents and accidents did not. Within the next month I was involved in two flying incidents, one of which redounded somewhat to my credit but the other certainly did not.

I took off at 6.30 one morning to carry out a high altitude photographic exercise some fifty miles away in Mohmand territory. It was a glorious morning such as often occurred immediately after the hot weather, cloudless and cool with unlimited visibility. A superb morning for high altitude flight; these high flying missions were not common and I was prepared to enjoy this one at 20,000 feet under such perfect conditions. Our aeroplanes had no oxygen breathing apparatus and 20,000 feet was about our limit without it. In fact most of us felt the effects of the rarefied air from about 15,000 feet upwards and pilots and air gunners kept a close watch on each others' behaviour.

As I climbed away from Risalpur to the north west, the snow covered peaks of the Himalayas far beyond the foothills were clearly visible although most of them were more than 100 miles away. Corporal Dobie, who was flying with me, tested the camera as we climbed, reported it to be functioning perfectly and then stood up and leaned over my shoulder to enjoy the magnificent view ahead. We tried to pick out Mount Everest, always a difficult peak to identify from that distance as it is surrounded by other peaks almost as high – Rakaposhi, Harmosh, Nanga Parbat and many more. We were too far away and it was not possible to identify the individual peaks with any certainty. Nevertheless the panorama ahead was spectacular.

We were so absorbed that we failed to notice that the radiator temperature was rising above normal and it was not until we had reached 18,000 feet that I realised that it was some twenty degrees above normal. Thinking this might be due to our steady climb, I wound the radiator right out to give maximum cooling and carried on. The temperature continued to rise and, at 19,000 feet, it was showing 90° on the gauge. Something was clearly wrong and I eased back the throttle and flew level to see what would happen. For a moment or two the needle steadied but then started to rise again towards boiling point.

'We must have a coolant leak,' I said to Dobie, 'We'll have to abandon the trip.'

Hardly were the words out than the temperature shot up to 100° and I knew that any moment the engine would seize. I slammed the throttle shut and whipped the Hart round in a turn back onto a heading for Risalpur which by this time was forty or more miles behind us. The engine was now ticking over but it felt rough and uneven and the temperature remained far too high. I knew that a Kestrel engine would seize up when only ticking over under such circumstances and so I reluctantly switched off and the propeller came to rest with one blade sticking up in front of me in an accusing sort of way. That motionless blade gave me an uncomfortable feeling and a dry taste in my mouth. There were no emergency landing grounds in that particular area and there was nothing for it but to head for home and see how far I could get.

I trimmed the aeroplane to glide at a steady 75 mph and told Dobie to tighten up his harness and chain and to keep his head well down to avoid creating unnecessary drag. Luck was with me to the extent that the wind, which was very light, was directly behind and so giving me a little help. By the time we had descended to 10,000 feet, I calculated that we were 20 miles from Risalpur and I started to look for likely landing places.

The country was reasonably flat but stony, with ugly outcrops of rock, dried up river beds – in every way thoroughly uninviting. A disused bombing range some five miles to the north of the aerodrome probably offered the best chance of putting the Hart down without injury to ourselves although there was little hope of avoiding damage to the aeroplane. I kept my eye on the bombing range as we sank lower and lower and also got a good idea of the wind direction from blowing sand on the ground.

At 5,000 feet, I began to realise that we were doing better than I had dared to hope and that there was a faint chance of reaching the aerodrome. I shouted to Dobie to get out the Verey pistol and as many red cartridges as he could find and to stand by to fire when I gave the order. Even if we failed to reach the aerodrome I wanted to alert the crash crew to the fact that we had come down in the vicinity.

My hopes continued to rise, and as 2,000 feet appeared on the altimeter I knew that I could reach the aerodrome. I did not, however, wish to go straight in and land down wind if it could be avoided. The Hart never appreciated a down wind landing and could be difficult. Furthermore, several other aircraft were flying in the vicinity and a down wind landing would create the greatest collision risk.

'How many red cartridges have you got?'

'Four, Sir,' said Dobie.

'Right. I want you to fire all of them when I tell you.'

I now reckoned that I could get half way down the west side of the aerodrome and then turn in to land across wind to the east. As we approached the north west corner at about 1,000 feet, I told Dobie to fire two cartridges in quick succession. Although expecting it, the first bang nearly made me jump out of my harness, and the red light curved over towards the aerodrome and went out before it reached the ground. The second followed five seconds later and I reckoned they must have been seen.

'Fire the third as I turn in, and the last one as we approach the boundary,' I said to Dobie.

At 400 feet I started my turn in and the third bang caught me by surprise as usual. Two Harts were stationary on the aerodrome and I prayed that they had seen my distress signal and would remain still. I had about 100 feet to spare as I straightened up for my final approach and the last red light soared away towards the hangars. As I was landing across wind, I put the left wing down and side slipped gently towards the wind direction to counteract the drift and get rid of my excess height – not very much after gliding for forty miles!

I brought the Hart out of the sideslip as we crossed the boundary and landed reasonably well on one wheel with the left wing down. I was a little concerned lest she 'weather-cocked' into wind with no engine to counter it, but the brakes were adequate to stop any tendency that way and we came to rest with the propeller still standing upright and quite useless.

It seemed strange to sit in the middle of the aerodrome in a completely silent aeroplane and, for a moment, I relaxed as an enormous sense of relief swept over me dispersing the tension of the last fifteen minutes.

'Well done, Sir,' said Corporal Dobie from the rear cockpit, tapping disrespectfully on my flying topee with one of his expended Verey cartridges.

We climbed down on to the grass as the fire tender roared up with its crew doubtless hiding some disappointment that their services were not needed. The engine cowling was heavily streaked with Glycol and it was obvious that the engine had lost most of its coolant. The Flight Sergeant reckoned that I had switched off only just in time to prevent the engine being wrecked beyond repair.

Dobie and I heaved our parachutes on to the fire tender and were given a lift back to the hangar as the A Flight airmen arrived with a tail trolley to push K 2095 back to my Flight. Luck had undoubtedly favoured me. It was one of the few days with the wind in the north; had it been in any other direction I could not possibly have reached the aerodrome. Had I been further away or at a lower height, it would also have been impossible, so my self congratulation was tempered by the knowledge that fortune had smiled on me that morning.

Fortune is, however, a fickle jade and she did not smile on me a few days later. On that occasion it was late in the morning and I was returning to the aerodrome from some exercise or other with LAC Galloway in the back. The midday heat haze had started to form, cutting visibility down to about one mile. The wind this time was from the south as I approached to land over the northern boundary. There were no other aeroplanes in sight and I chose the left side of the aerodrome in order to avoid landing directly towards the hangars.

I crossed the threshold and started to level out at, perhaps, ten feet when, to my horror, I spotted another aeroplane crossing the opposite boundary and heading straight towards me. Although it was a little hazy I could see that it had wings of equal span and a large circular engine. It was not a Hart and must, therefore, be a visitor who was landing in the wrong direction. It was in fact a Wapiti from Kohat. At the moment I spotted him, we were I suppose, about 700 yards apart and approaching each other at 150 mph. He had probably not seen me, concentrating as he was on landing at an unfamiliar aerodrome.

The first thought that flashed through my mind was that if I opened the throttle, abandoned my landing and started to climb, he might well do exactly the same and a mid air collision might result. In that split second, I decided that I had just enough speed, height and room to carry out a quick 'S' turn and land to the right of the visitor. More from reaction than any deliberate calculation, I turned quickly to the right and then

231

back to the left and levelled out some 50 yards away from my original line of approach. I did not, however, make allowance for an irrigation 'bund'. Certain areas of the aerodrome had small walls of earth, each about a foot high, running across them to contain irrigation water when particular areas were flooded to encourage the grass to grow. When I straightened out, the left wheel caught the 'bund' and, unbeknown to me at the time, bent the wheel slightly. I levelled out and touched down quite successfully but the bent wheel locked solid on landing. The effect was literally to trip me up at 70 mph with catastrophic results.

I have a vague recollection of the nose plunging down as we started to somersault, and watching fascinated as the propeller splintered into a thousand fragments. By that time the aeroplane was vertical, and I suppose some thought of self preservation made me decide to plunge down into the cockpit. I did not get far with that resolve as the violence of the somersault caused my straps to break and I flew out over the windscreen as if catapulted. I dimly remember hitting something which, in fact, was Galloway who had also been catapulted from the rear cockpit. We must have met in mid air as we hit the ground, locked in each other's arms, about ten feet in front of the aeroplane.

There was a moment's silence. I opened my eyes and Galloway was looking at me in a dazed fashion.

'Are we alive?' I said.

'Yes, I think so, and I don't think I'm hurt; how about you?' he replied in a whisper.

I sat up gingerly and tested my limbs. All seemed well and I struggled dizzily to my feet while Galloway did likewise. Apart from a few bruises we were completely unhurt which was miraculous considering the violence of the crash. The Hart was a forlorn sight. It had pitched right over on to its back, banged the top of the rudder on the ground and bounced back into a vertical position. There was no fire, but petrol was dripping from the tank in the damaged centre section on to the hot engine with a dangerous sizzling sound. I pulled Galloway hurriedly away from the wreckage as the fire tender rushed up and started to pump foam onto it.

A closer inspection before I was ordered into the ambulance by a Medical Orderly showed how fortunate it was that my straps had broken. The Hart had gone on to its back with such force that the centre section and my windscreen had both been crushed against the ground before the aeroplane bounced back. As my head would almost certainly have been above the windscreen, it would presumably have hit the ground with great force had I remained in the cockpit – and Galloway's fate would have been much the same.

The visiting pilot whom I had avoided with such disastrous results had seemed quite unaware of his error and had watched my performance with amazement. Perhaps he thought that was the way that we usually landed at Risalpur. He was a young officer who had recently arrived at Kohat and was on one of his early Wapiti flights. I did not speak to him but he was apparently marched in front of the Station Commander who gave him a short, sharp lecture on airmanship and sent him back to Kohat considerably chastened. I was not blamed for the accident but, nevertheless, I did feel, with the benefit of hindsight, that I should have taken a more sensible course than attempting to carry on with my landing. The rules of the air stated quite clearly that when two aircraft are approaching head on, each should turn to the right. I did indeed turn to the right, but should then have opened the throttle, abandoned my landing and climbed away. It was an expensive accident, but whatever may have been thought of my performance nothing was said, and for that I felt grateful, as I had certainly taught myself a lesson.

CHAPTER 16

INTO THE UNKNOWN

S hortly before Malcolm Mackay handed over A Flight to me we carried out together a most unusual flight in two Harts, a flight which took us to Gilgit. Gilgit was situated at the most northerly point of British India, astride the caravan route which ran from Chinese Turkestan through the Himalayas by various passes and defiles down to the plains of India. These camel caravans took weeks and months on their hazardous journey bringing carpets, rugs, skins and similar merchandise to sell to Indian merchants.

Several cases of bubonic plague in India during 1935 were

traced to infection spread by these itinerant traders and the purpose of our flight was to carry bubonic plague serum to Gilgit to inoculate all travellers in the hope of preventing the spread of the terrible disease. Although this was an emergency mission, it had to await favourable weather as Gilgit lay among some of the highest peaks in the Himalayan range and could only be approached by flying up the narrow gorge of the river Indus by accurate map reading. The task was allotted to us at Risalpur because the Hart was more suitable than the Wapiti, having a better performance and higher ceiling should difficulties be encountered.

It was impossible to obtain any weather report from the British Resident at Gilgit. His only means of communication with the Government at Peshawar was by wireless telegraphy which was notoriously unreliable due to the unpredictable effect of the mountains which surrounded him on all sides. It could sometimes take days to get a message through, and we were to experience this difficulty ourselves.

Malcolm decided that when the general meteorological conditions over Northern India were clear and calm we would fly off at dawn and reach our destination before the build up of cloud over the mountains reached dangerous proportions, which usually happened from midday onwards. If the weather deteriorated en route we would have no hesitation in turning back as there were no diversionary landing grounds where we could land. Keeping in visual touch with each other and with the ground were crucial requirements and we agreed that there would be no wandering about looking for holes in cloud through which to descend. One glance at the map and a quick count of the peaks which exceeded 25,000 feet in the vicinity of our route was sufficient to convince me of the wisdom of this decision. This was one flight for which one need feel no embarrassment at turning back, particularly as a day or two was hardly likely to make much difference to the spread of plague.

We were asked by the Government of India to take one of their officials to look into some Intelligence problem affecting

Gilgit. He was to travel with me while Malcolm carried a Wireless Operator who was, incidentally, an experienced engine fitter which might well prove to be a valuable bonus. As there were no fuel stocks at Gilgit, we decided to carry luggage containers on the bomb racks under each wing, one container to hold spare cans of petrol, the other to take our bedding rolls. The distance from Risalpur to Gilgit by the route we were to fly was about 240 miles, and although a Hart held just enough fuel for the return journey under normal conditions, there was no margin for error or diversion to avoid bad weather. Consequently, we decided to carry enough fuel in two gallon cans to ensure a good safety margin for the return journey.

We planned to make the flight, weather permitting, on the day after the serum arrived from some laboratories in, I think, Delhi. My passenger was to be a Mr Vickers who was stationed at Peshawar and I telephoned him to stand by and be ready to drive over to Risalpur on the evening prior to our take off so that I could fit him out with flying kit and show him over the Hart. He told me that he had done very little flying and was tremendously interested in this flight into the unknown. For his sake, I hoped it wouldn't be too rough among the mountains.

The serum duly arrived on a Wednesday afternoon, and as Northern India seemed to be in a fairly stable anti-cyclone at the time, Malcolm decided that we would take off at 6 am the following morning. The two Harts had already been prepared and it only remained for me to call up Mr Vickers. He came over for dinner in the Mess and Hukmud Khan prepared a bed for him in my bungalow as one of the rooms was vacant. He was a pleasant young man of about thirty and, although he would not say precisely what his mission in Gilgit was, he said enough to indicate that he was engaged in Government security work and was concerned about some violations of the frontier in the area to which we were going.

Thursday morning dawned bright and clear and at five minutes past six, Malcolm led the way across the aerodrome as we took off in formation. We climbed away to the north east and Malcolm set a course which would enable us to hit the Indus just before it entered the foothills of the Himalayas: from that point, we had to follow its twists and turns all the way to Gilgit. 10,000 feet was to be our cruising height, carefully chosen to keep us well above the high ground in the vicinity of the river but below any high cloud which might begin to form among the peaks as the sun mounted.

I flew in loose formation with Malcolm, on his starboard side, and we climbed steadily to 10,000 feet. I paid particular attention to my pressures and temperatures as any engine trouble in the later stages of this trip would be disastrous; the recent coolant leak and subsequent forced landing were all too fresh in my memory. All was well, however, and the Indus came into view after forty minutes as the towering mountains closed in upon us.

By this time, my passenger had overcome his initial nervousness and had risen from the comparative security of the small seat in the rear cockpit and was standing up, peering over my shoulder at the scenery but still firmly anchored to the floor by his chain which I had told him not to undo under any circumstances. Turbulent mountain conditions could easily cause an inexperienced passenger to be thrown out of a Hart. It had happened, and I didn't want to lose Vickers that way.

We followed the Indus due north for a while before it again turned north east straight towards the mountains. We appeared to be flying straight into a mountainous wall with row upon row of gigantic peaks stretching into the background as far as the eye could see which, with superb visibility, was more than 100 miles. Having studied the map carefully before we started, I knew that, in fact, the Indus wound its way up among these peaks to its source and, provided that we followed it meticulously and met no low cloud, there was no danger of flying into a mountain.

One hour after leaving Risalpur, and cruising at 140 mph at 10,000 ft, we found the ground rising steeply on either side of us. A few minutes later we were passing a majestic peak on the starboard side; this was Nanga Parbat shown on my map as 26,620 feet. A rough calculation from the map on my knee made it no more than 22 miles from our track and it seemed very much closer as its great snow covered cap towered above us.

Shortly after passing Nanga Parbat we flew into, or just above, the Indus gorge. For many miles the river cascades through a narrow defile with precipitous sides. The banks appear to come almost straight up from the river bed and rise to about 8,000 feet. There is then a narrow plateau on either side, perhaps a mile in width, after which the ground continues to rise sharply to the mighty peaks of the Karakoram range, among which Everest stands above them all.

Flying as we were at 10,000 feet directly over the river, we were some 2,000 feet above the narrow plateau which bordered it. The view from our fragile cockpits was awesome. Vertigo and nausea does not usually affect one in an aeroplane but looking down at the river tearing through the gorge two miles below and then at the mountains towering above, I had a distinct feeling of claustrophobia which I had never experienced before. I noticed that my passenger had quietly disappeared down into his cockpit again and I also felt a strong inclination to put my own seat down to its lowest position and concentrate on the instruments and on keeping station with Malcolm.

The weather remained clear except for a few woolly clouds beginning to form around some of the peaks, notably round the summit of Harmosh (24,720 feet) which came into view to the right of us. At this point, I tried to identify Everest which lay somewhere in the background behind Harmosh. It was not easy, lost as it is among other peaks, but eventually I spotted it, mainly because I had been told that it had an almost permanent plume of snow blowing from its summit. I pointed it out to Vickers who emerged from the protection of his cockpit to follow my pointing arm. Far away to the right a long smoky plume was blowing away to the south from a sharply pointed peak – the highest mountain in the world. I was so fascinated by the sight of it that I almost collided with Malcolm which brought me sharply back to the job in hand. No wonder they call this the roof of the world, I thought to myself.

Every two or three minutes I checked the various dials in the cockpit, almost apprehensively, but the Kestrel engine was running smoothly and steadily and the fuel consumption was normal. It was painfully obvious that a forced landing in the Indus gorge would probably be fatal, with the likelihood of the wreckage rolling down the precipitous banks into the torrent. If lucky enough to crash land without injury, the prospects of ever being found or rescued were negligible. The dials on the instrument panel assumed, therefore, a particular importance.

Exactly two hours had passed since taking off when I sighted Everest, and we were nearing our destination. We could now see sufficiently far ahead to know that the weather would be clear at Gilgit and no question of turning back would arise. Several miles ahead the gorge swung to the left and as we rounded the bend, it began to widen out and the pressure of the mountains on either side lessened somewhat. Malcolm rocked his wings, a signal to me that he was about to do something and, as I suspected, his nose went down slightly and he started to descend. I adjusted my throttle and followed suit, looking over my engine to catch my first glimpse of Gilgit.

Five minutes later, passing through 8,000 feet, I spotted the point at which a tributary joined the Indus from the east. The aerodrome had been built on the flat plateau which filled the 'V' shaped promontory between the two rivers, at 4,000 feet above sea level. Malcolm and I had previously agreed to break form-ation as we approached Gilgit in order to study the aerodrome independently as neither of us had seen it before. I therefore slowed down and stayed above him as he dived down to circuit height.

The aerodrome consisted of two runways in the form of a cross, each runway being some 600 yards in length, adequate for a Hart at 4,000 feet but not generous. The surface looked hard and flat but I had no doubt that it was pretty stony and rough. Three of the runway ends terminated at the edge of the cliffs forming the banks of two rivers, while the fourth end confronted a hill at least 1,000 feet high. A limp windsock hung near the intersection of the runways, and this indicated that what wind there was came from the north. I watched Malcolm's Hart, looking like a silver insect against the two fast flowing rivers as it slowly circled round and then turned in to land towards the north – over one precipice and towards the mountain at the far end of the runway. He touched down with a spurt of dust about thirty yards beyond the threshold and came to rest two thirds of the way along the strip.

It was my turn and, after ensuring that Vickers was secured, I joined the circuit and prepared to follow Malcolm who was now taxying down the other runway to leave me a clear approach. Mine was a bad approach. Allowing extra speed in case there was a sudden down-draught off the cliff face, and doubtless a little more for the altitude and the strange aerodrome, I found myself crossing the threshold of the runway at a speed nearer to 90 mph than 70. Under these circumstances a Hart, which was well streamlined, would float and float and float: any attempt to put it down prematurely would be to invite a series of bounces. I opened the throttle and motored quietly along the runway and went into another circuit. I could hardly fail to notice how close the mountain seemed as I turned away. The second approach was better and the landing reasonably smooth.

'Lost your nerve, I see,' said Malcolm as I climbed out of the cockpit a few moments later.

'Discretion is the better part of valour, particularly at Gilgit,' was the only rejoinder I could think of on the spur of the moment.

The British Resident, Mr Clarke, was there to meet us having ridden down from his Residency which was housed in an old fort several miles away. But before we could follow him

240

home, we had to refuel the Harts, secure them for the night and erect a portable aerial in an attempt to transmit an arrival message back to Risalpur. Vickers handed up the two gallon cans while I emptied them into the tanks through a chamois leather and funnel. That done, pickets were screwed into the hard ground under each wing tip and the tail. That was a tough job as the ground was like iron but fortunately Mr Clarke had a few coolies with him who were a great help. We secured the Harts to the pickets and put on the engine and cockpit covers. Corporal Dobie erected the portable aerial, connected it to his set and tried in vain to raise Risalpur. We could get no response whatsoever, but nobody was surprised and we knew that Risalpur would not be unduly alarmed if no message came through from us. The Resident confirmed that his successful transmissions were a matter of sheer luck.

'Try again on my set after dark, if you wish; the conditions are usually better.'

The Residency and the town, or village, of Gilgit lay several miles up the valley from the aerodrome which had been constructed on what seemed to be the only flat piece of ground for hundreds of miles. There were no roads, only tracks for the tough hill ponies, camels and donkeys. A string of ponies awaited us and after a cup of coffee which Mr Clarke had thoughtfully brought along in thermos flasks, we mounted and set off on the second part of the journey. The going was rough and slow along a track which clung to the mountain side high above the Indus. Eventually after an hour or more of jogging along, our little entourage emerged on to a small plain with plenty of well irrigated cultivation. In the centre stood the fort dominating the scene with the huts and houses of Gilgit clustered round it, as if for protection. It seemed unreal to see the Union Jack flying from the fort, surely the most isolated British outpost in the world. This was the spot where Marco Polo had introduced the game named after him in India, and it is still played in Gilgit on the hard stony ground by tribesmen mounted on their tough but extremely agile hill ponies.

I dismounted thankfully at the fort; khaki drill shorts do not make good riding breeches and my posterior had never become hardened to the saddle. It was more at home on a parachute cushion! As could be imagined, Mr Clarke had very few visitors and was delighted to see us. We spent a happy and convivial evening with him during which he regaled us with stories of the strange life he led. He was, he said, very much a volunteer for the post being something of a misogynist. The hunting and fishing among the mountains were apparently superb and he could occasionally trek as far as Kashmir, although it must have been a formidable journey from what I had seen of the intervening country.

'How do you get your supplies?' I asked him as I downed a very good John Haig chota peg. 'You seem to be very well supplied with at least one essential commodity.'

'Well, its not easy. I get my essential groceries by camel caravan from Peshawar once every six months and when the caravan returns to the plains, I send down my next order. This applies also to mail, newspapers and magazines which makes them all seven months old by the time I read them. Incidentally, I'm most grateful for the papers and mail which you've brought with you.'

Vickers, who knew of Clarke's isolation better than we did had made up a small pack which we managed to squeeze into one of our luggage containers.

'There is no shortage of meat, milk and good fresh vegetables,' Clarke went on, 'and so I don't do too badly.'

As we discovered that evening he lived quite well and we found plenty to eat and drink and spent a wonderfully cool night in the mountain air with the constant roar of the Indus in the background.

There was something unreal about the utter isolation of Gilgit and I well remember waking in the middle of that night and wondering how a cultured and intelligent man like Clarke could stand three years so completely cut off from family and friends with virtually no contact with the outside world.

242

An early start for the return journey was essential and we rose at 5 am intending to be airborne by 7 o'clock to avoid the gradual build up of clouds. I half regretted that it was such a beautiful morning and could happily have stayed another couple of days but that would have worried Risalpur as Corporal Dobie had been unable to get any message through. Mr Clarke again accompanied us to ensure that we left his little kingdom safely and we were soon removing the aircraft covers and screw pickets and carrying out our daily inspections. No flat tyres or coolant leaks, no damage to the fabric from stones and no frayed control wires. The empty petrol cans were left to be loaded onto the ponies. Clarke said they were much prized by his coolies and we were only too glad to leave them behind.

I was sorry for Corporal Dobie who had to start up both aeroplanes on the winding handles. I dare not let Vickers wind mine and the Gilgit natives certainly could not be trusted. Fortunately both engines started immediately and the cool morning air was filled with the staccato crackle of the exhausts as we warmed the engines up. With a wave from Mr Clarke and from all the cheerful coolies, Malcolm taxied away and I followed when his shower of small stones and cloud of dust settled. There was little or no wind and we decided to take off in the opposite direction to our landing, over the southern precipice with the mountain behind us.

Malcolm started his take off run while I waited at the side of the runway and watched his departure.

All went well until he was about ten feet off the ground. My heart stopped. A puff of black smoke came from his engine; the Hart faltered and then, to my horror, the nose went down and he disappeared from view over the precipice. I was stunned and dimly aware of Vickers thumping me on the back and shouting, 'Good God, he's gone over the cliff'.

I suppose about four seconds passed while I had visions of Malcolm and Dobie being smashed to pieces on the rocks 500 feet below, when suddenly the Hart reappeared climbing rapidly out of the abyss in the distance, silhouetted like a silver moth against the backdrop of the mountains.

'Whatever happened to him,' I wondered as both Vickers and I heaved sighs of relief. I wasn't certain, however, that he was yet out of trouble and I remained stationary at the side of the runway in case he wished to land again. He climbed up and round in a wide sweep, and as he came back over the aerodrome, a green Verey light curled out from the rear cockpit and fell towards us, signifying that all was well. The explanation, which I learned later, was simple but nevertheless could easily have been disastrous.

The Kestrel engine was sensitive to altitude and the Hart cockpit contained a mixture or 'altitude' control which was a small lever alongside the main throttle. When taking off from a high altitude aerodrome, we used this control judiciously to improve the mixture. Malcolm had overdone it and his engine had sputtered at the crucial moment when he left the ground. His correct reaction was to push the nose down to avoid the risk of stalling if the engine failed. As he had several hundred feet of space down to the river, he made use of it while he readjusted the mixture control. The engine picked up immediately, enabling him to climb away. It had given all four of us in the two Harts a nasty shock, and I made my own perfectly normal take off with some trepidation as the solid ground disappeared from below me giving way to the fearsome view of the Indus tearing through its rocky channel far below.

We formed up together at 2,000 feet above Gilgit and Malcom led me down in close formation for a farewell run across the aerodrome where Mr Clarke and his small party waved us on our way as we pulled up into a climb back to 10,000 feet. The weather was perfect with Everest standing out more sharply than on the previous day.

Probably because the more massive peaks were now behind us, the feeling of being closed in was less acute which made the journey home 'out of the unknown' much more enjoyable. It was still a relief, however, to reach the plains and relax one's anxious attention to the note of the engine. We left the Indus without any regret as it flowed on in a rapidly widening and muddy stream into the Punjab.

It was only 9.45 am when we landed, the homeward flight having taken two and a half hours, but it seemed the end of a long day to me as Vickers and I humped our parachutes back into the Flight office, called for a cup from the 'char wallah' squatting outside and listened to the tale of Malcolm's little problem. Remembering his comment when I overshot at Gilgit, I had to say,

'That makes us all square, I think.'

Just as we expected, no message had penetrated through to Risalpur and we were officially 'missing' for 24 hours but it had happened before and nobody had been particularly concerned. Accidents on these flights were fortunately rare but not unknown.

On another occasion, two Harts had flown to Kala Drosh, a remote landing ground to the west of Gilgit in Swat territory. The main feature of any flight to Drosh was a 14,000 foot Pass which had to be crossed. Not infrequently this Pass was in a cloud. The two Harts were on the return journey and forced to enter thick cloud to get over the Pass. Unfortunately there were heavy icing conditions in the clouds and both engines iced up and stopped. As luck would have it, both Harts, now widely separated, glided down accurately into the valley south of the Pass. The engine of one of them, flown by John Pope, picked up below cloud and he continued home without ever seeing the other aeroplane, flown by his Flight Commander, Joe Shaw.

Joe was less lucky. He too came out of cloud in the centre of the valley but his engine remained iced up and he had no alternative but to look for somewhere to land. Below him lay a solid white carpet of snow, but below it he knew there would be a boulder strewn river bed. He could do nothing but select the smoothest looking part of the snow carpet and put the Hart on to it, or into it, which he did skilfully. The Hart went straight over onto it's back and Joe Shaw and his air gunner were buried upside down below several feet of snow. They were almost uninjured and somehow or other managed to dig their way to the surface. They were found sometime later by villagers who had seen the crash and eventually were taken, somewhat battered and bruised, to the Wali of Swat who took them in and looked after them. It was about three days, during which aircraft searched the locality in vain for the crashed Hart, before word filtered through that the two airmen were safe. Not only had they had a miraculous escape but they had also been fortunate to fall into friendly hands.

Flights to Gilgit and Drosh were carried out infrequently, and not more than once or twice a year unless some emergency such as the one which prompted our flight arose. They were regarded as risky but were an essential part of our 'watch and ward' duties on the Frontier as well as being unparalleled experience for those who flew them.

CHAPTER 17

DECATHLON

S port played a large part in our life on the Frontier stations, partly because most of us had been brought up to play and enjoy games, partly because our flying demanded a high standard of physical fitness and partly because the climate and hours of work gave us plenty of leisure with few activities available to us other than sport. Risalpur was extremely well provided with tennis and squash courts, a swimming pool and cricket, football and hockey pitches laid out in various corners of the aerodrome. Limited-over cricket, which was to gain such popularity later in England, was played every evening then on the Indian stations and, although the rules and standard of play differed slightly from those of the Gillette and Benson and Hedges Cups, the principles were the same and the competition intense.

As the cool weather approached in October, 1935, somebody, and I cannot recall who it was, suggested that we should challenge the officers of Skinner's Horse, our Indian Cavalry regiment, to a Decathlon. This idea caught on with the result that a small committee was set up to plan the details of the competition. I call it a 'decathlon' because it eventually comprised ten separate events, but neither the events nor the manner in which they took place would have commended themselves to the International Olympic Committee.

Our committee decided that each team should consist of eight officers who would compete in all ten events, the whole competition to be concluded in one day, and a Sunday in late October was selected when some reasonably cool weather could be expected. The events selected were both varied and unusual, some being outdoor sports and some indoor. Bicycle polo, pistol shooting and swimming were planned for before breakfast, golf and clay pigeon shooting before lunch, tennis and squash racquets before dinner and snooker, darts and poker after dinner. The RAF team was to entertain Skinner's Horse to lunch, after which both teams would break up for a two hours rest. For dinner, the RAF would be the guests of Skinner's Horse and the final indoor events would take place in the cavalry mess. The prize was to be a barrel of draught Murree beer, paid for by the losers.

Selecting our team now became the problem. Should we go for eight all rounders or should we select those who were good at particular sports? It would be easy enough to find eight reasonably athletic young officers from the forty or so in the Mess but, in certain of the events such as clay pigeon shooting, we had nobody with any skill at all. It seemed sensible therefore to go all out to win those events for which we could produce competent performers, and our team was selected on that basis.

I was included in the team as a reasonably good golfer and tennis player with a certain devious skill at poker. We could muster two excellent pistol shots and three good swimmers but there was a great shortage of other skills. As we had no reason to believe that the officers of Skinner's Horse were any better endowed we prepared for the competition with quiet confidence.

The last Sunday in October was to be the great day, and it was a good one. Morning dawned cool and fresh; the temperature seemed unlikely to rise above about 75°, the team was as fit as it was ever likely to be and we were all set for a splendid but exhausting day. By 6 am I was pedalling down the road on my Japanese bicycle, which had cost me £1 when new and which was to be my mount for the first event on our opponents' parade ground. The RAF team was dressed in old flannel trousers tucked into our socks to protect our legs against the inevitable knocks and scrapes. Rugger shirts and Bombay bowlers completed the unofficial uniform. We were somewhat disconcerted to find our opponents smartly turned out in white polo breeches and helmets, but this was at once put down to a touch of 'gamesmanship'. Polo sticks being too long, too delicate and too expensive for this adaptation of the game, our weapons were to be hockey sticks, a distinct advantage to us who were totally unfamiliar with polo sticks. We had all agreed to play our full teams of eight a side for fifteen minutes each way, and the referee was a Captain from the Royal Corps of Signals imported as an impartial observer to judge the whole competition in return for a good dinner that evening.

The whistle blew and the game started, each team playing four forwards, three half backs and a full back who also performed as a goalkeeper. If there were any rules they were invented by the referee at the time and seemed designed merely to prevent dangerous play. Threatening behaviour with the stick, deliberate ramming of an opponent, abuse and any other form of ungentlemanly conduct were penalised with a free hit. Skinner's Horse went on to the attack from the start and within ten seconds our full back was lying in a heap of old iron vainly trying to prevent the ball from trickling slowly but inexorably through the posts. He failed and we were one goal down before most of our team had even moved.

I will draw a veil over that first half but we reached the interval with the score 4–0 to Skinner's and two broken bicycles to us. We were learning fast, however, and our blood was up. With the damaged machines replaced, a fierce second half commenced and within a minute Peter Hamley scored our first goal with the referee turning a blind eye to at least one obvious foul while Peter was scattering the opposition. Nevertheless we had to admit that the cavalrymen were much the more competent at this game. They scored two more goals and we managed to scramble another doubtful ball through the posts before the game ended 6–2 in favour of Skinner's Horse. Our confidence was a little shaken by this initial defeat as we cycled, or pushed our damaged steeds back to our own bungalows to bathe, change and treat various grazes and scratches with iodine.

By 7.30 am we were all back, this time at the RAF rifle range for the pistol competition. Each officer was permitted to use his own pistol or revolver. These were issued to all officers as personal weapons and, in the case of the RAF, they were either 0.45 Colt pistols or 0.38 Smith and Wesson revolvers. My own Colt was a good weapon which had served me well for several years and was used regularly.

Each competitor was to fire six aimed shots at 15 yards, followed by six shots at a 'snap' target which appeared for five seconds at a time, also at 15 yards. We made a good start and were leading when my own turn came as third member of the team. Two bulls, three inners and one outer was quite a respectable score for the aimed shots and I then hit the small figure as it popped up three times out of six shots. We kept our slight lead and were ahead by ten points half way through the competition. Our spirits were somewhat dampened when a tall Indian Lieutenant produced five bulls and hit the "snap" target four times. Fortunately our own crack shot was to come.

George Baker could not quite emulate the Indian officer's performance but he did get four bulls and two inners and then hit the other target four times. This was good enough to retain the lead which we held for the rest of the competition and went into breakfast level, with one victory apiece.

The next appointment was at the Nowshera Golf Club at 9.30 am. Four of us piled into my MG while John Cohu took the other half of the team to this attractive little course some six miles down the road from Risalpur. It had at that time sad memories for me as during an earlier pre-breakfast round, I had come across the body of a British Soldier belonging to the Duke of Wellington's Regiment who had been murdered and his body left in a bunker.

Our organising committee had decided upon foursomes over nine holes which was about as much as our tight schedule would allow. Should the four matches result in a tie, the individual scores would decide the outcome of the match. Peter Hamley and I, who had frequently played together, were the second pair and we disposed of our opponents comfortably to the tune of 3 and 2. It was a glorious morning, with brilliant sunshine and a cool breeze and Peter and I played well, finishing the nine holes in 40. By 11 o'clock we were all back in the clubhouse sinking the first Murree beer of the day with a good RAF victory of three matches to one in the bag. This was just as well as we knew that the next event, clay pigeon shooting, would be a walkover for Skinner's Horse.

Back to Risalpur we drove and stopped at a small range outside the cantonment where the soldiers practised their 'scatter gun' shooting. This range really had to be seen to be believed. In front of the firing position was an open, sandy space around which were half a dozen stone cairns some five feet in height. Behind each of these improvised shelters was hidden an Indian Soldier of Skinner's Horse. Each soldier was armed with a collection of clay pigeons. At a signal from a controller who was out of sight, one of the soldiers would hurl a clay pigeon into the air towards the centre of the open space.

Thus the targets came up at different angles and speeds without warning from any one of the half dozen throwing points. None of the RAF team had ever seen anything like this before and our performance was terrible. I had never been any good with a shot gun and managed to hit only one of the ten 'pigeons' which we were each allotted. My colleagues fared little better and the final result was 58–17 to our opponents. So bad was our shooting that it was a relief to know that the hidden soldiers had escaped unhurt; they emerged from behind their piles of stones grinning hugely at the victory of their officers.

By this time the temperature was rising into the seventies and we were all looking forward to the swimming event in our pool, with Pimms No 1 being handed round by the Mess staff before a good curry lunch at which we were to be the hosts. The swimming turned out to be more of a cooling exercise than a serious athletic event but nevertheless we were pleased to go one up in the competition. We had achieved a comfortable win by encouraging our opponents to concentrate on the Pimms at the expense of the swimming.

By mutual agreement a break of two hours after the heavy lunch gave a welcome opportunity to recuperate and I threw myself wearily on my charpoy with instructions to Hukmud Khan to wake me with a cup of tea at 4 o'clock. It was a warm and sultry afternoon; the hot weather seemed reluctant to leave us that year and I certainly needed little persuasion to fall asleep under the fan after reading less than one page of my novel. As usual Hukmud made plenty of noise, clattering the tea cups and clearing his throat to wake me up as he started to lay out clothes for tennis, the next event timed for 4.30 pm.

At this point we split our forces and played four squash matches and two doubles tennis games of three sets, all on the RAF courts. John Cohu, who was probably our best tennis player was to be my partner and we took on the number One Skinner's pair. This turned out to be quite our 'finest hour' of the day with a handsome victory of 6–1, 6–3, 6–2. As our second pair also won, the RAF team crept ahead by two events and we cooled down on the Mess lawn drinking cold nimboo parni while waiting for the more energetic squash players to finish. When the last sweating pair came wearily round the corner of the Mess, each team had won two of the squash matches but counting up the points gave victory to the cavalrymen which left us still one event up with the three indoor events to be played after dinner.

Dinner was to be a formal affair in the splendour of our opponents' Mess, but I wondered whether it need have been quite so formal as I climbed into my white mess kit. I was beginning to feel the effects of the long day of hard exercise, and it was by no means over. It was hardly worth using the MG as I pedalled slowly down to Skinner's Mess on my bicycle in the twilight of what had been a beautiful day. The evening had cooled rapidly after the heat of the day and it was a great relief not to have one's dress shirt sticking to one's back within minutes of putting it on. I was always impressed by how invigorated one felt as soon as the temperature dropped by ten or twenty degrees in India. By the time I walked into our hosts' Mess I felt fresh and ready for a good dinner and an entertaining evening. Being now one event to the good, we had reason to feel optimistic about pulling off the whole competition.

I made my way across the Mess hall, watched by the brooding buffalo and antelope heads peering down from the walls among the tattered remnants of Colours from bygone days wondering idly how much good British and Indian blood had been spilled in the collecting of all those trophies and battle relics. After saying my formal 'good evening' to the President of the Mess and being introduced to the Colonel, I joined the other members of the two teams and we discussed the days events over the pre-prandial sherry.

At 8 o'clock the dinner call was sounded by a trumpeter in the magnificent full dress of the Regiment from the hall and the President led us in to dinner. The candlelit table was a magnificent sight, laden with some of the finest silver I have ever seen. Some of the equestrian statues in particular were superb, mostly presented to the Regiment during the previous century. Some of the other pieces bore the stamp of having been 'liberated' in the many campaigns in which this famous cavalry regiment had taken part.

The dinner matched the surroundings and we were treated to quail for the main course, as if to rub in our hosts' success with the shot gun earlier in the day. The King's health was drunk in a vintage port which obviously came from a very good cellar indeed. The Indian Cavalry Regiments had always been noted for their wealth, Skinner's Horse being one of the richest. Their hospitality, particularly on this evening was certainly extremely generous and they had clearly set out to make the RAF feel thoroughly at home in their Mess.

After dinner the atmosphere in the ante-room was so pleasant and relaxed that there was almost a reluctance to get down to the serious business of the 'decathlon' again. The talk was almost entirely 'shop' and a topic of particular interest was the recent posthumous award of the Victoria Cross to an officer of the Guides Cavalry, a sister regiment to Skinner's Horse. This unique award in peacetime had been made as a result of an ambush at Mardan, north of Risalpur where a section of cavalry had been trapped by tribesmen in a defile. Thanks to the courage and leadership of the officer who received the award, the cavalrymen had fought their way out without heavy losses, but their officer lost his life. A Wapiti of 20 Squadron from Peshawar had been in the vicinity and had helped to identify and disperse the tribesmen, for which action Flying Officer Anderson had been awarded the Distinguished Flying Cross, also a rare award in peacetime.

We were dragged from our reminiscences by the team captains and the competition was renewed. Once again we split our teams to play both snooker and darts simultaneously. I opted for darts, being almost as bad with a billiard cue as with a shot gun. We were somewhat shattered to lose both events which reversed the tables and put Skinner's Horse one up with only the poker to be played. Well, we played a lot of liar dice in the evenings and we quite fancied ourselves for this final game. We played four tables of four players and the games swung back and forth for the last hour of the evening. Again we lost by three games to one, and our opponents had won the day by six events to four. It could not have been much closer and certainly not more enjoyable. We passed a few comments about the prowess of our opponents at indoor sports but the fact remained that we had been well and truly beaten.

It was after midnight: the competition had lasted for eighteen hours and we were full of good cheer but very weary as we took leave of our hosts, promising to send the barrel of Murree beer round in the morning.

The final high note was struck by George Baker as we left the Mess, most of us on our bicycles. George said farewell, took two steps forward to spring into the saddle, misjudged the distance and sprang right over his bicycle without touching the saddle and fell flat on his face on the gravel. He was picked up and dusted down by solicitous hosts and then made a second and more successful attempt to mount. We cycled slowly, wearily and somewhat unsteadily home regretting that tomorrow was a working day but feeling that we had invented a worthwhile competition to which we could challenge other units whenever we felt like a day of intense exercise.

CHAPTER 18
ZOGGING

We were fortunate to have as our Air Officer Commanding in India in 1935, Air Marshal Sir Edgar Ludlow-Hewitt. He was one of the pioneers of military aviation, a man of great experience and great charm. He was particularly respected by the young officers in the command for his insistance on flying himself round the Frontier stations during his tours of inspection. He flew his own Hart and was always accompanied by an airman who was the engine fitter of his aeroplane and who looked after it on the ground during his visits. As both the AOC and this airman stood well over six feet in height they tended to stick right out of the cockpits, well above any protection from the windscreen, which must have been quite uncomfortable at times.

Whenever the Air Marshal came up to the Frontier from his Delhi Headquarters it was usual for Risalpur to provide another Hart, with pilot and wireless operator, to escort him round. There were two very good reasons for this. Firstly, because he carried a fitter he had no wireless in his Hart and his escort acted as his communications link with the ground stations. Secondly, we were anxious not to lose him as the result of a forced landing in tribal territory and so it was the responsibility of the escort to keep a close eye on him and to be prepared to render help if he should get into difficulties. These were quite heavy responsibilities and only those pilots who were thoroughly experienced in Frontier flying were entrusted with the escort duty. The job was viewed with mixed feelings by most of us. On the one hand it was undoubtedly a privilege and the AOC was always most appreciative: on the other hand it meant a lot of waiting about while he was busy on a station with the constant worry that one's aeroplane or wireless might go unserviceable at a crucial moment or that the 'old man' might have an engine failure and crash in some inaccessible and hostile part of tribal territory and one would be powerless to help him.

There was, however, a further problem – not an intractable one but one which caused some pilots to do everything they could to avoid being selected for escort duty. The only way in which two Harts could communicate with each other was by 'zogging'. As I have explained in an earlier chapter, zogging consisted of transmitting morse code by arm signals over the side of the cockpit, a short arm stroke signifying a dot and a long stroke a dash. It was not difficult but required both concentration and practice. We did not use it very much in the normal course of our flying as other forms of signal were used in formation manoeuvres and there were few exercises in which pairs of Harts flew together and needed to communicate. Consequently one tended to become rusty in zogging although we were all required to practise it from time to time. The Air Marshal was a zogging expert and expected a similar standard from whomever escorted him on his journeys. It would be unfair to suggest that he delighted in conducting a form of 'trade test' of those who provided his escort. It would probably be more accurate to say that because he normally flew with an escort and needed to exchange messages frequently, he had plenty of practice in this particular art, set himself a high standard and rightly expected it from others.

The honour of providing the escort for the AOC's annual inspection of his stations on the Frontier fell to me in the autumn of 1935 with, fortunately, about two weeks warning – a necessary period in which to polish up my zogging. As wireless operator I selected LAC Galloway of my own Flight who often flew with me and, naturally, read morse expertly. He would have to check my reading of the AOC's messages. It might well require our combined resources if the weather was at all bumpy. Galloway and I practised assiduously for half an hour each day, usually sitting in the cockpits of two Harts some distance apart, either in the hangar or out on the tarmac. He was a great deal more competent than myself but after ten days or so I felt reasonably confident to interpret any messages sent to me. I was somewhat comforted by Joe Shaw, who had previously carried out this escort task, when he told me that the 'old man' zogged slowly and steadily and was particularly easy to read as he had a long arm which hung over the cockpit side like a chimp's!

I was due to fly over to Kohat on the morning of the 15th October where he would have carried out his inspection on the previous day. I was then to escort him to Risalpur where he would repeat the performance that morning. One incidental advantage was that I would avoid having to dress up in breeches and puttees for the station parade which would take place as soon as the Air Marshal landed.

The 15th October saw me up bright and early in order to be airborne by 6 o'clock. K 2095 had been polished and repolished as indeed had all the Harts on the station for this annual inspection. Donning my smartest suit of white overalls, a white linen helmet under the flying topee and a pair of Meyrowitz Luxor goggles, I checked the Hart over carefully while Galloway gave the wireless set a last ground test. I suppose I had a vague hope that a smart appearance might offset any deficiencies in my zogging. It was one of those crystal clear mornings, cool and fresh after the hot weather with the Himalayas standing out to the north as if only a few miles away. Risalpur looked immaculate, cleaned and painted for the AOC and I had a last look round my own Flight as I would only just about get back to it in time for the tour of inspection if he chose to include A Flight in his itinerary, which was never published in advance – probably never even known by anybody but himself.

We took off and flew quietly across the Peshawar Plain, climbing to 5,000 feet with a view to testing the wireless with Kohat, Risalpur and Peshawar to be on the safe side. I could feel rather than hear Galloway reeling out the 120 odd feet of copper aerial which trailed behind, steadied by a small lead weight. Halfway to Kohat he reported that reception was good and Kohat was expecting us to land at 6.50 am. The AOC, I was told, was scheduled to take off at 8 o'clock for the parade at Risalpur timed for 9 o'clock. That would give me just over an hour on the ground at Kohat to refuel and have any minor faults rectified. I might even get a cup of 'char and a wad' in lieu of breakfast which I was clearly going to miss.

We crossed the Kohat Pass and I looked down at the winding road, up and over the summit which was so familiar to me. It was completely deserted at that time in the morning; no buses were cooling off in the car park on the top before starting their descent. As always when returning to Kohat I looked down with nostalgia at the patch of green beyond the Pass as it came into view.

'If you are happy with the wireless, you can wind in the aerial,' I said to Galloway through my mouthpiece. A moment later, I could feel the vibration as he wound away at the reel for about two minutes before his head appeared at my shoulder with a 'thumbs up' sign. Reducing to half throttle I started a steady descent towards the aerodrome where the usual morning Wapiti activity was clearly visible. They were doubtless on their best behaviour with the AOC on the station probably having his breakfast in the Station Commander's bungalow. I too flew sedately, joining the circuit at 1,000 feet and sideslipping over the village and road onto the aerodrome.

A single Hart, but with an Air Marshal's pennant painted on its side, stood by itself on the tarmac and I was marshalled to a position alongside it by two airmen looking considerably smarter than usual. Pop Stemp came out to meet me and took me back to his office for a cup and chat while Galloway supervised the refuelling.

'Yesterday seemed to go quite well and the old man is in a good humour,' said Pop. 'He's very hot on the cookhouse and the dining hall this year but I think we came through the inspection pretty well. He's also hot on zogging so I hope you are ready for it.'

The AOC arrived at 7.45 and I was introduced to him.

'Your Hart is smarter than mine,' he said, looking at K 2095 shining in the sun. 'Keep well clear on my starboard side so that I can zog with my right arm if we need to exchange messages, and let Risalpur have my ETA* as early as you can.'

You could almost hear the sigh of relief from the Kohat men as both Harts started immediately in the usual cloud of blue smoke, and the AOC taxied out waving goodbye to the Station Commander. I followed him into the air and we climbed away towards the Pass. Ten minutes later I had calculated our arrival time at Risalpur as 8.55 am and Galloway got the message away and received acknowledgement. I relaxed. At least my Station Commander would not have to keep 500 men standing on parade in the hot sun for a long time awaiting the great man's arrival.

Hardly had the message been acknowledged when the wings

* Estimated Time of Arrival.

of the other Hart began to rock, a signal to me to close in to see what was wanted. I took up a position about two spans distant from the AOC and his arm came over the side of the cockpit. Galloway was ready to read with me as the long arm began to zog in a steady, very clear, slow rhythm.

'G O I N G D O W N S T A Y U P' was the message.

I could hardly believe my eyes, but the message was clear enough and Galloway confirmed it. Before I could ask for confirmation or even reply, the AOC had closed his throttle and the Hart had started to glide down. Hastily pulling back my own throttle, I followed him and looked quickly down. We had left the Kohat Pass behind and were over the Peshawar Plain. Then I realised that we were over a small emergency landing ground – one of the many dotted around the Frontier, but one which was seldom used as the aerodromes at Kohat, Peshawar and Risalpur were all within 40 miles of it.

'The AOC must be going to have a look at it,' I thought as we spiralled down. Mindful of his instructions to stay up and the fact that our trailing aerial was fully extended, I levelled out at 2,000 feet and watched him closely.

Lower and lower he went until it was apparent that he was doing a circuit to a downwind position as if preparing to land.

'Surely not,' I thought, knowing that Asgar Khel, which was the name of the landing ground, was regarded as unsuitable for Harts except in cases of emergency, 'unless he has some technical trouble in which case he would hardly have ordered me to stay up.'

I told Galloway to be ready to wind in the aerial as fast as he could if I had to land and I then dropped down another 500 feet. The other Hart turned into wind and, from its shadow on the ground, I could tell that it was very low. As it crossed the boundary of the landing ground there was a spurt of sand, followed by a long streamer of dust, and it had landed.

'In with the aerial,' I shouted to Galloway and started to dive down to get a closer view of what was happening. The other Hart had come to rest in the middle of the landing ground with its engine ticking over and the AOC was climbing out, but not so his passenger. In a moment all was clear as Sir Edgar proceeded to relieve himself behind the tailplane. I roared with laughter – and with relief – until I realised that I had just sent Risalpur an entirely false time of arrival. I flew over the landing ground and he waved to me with one hand, the other being otherwise occupied.

'They'll never believe this,' I said to Galloway, 'You'll have to back me up.' He could scarcely contain himself as he started to let the aerial out again.

We climbed up to 2,000 feet once more while the AOC was getting back into his cockpit and I thought about the revised message to send to my station. Various unsuitable messages flashed through my mind but eventually, after the other Hart took to the air again in a great cloud of dust, I told Galloway to say that the AOC had decided to inspect Asgar Khel and his revised ETA was 9.15 am. When he had climbed back to my altitude, I drew alongside him determined to indicate to him in some way that his actions had been, to say the least, irregular and had caused me a great deal of anxiety. When I was in position I zogged to him, 'YOUR NEW ETA IS 0915.'

I hoped that would tactfully show him that he had created some confusion. He smiled through his goggles and raised his hand in acknowledgement. I relaxed and drew away again as he set course for Risalpur. Fortunately Asgar Khel was not in tribal territory and there had been little risk of the Air Marshal being molested on the ground, but it was an extremely small landing ground – a mere 400 yards square – suitable only for general use by Wapitis. My chief had certainly demonstrated his proficiency as a pilot and had coped with the pocket handkerchief sized landing ground better than I would have done.

There were no more incidents and I was thankful to see Risalpur come into view dead ahead. I closed up a little in formation so that we could make a tidy arrival and Sir Edgar led me over the centre of the aerodrome before waving me to break away. My instructions were to go away and keep well clear of the station until the parade on the tarmac was over – in half an hour's time. I circled round and watched the AOC make a beautiful landing and come to rest in the middle of the landing area facing the station parade drawn up on the tarmac in front of the hangars.

My job was done and I flew off to have a look at the Indus where the Attock bridge carried the road and Frontier railway to Rawalpindi across it. Galloway reeled in his aerial for the last time and then produced the ubiquitous thermos flask, handing me a most welcome cup of coffee and a biscuit over my shoulder. The Indus was flowing fast and sparkling with the snow water still coming down from the high peaks of the Himalayas. The Frontier Mail was approaching Attock bridge, its black engine belching clouds of smoke from the old fashioned bell shaped funnel as it started on the last lap of its journey to Peshawar.

'Forty minutes late as usual,' I heard Galloway murmur into his speaking tube.

We returned home half an hour later. After checking that the parade had dispersed, I landed and parked the Hart on the end of my Flight line-up which, with all the other aeroplanes, was prepared for inspection. Later that morning the AOC walked through my Flight during his tour of the station, thanked me warmly for escorting him and apologised for upsetting my timing.

'I have never seen Asgar Khel before, and thought I would quickly check how you maintain it. It was excellent and I was greatly relieved,' he said looking straight at me without batting an eyelid.

The following morning I escorted him down to Chaklala, the aerodrome outside Rawalpindi where 5 Squadron had been accommodated in tents since the Quetta earthquake. We zogged hard all the way down the main line which runs as straight as a die from Nowshera to Rawalpindi and I felt quite exhausted by the time he landed at Chaklala and I flew low over the aerodrome to take my leave of him. He would fly back to Delhi unaccompanied as it was only when near the Frontier that we escorted him. The real reason for the unexpected landing at Asgar Khel was kept a close secret by Galloway and myself. If the AOC had divulged it to the Station Commander, he also kept it to himself.

Zogging was something of a dying art and this was one of the last occasions on which I practised it. Whereas it was no problem at 100 mph in a Wapiti, it was a considerable strain on the arm at 140 mph in a Hart and clearly became impossible in faster aeroplanes.

CHAPTER 19

LONG DISTANCE FLIGHT

In 1935 long distance flying was still very much in its infancy. Most of the military aircraft of the day were biplanes with ranges of a few hundred miles only and top speeds of less than 200 mph. It was the era of civilian pioneers such as Kingsford-Smith, Amy Johnson and Campbell Black, all of whom flew specially constructed or adapted aeroplanes in attempts to set up new speed and endurance records. It was also a time when the RAF was beginning to exploit the inherent flexibility of the aeroplane to reinforce distant parts of the Empire as a matter of routine instead of a somewhat hazardous adventure. A series of leap-frogging reinforcement flights was initiated in which a squadron from India would fly down to Singapore, its place in India being taken by a squadron from Iraq, and a home based squadron simultaneously reinforcing the Middle East.

Provided that there were no more urgent commitments, this exercise was practised annually and the squadrons in India took it in turn to reinforce Singapore, a Wapiti squadron one year followed by a Hart squadron the next year, and so on. As can be imagined, this was a highly popular and much sought after trip which usually took place towards the end of the year when the best flying weather could be expected in India and when the worst of the monsoon had passed through Burma and Malaya. The fact that the flight normally included a stay of about four weeks, including Christmas in Singapore, did nothing to lessen its attraction.

There had been no opportunity for me to go on this flight while at Kohat but, in 1935, it was the turn of 39 Squadron and so I was luckier than some who completed a full five year tour in India without ever having the chance to fly much beyond the Frontier. Being a Flight Commander, I also had the responsibility and satisfaction of leading my own Flight.

We were told in September that the Squadron had been selected to undertake the flight early in December, returning to India in mid January, 1936. We thus had three months warning but there was a great deal to be done in that time. In the first place it was a matter of pride for the selected squadron to take its full complement of twelve aeroplanes. Not only did this require 100% serviceability – a standard which was not easy to maintain (our usual serviceability on the Hart averaging 75%), but as each Hart would complete at least 80 hours flying during the round trip, it was essential to ensure that none fell due for a major inspection during its absence from Risalpur. Singapore was not equipped with Harts and did not hold the spares to undertake major overhauls, and so we were required to take our own airmen and sufficient spares and servicing equipment to be entirely self

266

supporting. For the three months prior to departure, it was therefore necessary to stagger the hours flown by each aeroplane so that they all reached the departure date with about 100 hours to go before becoming due for the next major inspection. The Flight Sergeants spent hours with graph paper and blunt pencils working out their servicing programme up to the day of departure, and woe betide any officer or airman who upset the calculations by having an accident or exceeding the allotted flying hours in the meantime!

Planning the route, the intermediate and overnight stops, accommodation and refuelling arrangements, fell to our Squadron Commander, Squadron Leader Butler and the three Flight Commanders, Joe Shaw, Owen Jones and myself. The outward flight was to take six days, the distance being about 4,000 miles, and ten intermediate stops were planned. In general this itinerary allowed two trips of about 3½ hours each per day except on the fourth day when only one stage was scheduled to allow a little latitude for any necessary work on the aeroplanes. It sounds leisurely progress by the standards of today when the 4,000 odd miles would probably be covered non-stop in less than seven hours. It was not, however, by any means leisurely when one remembers that the seven hours flying, often in fairly rough conditions and map reading every inch of the way, was punctuated by a refuelling stop in the heat of the day when the two man crews had to refuel their own aircraft from four gallon drums.

We planned the longest legs on the flight across India where the better aerodromes and facilities existed. Down through Burma, Siam and the Malay States, conditions were known to be very rugged, and so more time on the ground was allowed – a precaution which in the event proved wise indeed. It was decided that each Flight of the squadron would fly separately at thirty minute intervals to avoid congestion on the ground and to spread out the refuelling as much as possible. However, we planned to arrive tidily over Singapore in squadron formation with, we hoped, twelve aeroplanes.

The squadron was to be accompanied by a twin engined

267

Vickers Valentia troop carrier from the Bomber Transport Flight at Lahore. There would be room for twenty squadron airmen in it together with our main pack-up of spares and ground servicing equipment, and personal kit. Its load was very restricted and the selection of essential equipment posed quite a problem for the three Flight Sergeants who would happily have thrown in anything which might conceivably be useful. As the Valentia cruised at some 50 mph less than the Harts, it clearly could not keep up with the squadron. Slow though it was, it had more than double the range of a Hart. So we decided that it would take off each morning after the airmen had seen the squadron safely off the ground, overfly our midday refuelling stop, when there would be an opportunity to bring it down if we were in any trouble, and hopefully reach our next night stop before us so that our own airmen could receive us and deal with the Harts before nightfall.

The next problem to be solved was that of the maps to be used. The eyeball was the only navigational aid and map reading was the only method of navigation along the whole route. Whereas the maps of India were reasonably detailed and accurate, those of Burma, Siam and the Malay States were extremely sketchy and far from accurate. Photographic survey was in its infancy and little progress had then been made in map making from aerial photography. The sheer quantity of maps needed for 4,000 miles posed difficulties in the confined cockpit of a Hart. We rejected the idea of using maps on the scale of $\frac{1}{4}$ inch to a mile. According to my calculations, this would have required almost 30 yards of map. We finally settled on the 10 mile to one inch scale maps, and even this would need 33 feet of map. None of us was too happy about using this small scale. Perfectly adequate though it was in fine weather with good landmarks, the thought of finding an obscure landing ground like Mergui or Victoria Point in a monsoon storm leading three Harts in formation gave me a few qualms. In the end we compromised by having one set of the smaller scale maps for the pilot only in each aeroplane and a number of the larger scale ones of the potentially difficult areas in the rear cockpit with the air gunner who could produce them if needed. Even when using the smaller scale maps we could not afford the space to carry the complete set for the whole route and they would have been much too unwieldy in the cockpit – rather like trying to read *The Times* in the back of an open sports car at 80 mph!

With much labour and scissors and paste, we made up books of maps, one for each pilot. Each sheet was cut with the track to be flown as a black line down the centre with some 50 miles on either side of it. These sheets were about 10 inches wide and a foot or so long. They were pasted on to thin cardboard with eyelet holes at the top and then fastened together with large rings, making a book of 32 pages which could be turned over easily with gloved hands. One simply map-read down each page in sequence, propping the book between one's stomach and the top of the control column. Looking at the finished article, it seemed a hell of a long way to page 32 where Singapore stood out boldly, followed by an endless expanse of sea towards the East Indies. Somewhere about page 23 there was nothing but open sea. That was the Bay of Bengal and I was required to map read over nothing at all for about half an hour.

'Oh well,' I thought, 'it's too late to start worrying now. Even *I* ought to be able to hit the coast of Burma.'

What should we and what could we carry in each of the Harts then had to be considered. Obviously not very much but it had to be enough to be reasonably independent of the Valentia should it get into difficulties and be unable to give us full support. Each Flight needed to have a degree of independence in case we became separated, a not unlikely eventuality. The items considered most likely to be needed were a propeller, a spare wheel, a W/T* set and a selection of small engine spares. Special fittings were available for bolting a propeller and a wheel below the fuselage. I decided to take the propeller which was an awkward load as it stretched from a point in front of the tail skid, where it was perilously close to the ground, to a point

* Wireless Telegraphy.

269

behind the radiator; a long cumbersome load. The spare wheel was a snug fit almost directly below the centre of gravity so that the balance of the Hart was undisturbed. The spare W/T set had to be secured inside the tail while the collection of spares in the fourth aeroplane went into a pannier under one wing.

Each Hart was to be fitted with bomb racks for the journey as we needed them for our work in Singapore. On each of these racks we carried, for the journey, a streamlined metal supply-dropping container into which went overnight kit of the pilot and his air gunner plus a few items such as cockpit and engine covers, screw pickets and spare chamois leathers for straining the fuel. Bulk rather than weight was our chief problem and, when fully loaded, neither pilot nor gunner could move very much in the cockpits. This was where the spacious Wapiti cockpit scored over that of the Hart.

Preparations continued at an increasing tempo during October and November and we were told that our departure was to be on an unspecified day in December. I took the opportunity to carry out a couple of long cross country flights over unfamiliar country to the south east using the 10 mile to an inch maps. It was an unusual map as all our Frontier flying was done with larger scale maps, or with none at all as one became familiar with the territory. I found no great difficulty but realised that the central Indian landscape was relatively easy from a navigational point of view but the less well mapped parts of our route would clearly be much more difficult. During these training flights I took LAC Wesson, who was to fly with me to Singapore, and gave him some elementary instruction in map reading on the principle that four eyes were bound to be better than two if we lost ourselves. We were very remiss in failing to train our air gunners in the rudiments although the more senior among them became very competent of their own accord. Bearing in mind that these excellent airmen were not only gunners and bomb aimers when in the air but also full time fitters, riggers, armourers or electricians when on the ground, it would have been overloading them to add navigation to their other skills, particularly on their extra air gunners' pittance of sixpence per day.

As another useful preparatory exercise I sent each of the crews who were going on the flight to one or other of the emergency landing grounds dotted around the Frontier to refuel their Harts from the packed stocks of fuel held there. Each crew flew a circuitous route of about three hours duration, finally landing at one of the more remote aerodromes such as Drazinda, Bannu or Lachi. Using the standard funnel and a chamois leather to strain the fuel, the pilot and his air gunner had then to fill up their tanks from the four gallon cans taken from the packed stock. The chamois leather was a vital piece of equipment as much of the fuel on these landing grounds was contaminated and dirty due to the conditions under which it had to be stored. One had only to look at the dirt, rust and often water in the chamois leather after pouring a few cans through it to realise the danger of allowing unfiltered petrol to go into the tanks. A four gallon drum weighed more than thirty pounds and it was an exhausting exercise to lift them up to the top wing of a Hart and decant them into the tanks. We hoped not to have to do much refuelling personally but we all had to be fully prepared for it, and know the tricks of the trade.

The Outward Flight
In order to add a touch of realism to the reinforcement exercise, the squadron was to be given no more than 72 hours warning although we had been told that the flight would take place in December. The first few days of December passed and everybody became more and more twitchy, worried lest they should fall sick or that one of the Harts would need an engine change at the last moment or that an accident would put paid to somebody's chances of making the trip. Most of us were also anxious to spend Christmas in Singapore. Surely our headquarters in Delhi would not be unfeeling enough to leave the squadron stranded in some isolated outpost in Burma or Siam for Christmas Day.

271

We need not have worried. On 5th December, I was summoned to the Squadron Commander's office and he broke the news that we were to leave at dawn on the 8th and arrive at Seletar in Singapore at about midday on the 13th, if all went according to plan. Nothing remained to be done but give the aeroplanes a final polish and pack our various loads as securely as possible. The spare propeller which I had elected to carry was carefully swathed in fabric to prevent damage from stones and grit flung up from the wheels. Flying Officer Robins was carrying the spare wheel, Pilot Officer Devas the pack of spare parts and Sergeant Eyre the extra wireless set.

Squadron Leader Butler had decided to fly in C Flight which was a great relief to me. As the junior of the three Flight Commanders, I had expected him to lead my Flight, but he selected C Flight because Owen Jones, although senior in rank, had but recently joined the squadron after an engineering appointment and was, in consequence, inexperienced on the Hart. So it was decided that C Flight would go ahead to enable the Squadron Commander to arrive first at each destination, followed by B Flight with my A Flight bringing up the rear, all at our agreed intervals of thirty minutes.

The 8th December dawned clear and cold, so cold that a frost could not have been far away – an almost unheard of occurrence on the Frontier. Although the Frontier stations had gone into blue uniform for the winter, we were flying in khaki drill as we were moving into the tropics and we could not afford the space to carry unnecessary clothing. My bare knees were distinctly blue as I walked down from the Mess at 5.30 am with Hukmud Khan following with my luggage. Our Valentia was sitting on the tarmac running up its engines and looking for all the world like a pregnant hippo. Twelve immaculate Harts were lined up alongside it, several of them having engines warmed up by their fitters. The staccato crackling of the open exhausts of the Kestrels was accentuated by the cold morning air and the whole tarmac bustled with noisy and colourful activity as we prepared to leave on our long adventure.

Cameras were clicking in every direction and most of the station turned out to wish the squadron 'bon voyage and a Happy Christmas'. Promptly at 6 o'clock Squadron Leader Butler led C Flight out and took off in a good Flight formation, the highly polished cowlings and blue spinners and wheels reflecting the bright early morning sunshine. As a gesture to the well wishers he led the Flight round in a wide circuit and passed low over the aerodrome as he set an easterly course for Ambala.

Joe Shaw and B Flight left at 6.30 am without incident and just before 7 o'clock I led my Flight out to the south west corner of the aerodrome. By this time most of the spectators had drifted away to work or to breakfast. Our aeroplanes were heavy but not unduly so, not for example, as heavy as with a war load of two 500 lb bombs. My only problem in K 2093 was the additional drag of the spare propeller slung under my belly. However, if we had to have one Hart slower than the rest, it was right that the leader should be flying it. As B and C Flights had the same problem, our average speed over the whole distance was likely to be similar.

We climbed away from the aerodrome in close formation and levelled out at 4,000 feet. Looking back at the three red spinners churning round on either side of me was a splendid sight; we had at least made a clean start to the longest and most testing flight that any of us had ever made, and I allowed myself a few moments of personal satisfaction before I crossed my raised arms in a signal to ease out into a loose and comfortable formation. Each pilot had a set of maps and I wanted each of them to check my navigation in case we became separated in bad weather or in case I lost myself, which could easily happen during the next six days.

'All well and secure in the back?' I called out to Wesson.

'Not much room to move, but a good start and I have brought my rabbit's foot with me,' he replied, dangling the furry object over my shoulder.

It was an easy first leg across the plains of the Punjab in

perfect weather, for which I was grateful as it allowed me to settle quietly into the routine of the flight, getting used to the bulky book of maps on my lap, making notes of the route on my knee pad and checking the performance of K 2093. During take off and landing the book of maps had to be slid into a special canvas pocket by my right leg as they would otherwise restrict full use of the controls. It was a clumsy arrangement but the best we could contrive and worked quite well.

Three hours and twenty minutes after leaving Risalpur, Ambala came in sight. Ten minutes later we flew over the centre of the aerodrome, broke formation and landed independently. Ambala was the home of 28 Squadron, an Army Co-operation squadron equipped with Wapitis, and the airmen took us in hand, refuelled and checked over our Harts while the crews had tea and sandwiches in the squadron's offices. No snags arose and shortly after I landed, C Flight left on the second leg to Cawnpore. Our Valentia lumbered across while I was on the ground. It had been told that we had no technical problems and there was no need for it to land. It was clear, however, that it could not possibly reach Cawnpore before the leading elements of the squadron. This was largely because the professional help available at Ambala made our stay there unusually brief. It was the only RAF station on the route and was not, therefore, typical of later stops which were bound to be longer and more exhausting.

We were airborne again by midday and this leg to Cawnpore was much like the first, somewhat dull and uninteresting. The scenery across central India was monotonous – very flat, dry and dusty and I was glad to see Cawnpore appear after three and a quarter hours as the mental effort of map reading for almost seven hours was beginning to tell. Also it was bumpy and the book of maps bounced about disconcertingly. The aerodrome at this first night stop was the race course, close to the centre of the town. The grass area inside the oval of the white rails made a good aerodrome if a little small. As we circled round and broke formation, I counted eight Harts lined up beside the grandstand. So far so good.

Sideslipping in over the rails beside the winning post, I came to rest in the middle of the grass area. It was much smoother and greener than Risalpur and reminded me very much of a home aerodrome. Not unexpectedly there was no sign of the Valentia and it was another hour before it appeared over the horizon. By that time we had unloaded our own Harts much to the delight of the airmen in the Valentia who were weary after more than eight hours flying in the aeroplane. The whole party was spread over three or four hotels and none of us felt like doing anything more active than sinking a few beers, having dinner and going to bed. It had been a long day, Cawnpore offered few attractions and we had an early start in the morning.

The second day took us through Gaya to Calcutta, a much shorter flying day with less than five hours in the air and the promise of a long evening in India's eastern capital. Gaya, which I reached shortly before 10 o'clock in the morning, was the first time we had to refuel our own aeroplanes and it worked quite well. The fuel was carried to us by coolies in the ubiquitous four gallon can, millions of which were used all over India for carrying water. Wesson climbed up on to the top wing and I stood on the lower wing handing one can at a time up to him, keeping a close eye on the coolies who were not above banging a full can against the wing fabric. Wesson poured the fuel through a chamois leather inserted in a large funnel and then threw the empty can well clear onto the ground. Our only casualty was a coolie who walked under a descending can and collected it on his head. The tanks in the fuselage were easier to fill than the top tank and we completed the job in forty minutes – hardly a record but not too bad for a pilot and air gunner. Sergeant Eyre had a slight mishap and managed to tip two gallons over himself from the waist downwards which caused him to hop about a bit as the high octane petrol got through to him. During all this activity the Valentia droned overhead and a green Verey light went up to indicate that it could continue on its way to Calcutta. We looked up and thought about the troops doubtless enjoying a cool beer while we sweated away doing their jobs down below. Well, good luck to them; they would work hard enough and willingly if we ran into difficulties.

As they finished their refuelling, my Flight gathered round and we sat in the shade and ate sandwiches and drank coffee we had brought with us. I asked Flying Officer Robins to lead to Calcutta and I would take over from Sergeant Eyre and fly the 'arse end Charlie position' on the next leg. Since he smelled overpoweringly of petrol, we made him sit down wind while we ate our sandwiches and no smoking was the rule! When our turn came to take off, we said goodbye to the Shell representatives who had helped us to refuel and followed Robins into the air down the long wide strip which constituted Gaya aerodrome. It was pleasant to be able to relax out on the left wing of our loose formation, leaving the tedious map reading to somebody else for the time being. It was a short leg of less than two and a half hours and by 3 pm the vast muddy expanse of the Hooghli delta came into view with the sprawling city of Calcutta at its head. Our destination was Dum Dum, the city's civil airport used by the international airlines which at that time were beginning to pioneer their various routes to the Far East. Once again I was able to count eight Harts lined up on the airport as Robins led us across its centre in a shallow dive in close formation. We broke up and on this occasion I landed last on this, the largest aerodrome we had so far encountered. The Valentia had landed ten minutes before Squadron Leader Butler and so our own airmen were ready to meet us and take charge of the aeroplanes.

Two buses took us all into the city and I was appalled at the poverty and the slums through which we passed. It was a terrible introduction for a traveller and was not improved by the sacred cows which wandered at will through this Hindu city, lying on the pavements and befouling the streets. There was even a white cow lying on the steps of the Great Eastern

276

Hotel when the bus drew up to disembark most of us who were staying there. We carried our bags and bedding rolls very carefully round this beast in order not to disturb it and give offence. It would probably have been in the foyer had it been able to get through the swing doors.

The Great Eastern could be described as 'tropical Victorian' in its decor and furnishings. Heavy mahogany furniture interspersed with bamboo- and cane-seated chairs predominated. The rooms were huge and gloomy with dusty ceiling fans churning slowly round with that distinctive beat so familiar to all of us. However, it was comfortable and cool. The long solid bar with its brass rail was very British and the European habitués were intrigued with the horde of young airmen pausing for the night on their pioneering trip. There was little we could do in Calcutta in the short time available and, after a brief walk round, most of us repaired to the hotel for dinner, a few drinks and an early night.

The more interesting part of the flight started the following morning with the leg across the Bay of Bengal to Akyab on the coast of Burma. I resumed the lead and we took off at 7 o'clock. It was fine but there was more cloud than we had seen over India, a sure sign that we were approaching the area where the tail end of the monsoon might be encountered. I took the Flight up to 8,000 feet on this occasion, partly to get above a layer of well broken cloud and partly to give us more height should any difficulties arise over the open water. The Hooghli delta was a dreary expanse of mud and water, not unlike The Wash at low tide but very much larger. By the time we had crossed it I had a fairly good idea of the wind strength and direction and set a course out over the Bay of Bengal – the blank page of my book of maps.

We droned on over the open water with quite a number of ships visible through the clouds, mostly making for Calcutta. As there was nothing to do but maintain an accurate course, I was scribbling a few notes on my knee with my expensive Waterman fountain pen when a sudden jolt from an air pocket jerked the pen out of my hand and it disappeared over the side. I was extremely annoyed to lose my valuable pen and it was very stupid of me to have been using it.

The crossing took a little less than an hour, Chittagong being the point at which we were due to hit the coast. I led the Flight down through the broken cloud to 4,000 feet after about forty five minutes and the long flat coastline was just visible ahead. It resolved itself into sandy beaches, palm trees and mangrove swamps but no immediate sign of Chittagong. About five miles from the coast, Willie Devas, on my right, closed in and pointed out to his right. He put his left arm over the side of his cockpit and zogged 'C'. I turned ten degrees to starboard and we continued in towards the coast. A collection of low white buildings with red roofs began to appear and it was soon obvious that this was Chittagong. I was expecting a much larger and more imposing town but it was in fact an attractive looking series of clean buildings scattered along the shore among dense patches of jungle. Turning down the coast we followed the shoreline which brought us to Akyab in another hour.

Had I known then that my fighter Wing would be stationed there towards the end of World War II, I would undoubtedly have taken a greater interest in Akyab. The aerodrome had the appearance of an aircraft carrier, a single wide strip set on a plateau running parallel to the sea shore and very close to it. It was dusty but smooth and well drained as indeed it had to be. That part of Burma can have as much as 300 inches of rain in a year. After the dust and drabness of India, the green of the rich vegetation and the sparkling sea on the nearby beach made Akyab a delightful place that morning as we refuelled our Harts and drank coffee. We could not afford the time for a swim and had to resist the temptation to run down to the beach and wash away the smell of petrol.

A three engined Fokker monoplane belonging to Air France was on the aerodrome. The pilot, with his dark blue hat stuck on the back of his head, was sitting astride the centre engine cleaning a sparking plug with a wire brush, a lighted cigarette dangling from his mouth. Under the big wing his only passenger, an elderly lady who had a parrot in a cage beside her, was sitting quietly knitting. Such was airline travel to the Far East in 1935! We offered to help the Frenchman but he seemed perfectly content and totally oblivious of the fire hazard he was creating. He waved us on our way from his lofty perch with a cheerful 'merci bien, Messieurs. Bon Voyage'.

Two and a half hours later, after an uninteresting flight over the dense jungle of central Burma, we approached Rangoon, the outstanding feature of this capital city being, of course, the Shwe Dagon – the Golden Pagoda. Long before the city itself came into view I could see the afternoon sun glinting on the huge golden 'onion' which surmounts the temple. It is entirely covered with gold leaf, kept clean by the heavy rainfall, and shines like a lighthouse even in dull weather. This was a sight well worth studying and, as I was somewhat ahead of my landing time, I closed up the formation and we flew around and over the city several times before landing on the very rough, sloping aerodrome at Mingaladon. Once again the Valentia had beaten us and so our own airmen were ready to receive us and get on with the job of putting the Harts to bed for the night.

The Officers Mess of the 60th Rifles was my home for the night and most comfortable and hospitable it proved to be. The 60th was an old and famous regiment: it's Mess, not unlike that of Skinner's Horse was stuffed with the relics and loot of numerous campaigns: a veritable museum. With an hour or two of daylight left I was anxious to visit the Golden Pagoda, as were most of the officers in the squadron. Our hosts kindly fixed up transport for us and within an hour of landing we were climbing the broad steps of this famous Buddhist temple to leave our shoes at the top and enter the huge gilded doors. An immense figure of Buddha dominated the temple, encrusted with precious stones and gold filigree, gazing placidly down from his throne beneath the golden dome. The dome itself was disappointing when seen from the ground compared with the view from the air with the sun shining on it. This, I felt, was a

279

pity as it meant that very few of the believers ever had the chance to see the full beauty of their temple as I had seen it a couple of hours earlier.

Rangoon was the half way point of our flight and everything had gone well. No accidents and no serious unserviceability with any of the Harts, but we all knew that the more difficult part of the journey lay before us. For a moment it looked as if the difficulties would start the following morning. We woke to find Mingaladon shrouded in fog. As the sun came up, however, it was apparent that the fog was extremely thin and blue sky could be seen through it by 7 o'clock. It was to be a short day with one stage of three and a half hours only to Mergui in the southern extremity of Burma, so we could afford an hour or two's delay. By 7.30 the fog, although still thick at ground level was seen to be no more than fifty feet deep, and we decided to go. We took off independently and as I pulled sharply up through the mist into the clear blue sky, I was dazzled by the dome of Shwe Dagon sticking up through the fog and shining like a beacon. As I turned to the left to circle the aerodrome, first Robins, then Devas and finally Eyre popped up through the blanket of fog in quick succession like corks from a bottle.

This was to be an easy day, flying down the coastline of the Kra isthmus dividing Burma from Siam. The weather was good, broken cloud and bright sunshine, and this made my task of navigating down the coast easy. Mergui, when it appeared three and a half hours later, was easy to identify as the aerodrome stood out boldly as a bright green square completely surrounded by a dense forest of tall rubber trees. The approach to land needed a little care as the tall trees came right up to the edge of the landing area and created a significant down draught during the final fifty feet of approach. The whole squadron had landed by lunchtime and the Valentia brought the troops in over the trees half an hour later. This was an opportunity to spend a few extra hours in rectifying any minor faults before the final two days of the flight. My engine was misfiring occasionally with heart stopping puffs of blue smoke from the exhaust stubs in front of my face, usually when over a stretch of open water, and the fitter had all the plugs out finding two defective ones in the process which cured the trouble. Apart from an inefficient brake on Eyre's Hart we had no troubles and we covered up the aeroplanes at 4 o'clock for the night.

During the afternoon's work we were surrounded by interested spectators, mostly Burmese girls who made an attractive picture with their gaily patterned parasols, many with babies slung on their backs and nearly all smoking large Burma cheroots which, to my unaccustomed eyes, looked most incongruous. We did our best to keep them away from the petrol slopping about during refuelling but it wasn't very successful as they were treating the whole operation as a family party. Burma cheroots, the best of which were alleged to be rolled on the thigh of a Burmese maiden, were ridiculously cheap and I bought two large bundles tied round with some kind of vegetable twine for about two shillings – just the thing for Christmas in Singapore.

My host for the night at Mergui was an extraordinary man, a very large and extremely prosperous planter known locally as 'the uncrowned king of Burma', for reasons which I never discovered. Although originally an Englishman, he had spent most of his life in Burma, had no intention of ever returning to England and had gone native in a big way. He lived in a large and extremely untidy house close to the aerodrome with five Burmese wives and seemed completely happy. They tended to all his needs and all seemed equally fond of him. He generously offered one of them to me for the night and was in no way offended when I sought for some inadequate words to decline his generous offer. A Burmese wife was about the last thing I wanted before the last two days of the journey. I have often wondered what happened to him when the Japanese overran Burma seven years later. My guess is that, like a number of other men in his position whom I met, he was interned for a brief period and then released to carry on with his work under surveillance. Mergui boasted a small European club, housed in a tin hut and that evening was an occasion for a celebration by the handful of Europeans who came in from the surrounding district to meet us. It was a friendly and hospitable evening at their little club and we all carried away pleasant memories of Mergui and slightly thicker heads than we wanted under the circumstances.

A small incident enlivened our departure next morning. It had been decided on this occasion that the Valentia would leave first as we particularly wanted it to arrive first at our next night stop, which was Alor Star in Malaya. It had rained heavily during the night but cleared before the dawn. There was a considerable slope on the aerodrome and we had not been warned that the lower part became soft after heavy rain. The Valentia taxied off to the far end with its heavy load of airmen and equipment. As we watched it turn into wind, one wing dipped sharply and it came to rest in a slightly drunken attitude. Clearly the wheels on one side had bogged down. Fortunately neither the wing tip nor the propellers had touched the ground. The troops piled out of the Valentia and we aircrew ran across to the scene. The Valentia was well and truly bogged, its starboard wheels having sunk to axle level. The engines were switched off while a council of war took place.

With ropes, engine power and manpower we eventually pulled the big aeroplane out on to firmer ground. No damage had been done and the Valentia took off from another part of the aerodrome. It was a warning to the rest of us as the ground was very deceptive and any of us could have taxied a Hart straight into a soft patch without seeing it. Unlike the Valentia, a Hart would almost certainly have stood on its nose. Half an hour later I took my Flight off across wind on the higher part of the aerodrome and we continued on our way down the coast.

One slightly confusing aspect of this part of the journey was the presence of mangrove swamps along the coastline. On our maps these swamps were depicted as water whereas they appeared to be land when viewed from the air. Only when looking directly downwards could the water be detected between the mangroves. It was extremely difficult in consequence to see the shape and exact position of the coastline, not admittedly a serious problem in good weather but one that could make map reading not exactly easy in reduced visibility. On this occasion the weather was quite good with excellent visibility below a cloud layer at 4,000 feet. Nevertheless, it was apparent as we progressed southwards that we were catching up with the tail of the monsoon. Clouds were steadily increasing and storms of rain becoming more frequent.

The midday refuelling stop on the leg from Mergui was at Victoria Point which came into view after three hours pleasant and easy flying down the coast. We knew in advance that this was the smallest, roughest and generally most inhospitable aerodrome on the route. I did not like the look of it at all as we approached so I was happy to see the eight Harts of the other two Flights safely on the ground and drawn up in one corner of the small and irregularly shaped landing ground – it did not deserve the title 'aerodrome'.

I approached to land up the slope over a wet marshy area to seaward of the landing ground. Coming in as slowly as I dared with plenty of engine on, I was horrified to see a flock of large white birds rise up from the marsh in front of me when I was down to about thirty feet. My mind flashed back to the incident with the kitehawks at Kohat but, on this occasion, none of the geese, as they turned out to be, hit me. But the incident distracted my attention to the extent that I landed more heavily than I liked. The birds had been scattered for the following members of the Flight who all made good landings, much to my relief. The refuelling arrangements were as basic as the landing ground and it took us a long time to collect our fuel and hoist the cans up on to the wings. It was also getting hotter as we flew towards the equator, the midday temperature now being well into the eighties. It was a weary band of aircrew that stretched out in the shade of coconut palms for the sandwich lunch after the Harts had been filled up and checked over. We gave the Shell coolies the remains of the picnic before climbing back into the aeroplanes and taking off for Alor Star.

Alor Star, the capital of Kedah in the Malay States, was known to have a large aerodrome used by Imperial Airways and other airlines. As we flew steadily on down the coast, little did we know of the situation facing us. The weather deteriorated into storms of tropical rain and heavy accumulations of cumulus cloud. There was no question of trying to go above the clouds and I found myself forced down to 500 feet in order to keep the coastline in view. My three pilots closed up but maintained a respectful distance as there were some considerable air pockets below the clouds. Short of Alor Star the rain ceased and visibility improved under the low cloud base. It was a relief to see the aerodrome but, even from a distance, puddles were visible all over the surface. I was not unduly concerned because I could see Harts parked on the apron.

Alor Star had one all-weather tarmac runway laid down on one side of the grass surface, similar to that at Kohat. It was about 500 yards long and 40 feet wide with a camber and drainage channels on either side to take away heavy monsoon rain. It was one of the earliest and a far sighted attempt to produce an 'all-weather airfield'.

To my consternation, a large white cross in the centre of the grass area proclaimed that it was unserviceable and, as we circled round at 1,000 feet, I could see the signal displayed by the apron indicating that the runway only was in use. Had the wind been up and down that runway, all would have been well, but unfortunately it was gusting up to about 25 miles an hour dead across it.

Landing a Hart across wind was not the easiest of manoeuvres although quite practicable on a wide grass area with good brakes. After five days of landing in fairly rough conditions, our brakes, which were sensitive at the best of times, were far from efficient. Doubtful brakes coupled with a narrow cambered runway, bordered by drainage channels and a 25 mph cross-wind, had produced a landing problem which filled all four of us with foreboding. We completed two full circuits in formation while I pondered on the problem.

'If B and C Flights had no problems,' I thought, 'there is no reason why we should not cope without difficulty.'

What I did not know was that the wind had doubled in strength since the others had landed and the approach of another storm had produced strong gusts.

I broke the formation up and went round to land. It was bumpy on the approach with a lot of drift to the left. I therefore landed as gently as I could on one wheel with my right wing well down and with plenty of speed. The runway was smooth enough but the tendency to swing into wind to the right started as soon as I had the Hart firmly on its two wheels. My brakes were still quite efficient and, with the help of one short burst of throttle, I was able to keep her straight. But it took the whole of the runway, juggling with brakes and throttle, to come to rest. It had not been easy or comfortable and it was with some anxiety that I taxied off the strip at the far end and waited to see how the others fared.

Robins came in very steadily, landed well and appeared to have things well under control until he was half way down the strip. He then started to swing into wind because, as it transpired, his left brake was almost useless. He could not control the swing and, as always happened, it became tighter and tighter until finally his outside wing went down, scraped along the ground and bent upwards. This stopped him and he came to rest, half on and half off the runway with a wheel bogged down on the grass.

That was bad enough but worse was to come. Devas came in next, made an excellent approach, touched down smoothly and then started to swing towards Robins' damaged Hart. Realising the danger, he gave the engine a burst of throttle to stop the swing. That was successful but he overdid it and a swing developed in the opposite direction. He was now in serious trouble on the narrow strip of tarmac. The wind gusted under his tail, swung him right round and he ran off the tarmac. As he did so, the drainage ditch and waterlogged grass tipped up the Hart and it stood on its nose with a splintering crash as the propeller broke. There it stayed, bolt upright on the opposite of the runway to Robins' aeroplane and partially blocking the runway.

Sergeant Eyre, still aloft, was faced with a terrible dilemma. A storm was rapidly approaching. There was no alternative aerodrome and the grass surface was quite unfit to use. We could not move the two crashed and bogged Harts very quickly and we had to leave the decision as to what to do to Eyre himself. After two more circuits to sum up the position, he decided to land. There was plenty of room to pass between the two aeroplanes and, had the wind been up and down the runway, there would have been no problem. Apparently he knew that his brakes were still operating, or certainly had been at the midday stop, and he decided to have a go. The next storm was within five miles and so time was short. He succeeded splendidly. I held my breath as he shot between the two damaged aeroplanes and kept his own running straight to the far end where he pulled up behind me. I clapped my hands above my head in congratulation and he raised his hand in acknowledgement. But I felt very sick as I taxied in: half my Flight wrecked at the same time, and almost at the end of our long journey. It was heartbreaking but one simply could not blame either of the pilots. Eyre and I had been lucky to have had reasonable braking power to offset the cross-wind. The combination of circumstances had been too much for the Harts rather than the pilots and I doubt whether any of the squadron pilots would have done any better.

Within half an hour the damaged aeroplanes had been extricated from the soft ground and towed slowly to the tarmac to be surveyed by the Flight Sergeant and his technical airmen.

'By working all night and with a bit of luck,' he said to me, 'I think we can make one serviceable aeroplane out of the two by tomorrow. We can do nothing here about K 2134 as the wrecked propeller may have strained the engine and damaged the crankshaft. However,' he went on, 'we can take the undamaged port wing off K 2134 and replace the wrecked port wing on K 2054 with it. If all goes well tonight, Flying Officer Robins should be able to take off with you in the morning.'

As there was a direct rail link between Alor Star and Singapore, we decided that Willie Devas, with his air gunner and a fitter and a rigger, would have to dismantle his Hart, load it on to a rail car and bring it down to Singapore. As we would be there for four weeks, there was a chance that it could be repaired in time to fly back with the squadron.

And so the decision was made and the airmen went to work with a will. I went down to see them twice during the night and they were meeting the challenge of a 7 o'clock take off with time to spare. In fact the new wing was in place and correctly rigged by 4 am. We could not risk an air test with the aerodrome still waterlogged and a cross-wind still blowing dead across the runway, but this was of no great concern as Robins had done no other damage. The worst that was likely to happen was that K 2054 might tend to fly one wing low until some fine adjustment to the rigging could be applied in Singapore.

So an unhappy Willie Devas saw the three of us off that morning and I felt very sorry for him. He was determined, however, to join us with his wreckage within a week in the hope of having it in one piece again for the return flight.

The plan for this last day, 13th December, was a short trip by the three Flights separately to Taiping where we could refuel and prepare for the final leg to Singapore. Squadron Leader Butler wished the whole squadron to leave Taiping together and to arrive over Singapore in one neat formation. Unfortunately our troubles were not yet over. Leaving Devas in the care of the local Imperial Airways representative at Alor Star, who could not have been more helpful and sympathetic, we took off individually down that fateful runway.

The trip to Taiping took exactly one hour; the weather was good and it was a pleasant, relaxed flight. On our way we all kept a look out along the coast for any signs of the Southern

Cross. Kingsford-Smith, the Australian pioneer, had been missing in his three engined machine of that name for some time and it was thought that he had crashed off the coast of the Malay States. We, of course, saw nothing but I believe that a wheel or part of his undercarriage was subsequently found in that area.

Taiping was a pleasant little aerodrome, green but unexpectedly dry and hard compared with Alor Star and, by 9 o'clock the Harts, now reduced to eleven, were all neatly lined up beside the small square tarmac. On this occasion the Valentia came in so that our airmen could help with preparations for the final leg. There was no need for them to arrive in Singapore before us as we would be well looked after by the Seletar squadrons.

Our arrival at Seletar, the one and only RAF station on Singapore Island at that time, had been planned for 1 o'clock, three hours being allowed for the flight from Taiping which lay some 350 miles up country. The Squadron Leader took off at 10 o'clock, followed by the whole squadron in a long stream. After several wide circuits of Taiping, we had formed up into a loose formation, with the four Harts of B Flight over to the left of the Squadron Commander and my three Harts on his right. The first hour was uneventful and, for comfort, we kept well apart. But storm clouds were gathering ahead and an occasional flash of lightning could be seen high up in the heads of the cumulus cloud. As the sky darkened, we all closed in on the leading Flight and the CO took us down to 2,000 feet to keep in visual touch with the ground. There was no doubt that we were in for a severe tropical storm. It extended across our front as far as the eye could see in both directions. Going round it seemed out of the question which left only the alternatives of going through it or turning back to Taiping. We went on, plunging into a dense curtain of rain.

There was no question of maintaining any sort of squadron formation and so I reduced speed by about 10 miles per hour and moved out a few degrees to the right in order not to overrun the leading Flight. Robins and Eyre tucked themselves closely

288

in beside me but, even so, they were only just visible through the downpour. The sky grew darker and darker, accentuating the flashes of lightning which increased in frequency and intensity as we approached the centre of the storm. I caught the occasional glimpse of the jungle below with tufts of cloud sitting on the treetops and the rain thrashing down as only monsoon rain can. Map-reading was impossible and I could only concentrate on holding my course and hoping that we would be out of the storm before reaching Singapore.

A most uncomfortable half hour ensued but my two pilots stuck to me like glue and I was thankful that they were both experienced and undeterred by the conditions. Wesson was getting a good soaking in the rear cockpit as most of the water bouncing off the top wing went over my head and caught him full in the face.

'Get down and cover yourself with the cockpit cover; you can't help me at the moment,' I called out to him, putting my own seat down to its lowest position.

After forty minutes of this battering, when I calculated that we must be within twenty minutes or so of our destination, the rain slackened, it grew lighter ahead and we suddenly burst through into brilliant sunshine. The open sea lay below but the coast was no more than 3 miles away to the left. In my anxiety to avoid the remainder of the squadron, I had drifted some ten miles or so from our correct track. Altering course to make a landfall we were able to relax again, Robins and Eyre moving out into loose formation after the strain of the last forty minutes. There was no sign of the rest of the squadron whom I presumed were well ahead and to the left of me. Quite clearly our plans for a tidy squadron arrival over Singapore had gone awry and so I decided to hang back and revert to our procedure all along the route by arriving behind the other two Flights.

When we recrossed the coastline, it was obvious from the quantity of standing water in the fields that an immense amount of rain had fallen. A gentle steam was beginning to rise as the surface water started to evaporate in the humid air. In another few minutes the Straits of Johore, separating Singapore Island from the mainland, came into view and the causeway between the two lay dead ahead. After consulting my map – I was now on page 32 – I altered course for the position of Seletar aerodrome and signalled to Robins and Eyre to close up. If we had abandoned the squadron formation, at least A Flight would arrive in neat and tidy fashion. As the causeway disappeared below me, Seletar should have been in sight but I could see no signs of an aerodrome. The outstanding feature, five miles ahead, was a circular lake which did not appear on the map. Seletar was, at that time, the only aerodrome on the island – a large Royal Air Force station housing two torpedo bomber squadrons and a flying boat squadron and providing facilities for such airlines as had penetrated so far to the east. At least four more aerodromes were subsequently constructed at a much later date.

My eye caught the distant reflection of the sun on a wing and I spotted a Hart apparently descending to land in the lake ahead. By this time we were close enough to see that it was surrounded by hangars and, with a jolt, I realised that the lake was in fact Seletar – under water!

'Oh God, not again,' I said to Wesson. Don't panic, I thought to myself, there must be some answer to this one.

By this time, we were within two miles and the Hart which I had been watching landed in a cloud of spray; came to rest apparently undamaged and started to taxi to the perimeter.

'It's obviously hard underneath,' shouted Wesson. 'I can see more Harts standing over on the tarmac apron.'

What a relief!

'Count them as we fly over, will you?' I replied, putting the nose down into a gentle dive across the centre of the flooded aerodrome. Passing over at 1,000 feet I pulled up into a climb, crossed my hands as the breakaway signal and Robins and Eyre fell away on either side into a 'Prince of Wales feathers.'

Diving down to 1,000 feet again I joined the circuit and studied the landing area: it looked terrible but even during the short period since I first spotted it, the water had begun to drain away and grass was beginning to show in patches. Seletar was a perfect circle of about 1,000 yards diameter and domed like an inverted saucer. Large capacity monsoon drains were positioned at intervals of ten yards or so around the whole of the perimeter. The surface was so well graded that, after rain, every drain would be filling to capacity until the surface was dry. As the sub-surface was extremely hard, it remained virtually un-affected by the heaviest rain and could be guaranteed to be dry again within an hour of a storm. Nobody had informed us of these characteristics and so, understandably, the first sight of Seletar 'lake' was daunting, particularly after the unhappy ex-perience of the previous day at Alor Star.

However, reassured by the sight of the other Harts on the ground, I went in to land bearing in mind the need to keep the tail well down. I was slightly concerned for the safety of the spare propeller slung under my belly. It was well wrapped up but, even so, the propeller tips were delicate and might easily be damaged by mud and water. Well, so be it. There was nothing I could do but to land as carefully as possible. I selected what looked like a less wet area where the grass was showing above the water and, coming in a shade too fast, inevitably missed it, touching down in a good, deep puddle. Fountains of muddy water shot up above the wings on both sides, blinding me completely. No braking was necessary as the water pulled the Hart up in less than 100 yards. Water was dripping off everything as I came to rest. A great deal had shot up through the radiator opening below the engine and I could feel it slop-ping about on the floor of my cockpit. Remaining stationary, I watched Robins and Eyre come in behind me, both dis-appearing as they touched down like destroyers. We splashed our way slowly to the tarmac and fell into line with the other eight Harts of the squadron. A more muddy, bedraggled squadron I had never seen; so much for our intention of arriving in spick and span order. I wondered how our airmen would feel when they arrived and saw the sorry state of their aeroplanes which, only six days earlier, had left Risalpur in immaculate condition thanks to their hard work. Nevertheless we had made the long journey with one casualty and we hoped to have that back again before leaving for home. The outward flight had taken 28 hours and 45 minutes flying time which gave an average speed of a little more than 130 mph. We were tired but elated at what most of us regarded as a considerable achievement and also at the prospect of Christmas in the cosmopolitan atmosphere of Singapore, so different from the isolation of the North West Frontier where I had spent the previous three Christmases.

Christmas in Singapore
The Officers Mess at Seletar was a long, low, modern building standing on a bank overlooking the aerodrome with a fine view from the main windows out across the Johore Strait with the Supermarine Southampton flying boats riding at their moorings. All the visiting officers were put up in this Mess while our airmen had a most attractive palm leaf thatched barrack hut right on the shore of the Strait alongside the flying boat slipway. They were allowed to bathe from their hut although the water was sometimes far from clean. We were allocated half of one of the hangars for our maintainance work within 200 yards of the airmen's hut – nothing could have been more convenient or thoughtfully arranged.

Understandably our first wish was to see this great city of Singapore, and taste some of its well advertised delights – Raffles Hotel, the New World and the Old World and the Chinese restaurants. The list was long and time was short. The city lay across the island from Seletar, a journey of about 15 miles and transport was something of a problem. When discussing this on our first evening in the Mess, somebody said, 'Why don't you buy a car?'

'What, for less than four weeks?' I said.

However when this idea was developed, it was not quite as stupid as it sounded at first. Apparently second hand cars changed hands with remarkable rapidity and with very little loss of value.

The long and the short of it was that John Pope and I clubbed together and bought a white Morris Cowley saloon for £20 on the understanding that other members of the squadron shared the running costs and paid their fares into the city. Being all white, the car was at once christened 'the Milk Float' when a smiling Chinese delivered it to the Mess two days later and said he would be 'very happy' to buy it back before we left, which in fact he did, for £15. The Milk Float was extremely popular and whenever John and I were not taking full loads into the bright lights with us, we hired it out to other members of the squadron for a small charge with the result that, not only did John and I have free transport throughout our stay, but I believe we made a small profit out of the transaction.

I found Singapore a fascinating city. Although it has changed and expanded greatly since 1935 in so far as the buildings are concerned, the people, the waterfront and the Chinese quarters are still much as they were then. The astonishing cross section of people of all races was probably what created the greatest impression on me. A typical evening out, of which we had many, would start from the Mess at about 5 pm with a run into the city in the fully loaded Milk Float. We would window shop for an hour. It was three years since I had seen a modern shop and there was no end to the sights, sounds and smells of the shopping areas. At half past six we would foregather in the long bar at Raffles hotel, almost unchanged since the days of Sir Stamford Raffles himself. Many places in the Far East have been famous for their 'long bars' but none were better known than at Raffles. Gin slings, John Collins, Stengahs and Tiger beer – these were the particular specialities and we would spend a pleasant couple of hours cooling down under the slowly revolving ceiling fans with an evening breeze from the harbour coming through the palms in the garden.

The Milk Float would take us down to Chinatown for a meal in any one of the dozens of restaurants. Chinese food was another experience for me and I developed a taste for it which I have never lost. After the eternal curry and rice of India, the variety of Chinese dishes was astonishing. The need for a little exercise after dinner would sometimes point the Milk Float towards the Old World. I can best describe this as Singapore's answer to a 'Palais de Dance'. Rows of professional dancing partners or 'taxi dancers' occupied the tables nearest to the floor, girls of almost every nationality whose services could be hired for one dance at a time.

On entering the hall, one bought a book of ten tickets, each one of which entitled one to a dance with the hostess of one's choice. When asking her to dance, a ticket was handed to her and, at the end of the dance, she had to return to her table and await the next customer. No assignations, no drinks, nothing beyond the dance was allowed, so the system palled after a while. The girls were most attractive whether they were Chinese, Polynesian or European and they were, of course, superb dancers. But the whole thing was impersonal, commercial and lacked warmth and intimacy. It was an experience but one visit was quite enough and midnight found the Milk Float on its way back through the rubber trees and vegetable gardens to Seletar.

On the Sunday morning before Christmas, one of the Seletar officers said to me, 'Come down to the aerodrome and meet Princess Pearl; she's coming in from Holland in the KLM Douglas at 11.15.'

Princess Pearl was one of the pretty daughters of the White Rajah of Sarawak, and was on her way home to Borneo from a visit to London. She was a frequent visitor to the Seletar Mess and very popular with the officers, some of whom were quite disappointed when she later married Harry Roy, the London dance band leader. Promptly at 11.15 the silver Douglas DC2 came in to land. The forerunners of the famous Dakota, many of which are still flying 40 years later, the KLM DC2 had been christened 'The Flying Hotel' when, in the hands of those two famous aviators Parmentier and Moll, it had taken second place in the England to Australia race in 1934. This was the first time I had seen one and most impressive it was, setting entirely new standards of airline comfort, speed and reliability on world wide routes. While the Princess was clearing customs, I went aboard the aeroplane which seemed years ahead of anything I had seen with its retractable undercarriage, wing flaps and armchair comfort. Little did one know then that the Dakota was to become, surely, the most famous aircraft that has ever been built.

We gave Princess Pearl lunch in the ladies room in the Mess before she had to catch her connection to Sarawak where her father and earlier members of the Brooke family had reigned for many years in one of the most extraordinary episodes of the British Empire. It was no surprise to me that she was popular in the Mess: she was glamourous, sporting and wealthy, and very knowledgeable about flying. Before seeing her off that afternoon she asked to see one of our Harts which was as new to her as the DC2 had been to me. In spite of being Sunday afternoon, two of our airmen were working on my Hart and when this glamorous young woman climbed into it, one of them said in a quiet aside to me as we left,

'Will you be coming back with us, Sir?'

It sounds as if the sojourn in Singapore was one continuous round of pleasure but that was true only of the evenings. As soon as the Harts had been serviced after their gruelling journey, we were back in the air each day with a programme of flying which was quite unusual and very interesting. My own experience of flying over the sea was negligible and I had never flown before in exercises with the Navy. Practice bombing against a moving target towed behind a launch was one exercise which proved difficult and made us realise that it was not easy to hit a ship travelling at, say, 15 knots from a height of 6,000 feet. Our bomb aiming equipment was really quite inadequate for the purpose, and the results were disappointing. The Hart was much better for dive bombing and here my results were closer to those which I usually achieved back in India. The glassy surface of the sea reflecting the brilliant sunshine could be most misleading so that all of us spent some time low flying over the water to accustom ourselves to the strange conditions.

Several combined exercises were held in which the Harts worked with the torpedo bombers of 36 and 100 Squadrons in attacking ships of the Far East fleet, the Harts simulating bombing attacks from the higher altitudes while Vildebeestes carried out low level torpedo attacks. The tail end of the monsoon, which had given us such an unfriendly welcome, passed away to the south and we enjoyed almost perfect weather for the rest of our stay which helped to make the flying particularly enjoyable. After the grim austerity of the North West Frontier, I found great pleasure at the end of a flight and before landing in flying round the island, inspecting the big white P & O liners at anchor in the harbour, bound for Australia and London. The crowded junk harbour was always a scene of great activity and there were usually some interesting warships making their way up the Johore Strait to the Naval base. Whenever an aeroplane could be spared for half an hour, Robins, Eyre or I would take up one of our technical airmen for this 'round the houses' flight. They had very little opportunity to fly in the aeroplanes on which they lavished so many hours of hard work and it gave us a lot of pleasure to give them a conducted tour round Singapore. The Valentia was all right in its way but there was nothing like the rear cockpit of a Hart for getting an exciting impression of the island's many attractive features.

A few days before Christmas, Willie Devas arrived after a long and wearying train journey from Alor Star with his damaged aeroplane carefully packed on to an open platform truck. The truck was brought into a siding at Seletar, unloaded, and the Hart towed on its own wheels the few hundred yards to our hangar. It was a sorry sight: one lower wing crumpled and bent with the other missing, no propeller and many small fabric tears all over the fuselage and mainplanes.

'We have three weeks, including the Christmas holiday to get it flying again,' I said to the Flight Sergeant. 'Surely you'll never do it?'

He looked a little dubious.

'If the engine is undamaged and if we can find some wings, I think we can manage it. The chaps will have to work over Christmas but they won't mind that. They are not having a bad time here,' he added, 'I wish I could have had a trip like this as a young airman.'

The engine was out in a few hours and the Seletar workshops were able to check that the crankshaft had not been damaged by the shock it had received. The wings presented a serious problem. There were no Harts at Seletar and we naturally had no space to bring wings with us. It would take weeks if not months to get them by sea from our Depot at Karachi. In preference to that we would probably have despatched the damaged Hart back to Karachi by sea. But a solution was found. The Fleet Air Arm had some Osprey wings in storage. The Osprey was the naval variant of the Hart and a stock of spares was maintained in Singapore for squadrons disembarked from visiting carriers. Hart and Osprey wings were virtually identical, one minor difference being that those of the Osprey were finished in a darker, almost battleship grey dope as compared to our own silver finish. In fact, all the Singapore aeroplanes were painted in this darker colour and no silver dope was available. I think we had one small can with us, purely to repair small fabric tears during the journey.

The return flight was to begin on 10th January and it was 23rd of December when work started on the repair of K 2134. Allowing three days for flight testing and subsequent adjustments, the airmen had sixteen days, including all the holiday, to complete the work. It was decided that work should go on every morning except for Christmas Day which would allow the troops at least to have the afternoons and evenings free unless the programme fell behind schedule.

Christmas at Seletar was similar to that on any RAF station overseas; parties, Christmas draws, serving the airmen with their Christmas dinner, ridiculous sporting fixtures and the usual competition for the best decorated barrack block. One of my most vivid memories of that holiday was participating in a terrible game of rugby on Boxing Day. We visitors played against the crew of a visiting destroyer of the Royal Navy on the 'padang' in front of the Government buildings on the Singapore waterfront. Why we had to play in such a public place I never discovered but the game attracted a huge crowd and we were all encouraged to play a remarkably spirited game. 'Spirited' is the right word as I was told that the atmosphere inside the scrum, dominated by the fumes of Navy rum, was almost unbearable. I fortunately played in my usual position on the wing and spent most of the game endeavouring to bring down my powerful opponent who seemed permanently to have possession of the ball. The situation was not improved when, instead of lemons at half time, our opponents provided tots of rum for both teams and most of the spectators. I believe the Navy won 15–9 but my memory may well be at fault. The game was voted a success, but not to be repeated.

Work on K 2134 went very well. By New Year's Day the two wings had been installed, not without some difficulty as there were slight differences in the wing fittings from those of the standard Hart. With the holiday over, the work was soon finished and, on 7th January, the aeroplane was wheeled out for an engine test. It was an extraordinary sight with two silver wings and two grey ones, a mass of grey patches all over the fuselage and one odd wheel. However, there it was in one piece again and, hopefully, flyable. The engine test on the ground proved entirely satisfactory and I decided to give it an air test on the following morning.

LAC Hackney, who was the rigger on K 2134 and had done most of the repair work, came up with me so that he could observe any peculiarities in the rigging that might need adjustment. I hoped the test would be no more than a formality but my hopes were not to be fulfilled. She taxied smoothly and all the controls responded satisfactorily until I took off. Half way across the aerodrome I found myself having to push the stick farther and farther over to the right as the left wing tried to go down. Being lightly loaded, we were airborne quickly and I could keep her level at full throttle only with the stick hard over to the right. As soon as the speed reached 100 mph, I eased back the throttle which took a little of the pressure off the stick but I could not turn to the right without skidding round with excessive rudder.

A left hand circuit was in operation and so I allowed the aeroplane to turn gently to the left, but with the stick well over to the right. There was nothing for it but to continue round to the left in a gentle turn and to land again before anything more serious happened. We landed quite normally because, as soon as the throttle was closed, most of the pressure came off the stick, much to the relief of my aching arm.

'Sorry, Sir,' said Hackney, 'that won't do. I don't quite understand it because all the rigging tolerances are correct.'

We had a conference around the aeroplane which was clearly not fit to fly back to India in that state. Finally the Flight Sergeant, who was himself a rigger, said, 'There's no doubt that the fuselage is twisted. The wings are correctly rigged themselves and I've checked Hackney's work, but if their points of attachment to the fuselage have been slightly distorted by the crash, the whole structure will be out of alignment. We can strain the rigging wires a little and probably eradicate some of the wing down tendency, but nothing can be done here about a twisted fuselage.'

The airmen worked for two more hours and that afternoon I took the Hart up for a further test. There was a great improvement to the extent that no longer was it necessary to hold the left wing up continually. Pulling and straining the rigging wires had introduced another peculiarity. Although she would fly without having to hold a wing up, she did not fly straight. I had the odd feeling that she was crabbing along with the nose over to the left of centre. I took her up to 3,000 feet and flew as accurate a compass course as I could contrive. There was no doubt, and my passenger confirmed it, that I was looking through the right hand side of the windscreen and the nose of the Hart was offset a few degrees to the left when holding a straight course. And so we had the situation that the 'wings were flying straight but the fuselage was not' which seemed to confirm the Flight Sergeant's diagnosis that it was twisted. I completed a thorough but gentle test – no spinning or violent manoeurvres – and decided that, uncomfortable though it might be, K 2134 was safe enough to fly home. I also decided, not without reluctance, that perhaps I should fly it back myself as I was already becoming accustomed to its oddities. Our last few days were spent in packing up and loading the aeroplanes for the return flight. We put as little extra equipment as possible into K 2134 to ensure that she was as light as we could contrive in order to alleviate the strain on the pilot's arms. No more flying was done and all twelve Harts were spick and span – except for the blotchy appearance of the damaged one – by the morning of our departure. John Pope and I sold the Milk Float back to its original owner for the promised £15 after a final run into the city. We had done 350 miles at virtually no cost.

Return to India

In many respects the squadron was sorry to leave Singapore where we had all been made so welcome and where we had spent an enjoyable and most unusual Christmas. The return flight did not seem quite the adventure of the outward journey: the unknown had been challenged and conquered and, as we were flying back along the same route in accordance with the same timetable, we felt that we knew the problems.

Promptly at 10 o'clock on 10th January, Squadron Leader Butler took off into a cloudless blue sky, followed by the other eleven Harts. We formed up into squadron formation out over the sea and, in contrast to our arrival four weeks earlier, flew over Seletar in a neat farewell formation which we maintained over Singapore city and harbour before turning up country over the rubber plantations and dense jungle of Johore. The close formation was held for a further ten minutes by which time rubber plantations and scattered homesteads were giving way to thick jungle. Butler then waved us away and we returned to the separate Flights in loose formation which had been maintained during the outward journey. Being the rearmost Flight, I slowed down in order to reach Taiping well behind the others.

The pleadings of Willie Devas to fly his own aeroplane back had triumphed and so there he was in K 2134, flying slightly sideways on my left. Wesson and I were happily back in our own Hart but relieved of the encumbrance of the propeller under the belly. That was now turning steadily on K 2134. The only stipulation I had made in agreeing to Willie's plea was that, should his lame duck become too uncomfortable, we would all take turns and relieve Willie on various legs of the flight. There is nothing more tiring than flying an aeroplane for three hours which cannot be trimmed to fly 'hands off', and which has to have one wing held up or the nose held down continually.

That first day of the return journey was, in my opinion, the most pleasant and relaxing of the whole journey. The weather was perfect, the sea blue and the jungle green and more benign in appearance than reality. The temperature at 6,000 feet was around 60°F and the air smooth. Wesson could be heard through the speaking tube whistling quietly to himself. It was almost with reluctance that we broke formation and slipped down to land on the exceptionally green grass of Taiping. Even Alor Star, later that day, had relented and the aerodrome was firm and the wind light as I watched Willie Devas make a perfect three point landing as if to make amends for his earlier mishap on that short runway which this afternoon looked so innocuous. We spent a pleasant evening thanking our Imperial Airways hosts suitably for the great help they had given to Willie in getting his Hart on to the Singapore train. I spent the night in the house of Mr Jenkins, a Captain Kettle figure with a trim goatee beard, who was one of the airline's representatives and a most congenial host. It was a hot and sultry night but his

301

large open-plan wooden house, built on stilts, was airy and spacious.

Just before thanking my host and going off to bed he said, 'Would you like a Dutch wife?'

Thinking back to the earlier offer made to me in Mergui, I hesitated. Seeing my predicament, Jenkins roared with laughter, his goatee beard shaking with mirth.

'No, not that – I don't keep any of those lying about. A Dutch wife is a long bolster which we often put between our legs on a hot night to stop them sticking together with sweat.'

I grinned a bit sheepishly and accepted his offer on the basis of trying anything once. However, after a few experiments, I decided it was not for me: the sarong which many of us had adopted in lieu of pyjamas was the coolest and least irksome rig for such nights.

Four hours flying next day took us back to Mergui and another night with the 'uncrowned King of Burma' who did not, on this occasion, offer me another of his Burmese wives and so I was spared the embarrassment of turning him down twice in one month. John Pope and I strolled through the town in the evening and found a street which contained nothing but Buddhist temples; at least a dozen of them side by side. Each one was beautifully and ornately decorated with wood carving and through their open doors we could see Buddha sitting, faintly illuminated by candlelight with his eyes glowing. These temples gave the impression of great wealth which contrasted strangely with the rest of Mergui which was obviously not a place of great wealth. John and I did not venture into any of the temples, even with our shoes off: we felt it might give offence, although the Burmese were so friendly and cheerful that I am sure it would not have done so – most attractive people for whom the arrival and departure of a whole noisy squadron was an event of almost carnival proportions.

The short flight to Rangoon was uneventful, the glittering golden dome of Shwe Dagon coming into view from thirty miles away. The 60th Rifles once again gave our officers a comfortable and hospitable night during which Squadron Leader Butler presented the regiment with a silver table model of a Hart. After refuelling at Akyab and an hour's delay while Sergeant Eyre's plugs were cleaned, I was quite sorry to turn west at Chittagong and leave the green countryside of Burma to head out across the Bay of Bengal for India once more. I took the Flight up to 10,000 feet again over the water to give that small additional chance of reaching land if anything went wrong, particularly as Eyre's engine seemed to have developed a tendency to oil up. My lost Waterman fountain pen still lay somewhere far below but it had been replaced very cheaply in Singapore and the replacement was securely buttoned in my shirt pocket. That particular lesson had been well learned.

The muddy, sluggish waters of the Hooghli delta came into view on time and we began a gentle descent towards Calcutta. Reducing the engine revs, I started to wind in the radiator with the large hand wheel on my left. It jammed and I could move the radiator neither in nor out. For some reason it had jammed in its runners below the engine and there was nothing to be done about it. Fortunately it was in the half way position and there was no risk of the engine boiling on the way down to Dum Dum, now less than half an hour away. The airmen found themselves busy during that overnight stop. One of the C Flight Harts had picked up a stone which had damaged the tip of its propeller. This had to be changed for one of the spare ones. My radiator fault was quite straightforward but it took more than an hour to rectify. The Hart radiator was held in position in its runners by strong, cotton covered elastics, one of which had broken on my radiator, causing it to jam. We were carrying spare elastic and the trouble was put right before nightfall. All the aeroplanes were beginning to show the effects of a long period away from their well equipped home base and an increasing number of temporary repairs were needed at each stop. However, with only two more days to go and twelve still in the air, we kept our fingers crossed against any major trouble.

303

After the cosmopolitan pleasures of Singapore, Calcutta offered little diversion that night. Most of us were pretty well broke and also beginning to feel the effect of long days of concentrated flying. That day's flight from Rangoon to Calcutta, with seven hours in the air and the refuelling at Akyab in the middle of the morning had, in fact, proved to be the longest and in many ways the most arduous of the whole flight. So we were content to stay in the hotel and discuss our experiences over a few jars of beer before turning in. Until that discussion, I hadn't realised how many incidents there had been which could have resulted in more accidents than we had had. Bill Brackenbury had a brake seizure on one wheel, at Victoria Point which had swung him round and a wing had just touched the ground but no damage resulted. A tail skid had fractured at Rangoon but, fortuitously, the bottom of the rudder had not touched the ground, and we carried a spare skid. Finally, at Akyab George Brown had accidentally dropped an empty petrol drum from the top wing which had knocked a hole in his lower wing. He had managed to tape it over to get him to Calcutta. We had undoubtedly had our incidents but they were of the kind to be expected when taking twelve quite fragile high performance machines through so many rough and poorly developed landing grounds (some of them were not fit to be classed as aerodromes).

I asked Willie Devas to lead on the next leg to Gaya and we went up to 11,000 feet to see whether map reading on the small scale maps was any easier at high altitude. From a position behind Willie, I could see quite clearly that K 2134 was undoubtedly crabbing along with its nose well to the left of centre. As I said to him when we landed, 'You'll never learn to fly straight again after this!'

'I'm getting used to it, and the view ahead is much better,' was his reply.

Map reading certainly was easier at 11,000 feet in the clear conditions over central India, but it was also intensely cold in our tropical kit and that evening a few comments about brass monkeys and the unnecessary freezing of certain parts of the anatomy were bandied about. When I rejoined with the comment that our average speed had been much higher, somebody replied:

'What's the hurry anyway; we've five years to do out here.'

There seemed to be no answer to that, so I let the matter drop.

Squadron Leader Butler had decided that we would fly as a complete squadron throughout the last day so that we could arrive at the RAF station at Ambala, and finally back at Risalpur in good order. Whereas this relieved me of any need to navigate, the relief was to some extent offset by the effort of having to maintain, however loosely, a squadron formation for more than six hours. All the way to Ambala we flew in Flights line astern, each Flight stepped down by a few hundred feet from that ahead to avoid buffeting from the slipstream. Flying westward as we were, the sun was not in our eyes and this position was comfortable: I was able to keep B Flight just above my top wing and some 100 yards ahead until we closed up into a squadron V formation about 30 miles short of Ambala, cruising over the centre of the aerodrome in very respectable shape at 2,000 feet.

What a pleasure it was to have the mid morning refuelling carried out by airmen from tankers instead of having to hump those dreaded cans up onto the top wing ourselves. We were able to go down to the 28 Squadron Mess to have an early lunch before the final leg of our journey, timed to start at midday.

During the afternoon the country below began to take on a more familiar look as we entered the Punjab. Two hours after leaving Ambala, we passed Rawalpindi with the Murree hills plainly visible to the north. It was the first time I had seen snow over the area where the Hill Depot at Lower Topa lay. It was getting much colder in the cockpit too and twice in the past hour I had wound the radiator in a couple of notches to keep the engine temperature up. The khaki drill which had been our dress throughout, was becoming inappropriate and I was looking forward to at least two months of cool weather in blue uniform. It is only when one has experienced climate with little seasonal change, such as Singapore, that one appreciates the rotation of seasons to which one had become accustomed at home. By the time we crossed the Indus near Attock bridge, I could feel the first goose pimples of the winter under my overalls.

Attock was the point at which we had been told to close up into squadron formation for the final run into Risalpur some 30 miles ahead. The familiar straight, dusty road to Peshawar lay below as I watched Joe Shaw move to the left with B Flight. I took A Flight to the right and accelerated slightly to catch up the leaders. The air was calm and smooth, excellent for formation flying, as the Squadron Leader led us in a gentle descent to cross the centre of Risalpur at 2,000 feet. It may seem strange to call Risalpur 'home', but that is how we all regarded it after 38 days away and a great deal of flying to put in our log books. The return flight had taken 29 hours and 20 minutes, exactly 35 minutes longer than the outward trip. This gave an overall average speed of 133 mph. Owing to the debacle at Alor Star, we had managed to fly only eleven Harts into Singapore but we had the satisfaction of getting all twelve back again and, even if two mainplanes had been left on the scrap heap at Seletar, this was a successful conclusion to the whole exercise. As we taxied in towards our hangar, we could see a large banner displayed, 'Well done 39 – Welcome home.' Most of the station had turned out to see us arrive but perhaps the nicest gesture was a pat on my helmet from Wesson in the back seat as the propeller finally came to rest. He had been the greatest support and we shook hands as we wearily climbed down from our cockpits.

It only remained to spin the yarns, count up the many lessons learned, clean up the aeroplanes and return to our normal work of policing the Frontier. Willie Devas had had a somewhat uncomfortable flight in K 2134 but he coped very well with its peculiarities. When our riggers got down to work on it, they found considerable distortion in the fuselage which was beyond Risalpur's resources to rectify. In due course, Willie flew it down to the Aircraft Depot at Karachi and returned with a new

Hart. Later we heard that K 2134 had been written off and stripped down for spares, but the important thing was that we had brought her back safely from Singapore.

CHAPTER 20

LAST OF THE SUMMER HEAT

The period November to March in India was always a great time for sport. It was cool enough for football and hockey, and for rugby wherever sufficient grass existed to make an acceptable pitch. Tennis and squash racquets on open air courts continued throughout the year. Indoor squash courts would have been quite unbearable during hot weather. In addition there was golf of extremely variable quality and rough shooting for those who were sufficiently patient and skilful enough to hit the fast, high flying quail and snipe which abounded in the rocky sandhills bordering the 'Vale of Peshawar'. This high flown name for a barren stony plain with, admittedly, some areas of cultivation and a few stunted trees, always amused me but it was probably no more unsuitable than the name of the principal road in the cantonment at Peshawar – The Mall. For the really keen horseman who was happy to chase a rag soaked in aniseed, the Peshawar Vale Drag hunted almost daily during these pleasant months.

After a particularly successful athletics meeting during which we won the Patiala Trophy from Kohat and Peshawar, I said to my colleagues one evening,

'It seems a pity to break up our track team which has done so well. Why don't we go pot hunting during the next two months?'

Most of the Army brigades and smaller units scattered around the Frontier held annual sports days at this time of the year and many included invitation races and relays in their programmes to add interest to the day's events. My idea caught on and six of us who could perform at varying distances from one hundred yards to a mile, banded together and entered for a number of these invitation races at Nowshera, Peshawar, Landi Kotal, Bannu and elsewhere.

The team appeared in a smart strip of black vests and shorts with a white stripe, made up by our Risalpur 'dhersi' (tailor). Our favourite event was a mixed relay event such as 2 × 200 yards and 2 × 440 yards at which we found ourselves almost unbeatable with the result that we gained quite a reputation. It was a highly successful 'pot hunting' venture and the total bag at the end of several weeks and half a dozen meetings amounted to no less than thirty three cups, tankards and medals. We finished our round of events on 1st April after the last, and one of the most successful meetings, at Landi Kotal, which was the home of the garrison responsible for the security of the Khyber Pass. Although I was not to know it at the time, that was the last competitive half mile race I ever ran – and incidentally won in 2 minutes 3 seconds on a 'mutti' track.

At the end of the meeting, our small team drove down the

Khyber Pass to Peshawar in the cool of the evening, past the forbidding exterior of Jamrud Fort which stood sentinel over the entrance to the Pass. Even in the clear light of the sun setting behind us, there was a menacing look to the blue hills on either side – the dangerous Tirah to the south and Mohmand territory, the scene of so many operations, to the north.

'This is one road off which we do not stray,' I said to Dan Carew beside me in the MG.

'I agree. There have been some nasty incidents on this road. Isn't that where Molly Ellis was taken from Kohat in 1923?'

'Yes, and its also where George Shakespeare crashed some years ago: not a nice area.'

Tired after our labours on the running track we stopped at the Peshawar Club and had a few drinks followed by an excellent dinner to celebrate the end of our season of 'pot hunting'. Dan Carew was the toast of the party having won eleven of the thirty three trophies including six personal victories in invitation sprint events. He was a magnificent sprinter and, given a good track and favourable conditions, could get very close to the 10 second mark for 100 yards. It was quite a sight to see him streaking through the field on the last leg of a sprint relay.

Winter was over. Early April saw the thermometer rising higher every day and it was soon apparent that 1936 was going to produce a long and very hot summer. Although I say summer, in fact the seasons in India were never alluded to as winter, summer, etc, but always as 'the hot weather' and 'the cold weather'. Why this was so, I have never fully understood although the expression 'winter' does seem somewhat inappropriate in the tropics. Equally the term 'summer' to our British way of thinking, connotes warm, pleasant weather, far removed from the blistering and unrelenting heat on the plains of India. In England we all prefer the summer. In India, particularly in 1936, we undoubtedly preferred the 'cold weather'.

By the end of April, the midday temperature was getting up to the 100° mark. By mid May, it was approaching 110° and in

June it climbed in the 120°s. This was a hateful period. Flying, even at six o'clock in the morning, was exhausting and uncomfortable and it was hell for the airmen working on the aeroplanes inside the hangars with no cooling of any kind. The pace of everything and everybody slowed noticeably, tempers were short and even after changing clothes as often as five times a day, one was permanently bathed in sweat. Even the luke warm water in the swimming pool afforded little relief.

Whether the athletic activity had weakened my resistance or not, I do not know, but in June, I fell ill at the very hottest period of that dreadful hot weather. Diagnosis of tropical diseases was, at that time, an even less exact science than it is today, but it was thought that I had sandfly fever. Whatever it was, it produced a raging fever with an astronomical temperature for a few days. I was incarcerated in bed in my bungalow as there was no hospital nearer than Peshawar and that was only used for serious and dangerous illnesses. The station sick quarters at Risalpur were not designed to keep patients in bed except for a brief moment en route to Peshawar hospital and so Dick Stewart, the medical officer, had no alternative but to entrust me to the tender care of Hukmud Khan.

I tossed and turned in the sweltering little room on the charpoy which got harder every hour for a week before the fever abated leaving me a pale and shaking wreck. What one would have given for some form of refrigeration or air-conditioning, but all that was years away. The ceiling fan churned the hot air around while Hukmud did his best to cool the room by pouring buckets of water over the split bamboo screens which hung down in front of the verandah. This produced some cooling by evaporation, but the effect of reducing the temperature from 120° to, say, 115°; was hardly worth his effort. He produced a large wooden ice box, placed it in the bathroom and ordered a 'maund' of ice to be delivered each day. This helped a lot although it had all melted and run away down the bathroom drainage channel by mid afternoon. We were then thrown back upon the resources of the 'chargil'. A 'chargil' was a large

311

earthenware waterpot kept filled with water on the verandah. Evaporation through the pottery surface had a cooling effect on the water and one of these chargils was kept on every bungalow verandah. Hukmud was a tower of strength and he must have suffered considerably himself as Indians dislike the intense heat almost as much as Europeans. It was not unusual to see Hukmud sweating as much as I was at times.

The worst was not over. As the fever abated, I developed jaundice and turned a sickly shade of yellow. The most upsetting part of jaundice was the intense feeling of depression which set in. Confined to my bungalow for a further week or more, I must have been unapproachable and poor Hukmud suffered even more, this time from my irritability.

Military doctors in India at that time did their best but they were severely restricted, not so much by the inadequacy of medical knowledge of the more obscure tropical diseases, but by the paucity of their equipment and facilities. It was not uncommon at Risalpur, for instance, for patients to be asked to take their own medicine bottles, cotton wool and even bandages along to the sick quarters when reporting sick. The number of HP sauce bottles to be found in barrack rooms and bungalows filled with various kinds of medicine was legion and it was a source of considerable embarrassment to the few hard worked doctors.

For some reason, perhaps the excessive heat, that summer of 1936 produced more illness among airmen and officers than usual, and I was certainly not the only sufferer sweating on his lonely charpoy through the interminably long days and nights. The few wives of the married officers who had not left the plains for the hot weather were kindness itself in visiting the sick bachelors, bringing fruit, books and, what was much more important, some cheerful comfort and encouragement. During one of these visits, Betty Marshall pressed me to join her husband and herself for some sick leave at a bungalow in Gulmarg which they had taken for the month of July.

'There's masses of room, and you'll be company for my sister,' she said.

312

It was an attractive offer on two counts: Dick Stewart had insisted that I get away into a cool climate for at least a short spell.

'I will not pass you fit to fly until you have had a holiday away from this awful heat.'

That was his ultimatum and I felt in no condition to challenge it. The second attraction was Betty's sister, Kathleen, who was a pretty eighteen year old who had somehow outstayed the usual fishing fleet period and had continued to live with the Marshalls through the hot weather. With all these pressures upon a sickly convalescent, what could he do but gratefully accept Betty's invitation? In any case, the depressing effect of jaundice made me most reluctant to go away on holiday by myself. If I could not throw myself back into a job of work again, then I felt that the company of friends on holiday was essential.

Early July came and Dick Stewart pronounced me fit to go away in spite of the sickly shade of yellow which was a frequent cause of comment in the Mess. 'Chinese Lee' and 'a throwback to your ancestors' were among the politest shafts of wit. Hukmud Khan needed a holiday after his weeks of attention to my wants and, as the Marshalls had their own bearer with them in Kashmir, there was no need for me to take mine. The thought of another drive up there in the MG was too much and so I decided to leave the car in a Rawalpindi garage for some work to be done on it while I took a seat in a taxi up to Kashmir.

Hukmud was a Pathan from a village north of the Khyber and had not been home for twelve months or more. When telling him of my plans, I asked him what he did on his holidays at home.

He said, 'I shoot, sahib.'

Jocularly I replied, 'I hope you don't shoot at aeroplanes, Hukmud.'

'Yes, sahib, but they are too fast: too high: very difficult.'

I was horrified.

'You mean you shoot at me, up there?'

313

'No, sahib, not at you: at aeroplanes.'

There seemed no suitable rejoinder to this as I digested our conversation. I suppose his attitude was not all that illogical. After all, I could well be sent out to bomb his village because his old father had overstepped the mark in some blood feud with a neighbouring village. What more reasonable that the old man — and his son, Hukmud, if he happened to be at home – should shoot back at the bombers. He did not seem to identify me with one of those aeroplanes at which he occasionally loosed off his ancient 'bandook'. Still, I was a bit taken aback by his revelation.

What a relief it was to pick up my sick bed, pack it into the back of the MG and set off bright and early one morning for Rawalpindi. It was hot and clammy and I felt weak and lethargic. The jaundice was clearly going to take time to shake off but the prospect of the invigorating climb into the mountains was already beginning to have its effect as I left Nowshera behind, pulled down my goggles against the dust and set off down the Frontier road.

At Rawalpindi, the Morris agents took over the car to give it a top overhaul while I was away. My bonus was free garaging for at least a fortnight. My taxi seat was booked for the following morning which allowed me a cool and comfortable night at Flashmans hotel. Although air conditioning had not yet arrived, Flashmans at least had refrigerators and the rooms were as well cooled as was possible with ceiling and table fans. It was certainly a great deal cooler than 46 Bungalow at Risalpur and I spent the first comfortable night for many weeks.

Punctually at 7 o'clock the following morning, a yellow Chevrolet taxi drew up at the front door. It was an open tourer with a somewhat dilapidated hood raised and a cheerful Sikh driver wearing a bright yellow 'puggaree' to match his vehicle. I had two companions for the journey to Srinagar, an Indian doctor, Dr Ram, who was in the front seat and a British civilian from the Government offices in Rawalpindi. Our bedrolls were packed between the mudguards and the bonnet and our suitcases piled on to a luggage grid at the rear. It all looked pretty insecure but nobody seemed particularly worried and we set off after introducing ourselves. Our driver, Amarit Singh, drove with the panache common to all Sikh drivers, but he drove well and knew the road intimately. After a period of driving from the back seat and hoping that we would not meet another Sikh, also driving with panache on one of the hairpin bends on the Murree road, I stopped worrying and started to enjoy the magnificent scenery and the rapidly cooling air. Murree and the Hill Depot at Lower Topa dropped astern and we plunged down to a long twisting road to the frontier post at Domel. Although I missed my MG, the large taxi was far more comfortable and rode the ruts and potholes much better. The various dried up river beds were just as bad as during my previous journey but the Chevrolet had twice the ground clearance of the MG and crashed its way over them, our driver having complete disregard for his springs and tyres while we passengers clung on to our hats and watched the luggage fearfully. The river bed which had caused my downfall a year ago was still the worst of them, so bad that even Amarit Singh slowed down and treated it with some respect.

As we chatted between spine shaking bumps Dr Ram looked at me.

'You have jaundice, I think?'

'Yes,' I replied, 'I'm going to Gulmarg to recover.'

'Ah well,' he said, 'the Kashmir air will soon put you right – the best mecidine in the world.'

This was cheering news and confirmed Dick Stewart's opinion.

Strinagar was reached at 5 o'clock where a night at the Club had been arranged for me before going on to Gulmarg the following day. My bedroll was covered with dust and dirt which had penetrated everywhere. Although the Club servants were very good and cleaned me up as best they could, I missed Hukmud Khan's attention and even regretted giving him his 'shooting' holiday.

The Club ordered a very battered Kashmiri taxi to take me up to Ferozpur the following morning from where the now familiar pony trek through the pine forest to Gulmarg started. Considering the appalling state of the road up to Kashmir, my journey had been reasonably comfortable and sharing the cost as far as Srinagar with my two travelling companions had made it considerably cheaper than bringing the MG. By midday I reached the Marshall's bungalow after pausing at Nedou's hotel to discover its whereabouts. It was distinctly chilly in the Gulmarg valley as the sun had not broken through that morning. My porters were swathed in head cloths and old Army greatcoats in spite of their exertions and I had donned two sweaters on the way up. But it was a grand feeling to have goose pimples again and to breathe in the cold, pine scented air. Even the yellow from my skin seemed to have started to fade and the Marshalls were kind enough not to draw attention to it.

Their bungalow, a comfortable log cabin like all the others in the valley, lay half a mile from the hotel, backing on to the pine forest and facing down across the fourteenth fairway of the golf course towards the river. A big log fire was burning in an open grate in the sitting room, fed from a huge pile of pine logs stacked behind the cabin.

'You look much better than we expected,' was Betty's comforting greeting. 'This air, good food and plenty of exercise will get you fit in no time.'

She was right. The Marshalls did not play golf and so I had not brought my clubs. We spent most of our days for the two weeks of my stay trekking and climbing through the forests and mountains. Bill Marshall and I took it in turns to carry a rifle on all these outings. It was not safe to be without one as the possibility always existed of coming face to face with a brown bear. It was unusual but not unknown for them to come down as low as the valley in the summer months and they were shy animals who would not attack human beings unless provoked, frightened or wounded – but you never knew when you might come across one and it was wise to be prepared. In fact we did

316

not see a bear during the whole fortnight: only monkeys and various species of deer. Trekking, and certainly climbing, were exhausting pastimes at this altitude of more than 10,000 feet but I was getting stronger every day. Some evenings were spent dining and dancing at Nedou's where there were always plenty of other friends from the plains. When too tired after the day's walking to struggle over to the hotel, poker and drinks round the log fire passed the evening most happily. Young Kathleen's education was enhanced, or perhaps advanced is the right word, by learning the intricacies of liar dice in the evenings, by learning to fire a rifle with considerable accuracy during our walks and by starting to play golf under my inexpert guidance on the rabbit's course.

Three days before it was time for me to leave the Marshalls a telegram arrived from Risalpur. How telegrams reached Gulmarg I never discovered but it must have been a lengthy and tortuous business as this one took four days to arrive at the bungalow. It said simply, 'Selected for CFS course commencing January.' Wonderful news which called for a celebration dinner for my hosts at Nedou's that evening.

Being near the end of my fourth year out of Cranwell, I was due to specialise in either engineering, armament, navigation or signals. Any one of these specialisations would have meant leaving flying for a long period which I was most reluctant to do at the time. There was, however, one escape route and that was to apply to become a flying instructor which, although it might be disadvantageous to my promotion prospects, would ensure that I carried on flying. Turning a blind eye to the future, I had put in my application for the instructors course at the Central Flying School, then at Upavon on Salisbury Plain. As this coincided with the early days of the expansion of the RAF to match Hitler's rise to power, flying instructors were badly needed and so my application was accepted.

That telegram was just what was needed to complete my convalescence. The remaining few weeks of that trying hot weather were almost welcome as I took my leave of Bill, Betty and Kathleen and made my way back to Risalpur with a last look at that beautiful valley of Gulmarg over the rump of a hill pony.

Perhaps, I thought, as I collected my MG in Rawalpindi, it had been unwise to spend quite a sum on the overhaul as I would now have to sell it in less than four months. On the other hand, Ghulam Sarwar of Peshawar, had offered to give me a credit note against a new car at home and the work done on it would undoubtedly enhance its value. Whether it was that overhaul or my frame of mind, I don't know, but the little car had never run more sweetly than it did on that journey up the Frontier road from Rawalpindi to Risalpur.

CHAPTER 21

'THERE'S A TROOPSHIP JUST LEAVING BOMBAY'

Before World War II all trooping, or the movement of sailors, soldiers and airmen to and from overseas theatres was carried out entirely by sea in a fleet of half a dozen troopships operated for the Government by a commercial shipping line. These ships, of around 15,000 tons, were mostly named after English counties such as *Somersetshire, Dorsetshire, Devonshire, Oxfordshire* – painted white with a wide blue band running horizontally around them – for all the world like a packet of a famous brand of margarine at that time. There were few servicemen who did not experience the discomfort, the tough crowded conditions, the smell and the unappetising food of these ships during their careers. Their reputation was infamous and deservedly so.

At least the Government had the humanity not to send men and families into the tropics in these ships during the hot weather. That would have been totally unbearable: they were bad enough when the climate was reasonably cool during what came to be known as 'the trooping season'. As far as India was concerned, this lasted from October to March during which period there was always one, and sometimes two, troopships reserved primarily for the RAF. The remainder, numbering up to about half a dozen each year were Army troopships in which individual airmen might be shipped. Karachi and Bombay were the Indian ports used for trooping and Southampton was the usual home port. A lucky few whose postings did not marry up with the troopship timetable would be given passages in P & O or other passenger liners. Being expensive, these were not popular with the authorities, but they delighted the individuals as my outward trip in the SS *California* had pleased me. Many a subterfuge was dreamed up to avoid passage by troopship but most of them failed. Senior officers and their families were the most likely to succeed because the troopships had extremely limited accommodation for those who rated rather more spacious and comfortable quarters than junior officers and airmen.

In order to be available for the CFS course in early January it was essential for me to leave India during the first half of November if I was to get the month's leave to which I was entitled. The RAF troopship, with its home draft of airmen was timed to sail from Karachi towards the end of November and would, therefore, be too late for my timetable. When I heard this news in September, I had visions of completing my Indian tour in style with a first class passage in one of those fine P & O ships homeward bound from Australia. Disillusion was not long in coming when the Adjutant called me into his office and said, 'Bad luck, you've been allotted a passage in the *Somersetshire*.

She is taking the 10th Hussars home from Karachi on the 8th November. I came out in her so I say again, bad luck. However you should get at least six weeks leave before your course starts at Upavon in mid January.'

'Oh well,' I said, 'at least I will be going in the right direction and even the 10th Hussars won't have their horses on board.'

'Don't be too sure of that' was his parting shot.

As about a quarter of the station changed over during each trooping season and as most of those changing over came and went in the same RAF troopship, the upheaval was considerable. Nevertheless it meant stability for the rest of the year which ensured continuity and was, in many ways, preferable to the unending trickle of comings and goings which became the pattern with air trooping in later years. It also gave the excuse for a tremendous farewell party when all those going home by whatever ships were well and truly 'seen off' by those remaining.

This boat party in 1936 was held at the end of October as a small number of airmen were to be in the *Somersetshire* with me, the main draft going in the *Dorsetshire* on the 20th November. It was much too large a party to hold in a canteen and so one of the squadron hangars was cleared of aeroplanes for the night, decorated, with a band rostrum at one end and a large bar at the other. The centre-piece consisted of a splendid plywood mock up of a troopship, on the deck of which all those who were going home had to congregate at some point during the party and receive a cheerful and alcoholic farewell, being towed out of the hangar on to the tarmac accompanied by clouds of black smoke from the funnel.

Before the party, an attractive and clever memento was produced by an airman in the Photographic Section. He had drawn a picture of the *Dorsetshire* and in every porthole and along the deck rails he had glued tiny photographs of all those leaving Risalpur. This completed drawing was photographed and the prints sold for a few annas. Every man in the ship was clearly recognisable and so popular was it that several reprints were demanded. I was very sorry not to be going in the *Dorsetshire* myself but it would have meant losing most of my home leave.

Like every party for all ranks, the preponderance of men over women was enormous, probably 600 men and 80 women on this occasion. Consequently the poor girls were danced off their feet while the men spent most of the evening propped up against the bar at the end of the hangar opposite to the band. The dance band of the Duke of Wellington's regiment from Nowshera had been hired for the occasion – probably the best dance band in the district. Our own station dance band filled in the gaps with the half dozen foxtrots and charlestons which comprised its somewhat limited repertoire. Like every one of those boat parties, this one produced the usual mixture of sincerity and hypocrisy. Many an airman, full of Murree beer, showed the deepest regret at saying goodbye to an NCO or an officer whose guts he had hated for years. All rancour seemed to have been put aside for this great evening – not that there was ever very much in an isolated community like Risalpur where good relationships were so important. Even that 'arch fiend' the Station Warrant Officer became a warm and kindly man as he unbent and lifted his elbow with some of his problem airmen.

At the height of the party, all those who were going home were invited to climb aboard the wooden troopship and to sing the traditional song:

> 'There's a troopship just leaving Bombay,
>   Bound for a Blighty shore,
> Heavily laden with time expired men
>   Bound for the land they adore.'

This opening verse was followed by many more, mostly unprintable, whereupon a mighty cloud of black smoke belched from the cardboard funnel and, with a great cheer, the vessel moved out of the hangar and on to the tarmac.

'Don't stand too close to the funnel,' said Bill Marshall, 'or you'll have your Mess kit ruined with soot.'

Just in time – as a cloud of soot was precipitated skywards which smothered most of us. We disembarked and rejoined the party.

This was the one occasion in the year when the rule that officers should not remain at a troops' dance for more than two hours was always broken. It was about 2 am when I walked back towards 46 Bungalow, the exciting prospect of going home perhaps a little dimmed by regret at leaving so many friends whom I might never see again. With the diminishing thump, thump of the Duke's band beating out 'Red Sails in the Sunset' behind me, I reached the Mess where a small group was standing round the entrance, all looking up towards the roof.

'What goes on?' I enquired.

'It's only Roger,' somebody replied, 'but he looks pretty dangerous this time.'

In the darkness above was the dim outline of a figure standing on his head or his hands on the roof guttering, quite steady and motionless. We were all accustomed to Roger Maw's antics. He had the unusual habit that, when he had had a few drinks, he would go quietly into a corner and stand on his head, sometimes for ten minutes or longer. For some extraordinary and quite inexplicable reason he seemed to be steadier on his head under these circumstances than on his feet. No medical reason for this strange inversion could be offered by Dick Stewart and his medical colleagues, and we generally accepted it as a quirk of heredity.

On many occasions, I had seen Roger standing quietly and unobtrusively on his head in a corner of the Mess anteroom after dinner, with a tankard of beer standing beside him and people walking past without a glance. But this time he had excelled himself. He had found a 'mali's' (gardener's) ladder in the garden, climbed on to the low roof of the Mess and there he was, standing on his hands on the guttering. Nobody was worried about his ability to do this but everybody clustered round was concerned about the strength of the gutters. If they collapsed, Roger would probably break his neck on the drive below.

Consequently the small group was ready to break his fall should he come crashing down. All was well, however, when a few minutes later Roger returned to his feet, found a ladder and descended steadily enough to the ground.

'Very pleasant up there – best part of the evening,' was Roger's only comment as we all drifted off to bed. It had been a good party.

Seven days later, on a cool bright morning, I was standing on the platform of Nowshera station waiting for the Frontier Mail, which made its first stop at Nowshera on its long journey from Peshawar to Karachi. A somewhat dejected Hukmud Khan was sitting on my luggage, waiting to accompany me down to the troopship and see me on my way. No other officers, but five airmen from Risalpur were travelling in the *Somersetshire* and so I found myself in charge of a small, but very cheerful homeward bound party.

The familiar column of black smoke appeared in the distance and five minutes later, the famous Frontier Mail puffed into sight – a mere fifteen minutes late. With its bell tolling and the great cow catcher on the front gleaming in the sun, the black engine ground to a halt with much screeching of tortured metal, clouds of steam, sparks and dense smoke. The usual pandemonium broke out as 'Soda water wallahs' shouted at passengers to buy their mineral waters, sweetmeat traders hawked their sticky cakes, porters hurled luggage about and everybody said goodbye to everybody else. If a large number of people were departing on one train, it was customary to transport the Mess bar, complete with stewards, down to the station, set it up on the platform and have a farewell party. It had not happened on this occasion but the Dukes, who had a large contingent going in the *Somersetshire*, had not only brought their bar down but the regimental band as well. The noise had to be heard to be believed and the normal five minutes stop stretched to twenty minutes before the train was allowed to leave to the strains of 'Auld Lang Syne'. The sight of three

Harts flying overhead was my last glimpse of life on the Frontier as we puffed away towards Attock bridge and the Indus.

It was a much faster and more comfortable journey than the one from Karachi in a troop train almost four years earlier, but there were some similarities. Despite the fact that the Frontier Mail was one of India's crack expresses (sic!), many of the passengers still depended for their meals on food sellers lined up on the platform at the many stopping places. Whenever we stopped, Hukmud would rush along the track and attend to my wants, occasionally being caught by the train starting again and having to remain with me until the next stop. Realising that this would be my last opportunity to enjoy the attentions of my personal servant, I took full advantage of Hukmad's determination to see me off in good style. But I did not forget to ensure that he also looked after my five Risalpur airmen who were travelling second class some way down the train. He could – and indeed did – see that they were not swindled by the rogues who set up their stalls especially to catch the travellers on the Frontier Mail.

The bleak featureless Sind desert was crossed at a rattling pace with no stops. Having acquired a second engine somewhere along the route, we made up some of the lost time, with dense clouds of black smoke and showers of sparks, until Karachi eventually came into view, flat, dusty and attractive only because it was the departure point for home.

His Majesty's Transport (HMT) *Somersetshire* was a welcome sight by the quayside, gleaming white in the sunshine with the wide blue band around the waistline to identify her in a similar way to that of hospital ships. A thin line of soldiers was moving slowly up the gangway, each one humping his kitbag and webbing equipment, but every one looking happy except perhaps for a few. There were always one or two who had got themselves into the hands of the notorious Indian moneylenders in spite of the strictest instructions constantly repeated to all of us. These 'banyirs' would suck an unfortunate Serviceman dry with stupendous interest rates which often rose

325

to over 100% in a short time. It was a court martial offence to be caught using them and it was not an uncommon sight to see these gentlemen waiting on the quayside in an endeavour to catch any of their clients who were attempting to skip the country without settling up. Hence the occasional fearful glance over his should from a guilty passenger trying to get up the gangway as quickly as possible.

It was time to say goodbye to Hukmud Khan. He had met me on this same quayside at Karachi nearly four years earlier. It seemed a very long time ago and he had stayed with me throughout, at Kohat, at Miramshah and at Risalpur. He had doubtless saved me on countless occasions from dishonest tradesmen and from thieving fingers which were always ready to rob the sahib when he was careless. He had given me a good knowledge of the Urdu language and I like to think that he benefitted from his time with me. I certainly taught him English, how to drive a car and to play tennis at which game he was, like many Indians, very good. Before leaving Risalpur I had given him his 'chits', or references, which were amongst a bearer's most valued possessions, and also a farewell tip which, although it did not seem unduly generous, was in fact the equivalent of three months wages. So it only remained for us to shake hands and depart on our ways. I never saw Hukmud again but I did enquire after him some thirty years later when passing through Karachi in 1966, from an old bearer in the Mess who had known him. It saddened me to hear that he had lost a leg through phlebitis somewhere up on the Frontier many years after I had left.

The *Somersetshire* was a large ship, but even so, a huge number of troops seemed to be embarking, many of them with families but not, I was pleased to see with their horses. When eventually shown to my cabin, I fully understood how so many troops could be embarked. I did not measure the cabin, but 8 feet by 6 feet would be an exaggeration, and I found myself sharing it with three Hussar subalterns. There were upper and lower bunks on either side of a central gangway with one wardrobe at the end and a wash basin crammed in beside the door. It did not take us long to find out that only one person could dress, undress or change at a time in the 6 foot by 3 foot gangway. As we dined in Mess kit every night, we were compelled to work out a complicated and exact roster for all our changes of clothes, and this often necessitated one person starting to change for dinner as early as 5.30 pm. However, my cabin companions couldn't have been more pleasant and the situation produced more humour than irritation. The only occasion on which our tolerance was sorely tried was in a storm in the middle of the night. The *Somersetshire* was playing up a bit and the door of the cabinet holding a chamber pot flew open sending the pot scudding across the floor. That would not have mattered had the pot been empty, but it was not!

If the officers' quarters were cramped, those for the troops and the families were basic. Part of the ship was divided into large open troop decks. Each of these spaces accommodated fifty or more soldiers and airmen with hammocks slung Navy fashion and a small area for each man's kit. The men could tolerate these conditions for the short duration of the voyage, particularly if they were homeward bound, but the families were even more basically treated. They were accommodated in much the same fashion except that some concession to privacy was made by dividing the space allotted to one family from its neighbours by canvas screens. The heat and smell in these confined spaces was most unpleasant and one did not have to be aboard long to understand why trooping to the tropics was confined to the cooler months of the year. Washing and toilet facilities and feeding were equally spartan but always clean and adequate.

All troopships were run on strict military lines: they had to be or unmentionable squalor would have resulted in no time. There was always an OC Troops on board while all junior officers and NCOs took turns to perform set duties, such as Orderly Officer, Orderly Sergeant, etc. Even meals were parades with officers wearing mess dress nightly for dinner.

327

With boat drills, fire drills, Captains rounds and other parades invented to keep everybody occupied, there was little leisure, and the whole voyage was vastly different from the comfort and luxury of a P & O liner. No wonder officers pulled every string they could to obtain a private passage.

My own turn to be Orderly Officer came at the end of the first week as we entered the Red Sea, the hottest part of the voyage but reasonably tolerable while on deck. I did my rounds, one by day and one at night and found the atmosphere on the lower decks almost more than I could bear. The ship was rolling considerably in a heavy swell. Many of the families were feeling ill and I didn't feel so good myself by the time I reached my cabin, still in Mess kit at 2 am. It was an experience but not one that I was anxious to repeat. The five airmen from Risalpur had managed to stay together at one end of the troop deck. They were immediately labelled 'the Brylcreem Boys' by the soldiers who said that they always smelled of petrol and oil.

'Better than smelling permanently of horse manure,' seemed to be their favourite rejoinder. They had all completed a full five years tour overseas, were still bachelors and took a certain pride in being the only airmen in the ship. I made it my business to meet them each day somewhere on deck to discuss their problems, but they were a cheerful and happy bunch with good home postings to look forward to and families to rejoin after a very long absence for men still in their twenties.

The passage of the Suez Canal was always interesting in a large ship which seemed literally to be sailing over the desert. On this occasion, a lot of amusement was caused when it was announced over our public address system that we would shortly pass our sister ship, the *Dorsetshire*, then outward bound. She was in a south bound convoy waiting in the Great Bitter Lake until our northbound convoy had passed. We were taken within 200 yards of the *Dorsetshire* which produced loud cheers and catcalls, and shouts of 'poor b——s' etc from our homeward bound troops, accompanied by scores of unwanted Bombay bowlers and other types of topee being hurled into the water to emphasise that they were no longer needed. I often wonder how many thousands of topees were washed up annually on the banks of the canal to be salvaged, carefully dried and worn by Arabs.

Port Said was the only stopping place on the voyage, when everybody was allowed ashore for four hours to buy their final gifts for home from Simon Artz. As usual the ship was surrounded by the boys diving for annas, the 'gulli-gulli' men and those selling the inevitable 'feelthy pictures.' This was the point at which both the Army and the RAF discarded tropical uniform and donned khaki or blue home dress. It gave one a great sensation of nearing home with the last of the heat, sand and dirt left behind.

And so the voyage continued, past Malta and the Rock of Gibraltar, out into the Atlantic and up to the Bay of Biscay. It was cold and rough in the Bay and there was a lot more sea sickness on the troop decks. The families suffered particularly, as the cold November winds kept them below decks in their cramped and uncomfortable quarters. But the Bay was soon left behind and we entered the Channel in calm, sunny weather which brought everybody out to catch that first, exciting glimpse of England.

Britain at that moment was in a turmoil – a turmoil which had hardly filtered through to the distant North West Frontier owing to the lack of communications. But, by the time the *Somersetshire* reached the English Channel, all on board were full of the rumours concerning King Edward VIII and Mrs Simpson. The newspapers were to remain silent until a few days after we landed but there were countless rumours and speculation as to whether the Monarchy would fall or whether the King would marry Mrs Simpson and remain on the throne. The fact that I had previously heard no whisper of these happenings shows more clearly than anything how completely isolated from world events we had been on the North West Frontier of India.

All these rumours served to heighten the interest caused by

the news, as we steamed up the Channel, that the ship was to be met at Southampton by their Royal Highnesses the Duke and Duchess of Gloucester, at midday on the 27th November. The 10th Hussars was the Duke's own regiment but we few airmen were able to look forward to basking in the reflected glory of a Royal welcome home. It was also a great day for me as the news came through that I had been promoted to Flight Lieutenant. This was a considerable surprise, much earlier than I could possibly have expected. Again it revealed the isolation of the life I had been living. Little real knowledge of the speed and extent of the expansion of the RAF had filtered through, but my early promotion was one extremely welcome result of that expansion, and it also explained why I had been selected as a flying instructor so readily.

Nobody was late rising on that last morning as our troopship moved slowly up the Solent at breakfast time, passing the *Mauretania* outward bound for New York. The last morning inspection was particularly rigorous as the troop decks and cabins had to be left spick and span.

Punctually at midday, we were warped alongside the quay on which the Army band was playing 'Home Sweet Home'. No sooner had the gangway been lowered than a Royal Daimler appeared and the Duke and Duchess came up the gangway, cheered by those lining the rails. They showed no sign of the strain which they must have been under as the Duke spoke a few words of welcome at a brief reception held in the main saloon. He and the Duchess knew most of the officers of his regiment but the few other officers on board, like myself, were presented and welcomed home. The visit was a nice gesture and greatly appreciated.

Special trains for London were at the quayside station and, by mid afternoon, the Frontier had almost faded from memory.